Lecture Notes in Computer Science 4716

Commenced Publication in 1973
Founding and Former Series Editors:
Gerhard Goos, Juris Hartmanis, and Jan van Leeuwen

Editorial Board

Bertrand Meyer   Mathai Joseph (Eds.)

Software Engineering Approaches for Offshore and Outsourced Development

First International Conference, SEAFOOD 2007
Zurich, Switzerland, February 5-6, 2007
Revised Papers

 Springer

Volume Editors

Bertrand Meyer
ETH Zurich, Department of Computer Science
RZ Building, Clausiusstr. 59, 8092 Zurich, Switzerland
E-mail: bertrand.meyer@inf.ethz.ch

Mathai Joseph
Tata Consultancy Services
1 Mangaldas Road, Pune 411 001, India
E-mail: m.joseph@tcs.com

Library of Congress Control Number: 2007936130

CR Subject Classification (1998): D.2, K.6, K.4.2, J.1

LNCS Sublibrary: SL 2 – Programming and Software Engineering

ISSN   0302-9743
ISBN-10   3-540-75541-1 Springer Berlin Heidelberg New York
ISBN-13   978-3-540-75541-8 Springer Berlin Heidelberg New York

Springer is a part of Springer Science+Business Media

springer.com

© Springer-Verlag Berlin Heidelberg 2007

Typesetting: Camera-ready by author, data conversion by Scientific Publishing Services, Chennai, India
Printed on acid-free paper   SPIN: 12171392   06/3180   5 4 3 2 1 0

Preface

SEAFOOD for Thought

Headline-grabbing though it may be, the software industry's large-scale allocation of work to developing countries has not so far generated much technical analysis. Attention is usually limited to the possible political and economic consequences, in particular the fears of loss of employment in the West. The aim of the present volume is different. We recognize that offshore development is here to stay, and not just a result of cost considerations. It is – more accurately – a form of distributed development, relying on advances in communications to let the software industry, in our globalized world, benefit from the wide distribution of human talent. But it is also the source of a new set of challenges, to which accepted software engineering principles and techniques have not completely prepared us. Producing high-quality software on time and within budget is hard enough when the QA team is across the aisle from the core developers, and the customers across the street; what then when the bulk of the development team is across an ocean or two?

The first SEAFOOD – Software Engineering Advances For Outsourced and Offshore Development – conference (prompted by an earlier article[1]) was an attempt not only to bring software engineering to outsourcing but also to bring outsourcing into the collective consciousness of the software engineering community. This is beneficial to both sides: successful outsourcing requires strong software engineering guidance, but research in the field must for its part account for the new world of software development. Whatever direction outsourcing takes in the coming years, we will never be just in one location any more.

SEAFOOD was held at ETH Zurich on 5–6 February 2007 and provided an opportunity for participants from academia and industry to confront experiences, ideas and proposals. The articles that follow are the result of this encounter. As can be expected of the first conference in such a novel field, we are still in the process of defining what constitutes a proper object of study on the topic; but the contributions already show a number of promising developments, which we are sure will be taken further in future conferences, starting from SEAFOOD 2008 to be held in the same venue in the first week of July 2008. The conference site at http://seafood.ethz.ch includes information on this conference, as well as past and future SEAFOOD events.

We hope that you will enjoy the results of SEAFOOD 2007 and that this volume will give you many useful ideas to understand and improve the engineering of outsourced software.

---

[1] Bertrand Meyer: Offshore Development: The Unspoken Revolution in Software Engineering, IEEE Computer, January 2006, pages 124, 122-123.

Many people contributed to making SEAFOOD 2007 a success. We are particularly grateful to the authors who submitted their work in a new and quickly evolving area; to the Program Committee members who reviewed the papers in time and through sometimes extensive discussions. (We extend our special wishes to Gio Wiederhold, who suffered an accident while in Zurich.) The role of Andrei Voronkov's excellent EasyChair conference system is gratefully acknowledged.

The conference benefited from four outstanding keynote presentations by Krishnamurti Ananthkrishnan, Chief Technology Officer of Tata Consultancy Services, Stuart Feldman, Vice President for computer science of IBM, Watts Humphrey from the Software Engineering Institute and Andrey Terekhov, from the State University of Saint Petersburg.

Martin Nordio from ETH played a key role in organizing the conference and helping prepare this volume; we are also grateful to Claudia Günthart for outstanding organizational support and to Christian Hunziker from ELCA for his work in publicizing the conference throughout Switzerland.

August 2008   Mathai Joseph
                                                           Bertrand Meyer

Organization

Program Co-chairs

Mathai Joseph, Tata Consultancy Services, India
Bertrand Meyer, ETH Zurich, Switzerland and Eiffel Software, California, USA

Program Committee

Manfred Broy, Technische Universität München, Germany
Kokichi Futatsugi, JAIST, Japan
Victor Gergel University of Nizhnyi-Novgorod, Russia
Koichi Kishida, SRA Key-Tech Lab, Japan
Qiaoyun Li, Motorola, USA
Mingshu Li, Chinese Academy of Sciences, China
Andrey Terekhov, State University of Saint Petersburg and TEPKOM, Russia
Gio Wiederhold, Stanford University, USA

Publicity Chair

Christian Hunziker, ELCA, Switzerland

Organizing Committee

Claudia Günthart, ETH Zurich, Switzerland
Martin Nordio, ETH Zurich, Switzerland

Table of Contents

Offshore Software Development:
Transferring Research Findings into the Classroom

Kay Berkling[1], Michael Geisser[2], Tobias Hildenbrand[2], and Franz Rothlauf[2]

[1] Caribbean Artificial Intelligence Group CAIG, Polytechnic University of Puerto Rico,
Electrical and Computer Engineering and Computer Science Department, 377 Ponce de Leon
Ave, Hato Rey, PR 00918, Puerto Rico
kay@berkling.com
[2] Lehrstuhl für ABWL und Wirtschaftsinformatik, Universität Mannheim,
D-68131 Mannheim, Germany
{geisser,hildenbrand,rothlauf}@uni-mannheim.de

Abstract. Distributed software projects are becoming increasingly commonplace in industry. Yet, software engineering education rarely graduates students with the necessary skills and hands-on experience that are particular to off-shore software development projects. Three key areas in successful off-shore software development projects are well documented in the literature as communication, knowledge management, as well as project and process management. This paper maps tasks within each of these three areas to functions that have to be provided by remote collaboration platforms and tools that distributed projects rely on. A case-study of an off-shore requirements engineering class experience between a Master course of Polytechnic University of Puerto Rico and a customer in a Swiss financial institution shows a correlation between areas of learning by the students and functionalities covered with the tools used in the classroom. The paper identifies additional tools, developed by the authors, which will provide additional functionalities in the deficient areas to increase the learning and preparation of the students for off-shore software development projects.

Keywords: Offshore Software Development, Distributed and Global Software Development, Software Engineering Education, Development Tools, Collaborative Software Development, Requirements Engineering, Traceability.

1 Introduction

1.1 The Fundamental Problem of Global and Offshore Software Development

Software development projects have never been easy to manage or predict in terms of cost, quality, or time to delivery. While a variety of methodologies exist to estimate cost and manage projects, still far more than half of all IT projects "fail" because of budget overruns, high maintenance costs or mismatch between desired and delivered functionality [31]. Such failures can in part be attributed to non-standard processes but are often due to inadequate communication between the parties involved [17].

B. Meyer and M. Joseph (Eds.): SEAFOOD 2007, LNCS 4716, pp. 1–18, 2007.
© Springer-Verlag Berlin Heidelberg 2007

In the last five years there has been a major increase in efforts to outsource software development to offshore locations such as India, China or Russia in order to cut the development costs [24]. According to Gartner, worldwide spending on offshore research and development will increase by a factor of 9 to ultimately $12 billion by 2010 and application development services will reach expenditures of $50 billion dollar [23]. On paper, the savings for projects that can be outsourced to economically advantageous locations look fabulous. The reality, however, is much less documented and shows that the challenges already faced by local projects are even enhanced by distance. The lack of effective communication due to distance, culture and language issues may well cause damage to projects that outweigh any potential savings of off-shoring development.

Computer science graduates who enter this global work environment are generally ill-prepared for these aspects of their future job. Few computer science curricula contain components to train their students in offshore development practices and related special considerations [10,27]. Yet, experience and skills in IT Management of global software development projects are essential to the success of offshore projects.

1.2 Objective and Methodology

The overall objective of this paper is twofold: First, the teaching methods used for offshore development education we present shall be replicable and reusable in various international university contexts. Second, by using methods and tools satisfying realistic offshore requirements, our basic approach will eventually be transferable and applicable in industry. Therefore, our work aims at making both a short-term and a long-term contribution to the improvement of offshore software development (OSD) practices: Through better education as well as methodological and tool support.

Analyses of the state-of-the-art in OSD practices, especially concerning software engineering (SE) methods and tools applied, yield three major categories of problems that need to be addressed – also in the classroom: communication, knowledge management, as well as project and process management [14]. The authors propose a combination of commonly used commercial and open source tools to provide the supporting functionality to improve performance of offshore projects in each of these three areas. Tools are chosen to be deployed in the classroom and support distributed educational software projects within semi-commercial settings, i.e. with a real customer. The classroom experience is designed to provide feedback with respect to accomplishing learning objectives and measuring the usefulness of the proposed supporting functionalities within real OSD scenarios.

The rest of this paper is organized as follows: Section 2 discusses current issues in OSD and presents major requirements for tools to support these scenarios. Section 3 describes the teaching environment for a SE course that is used as a baseline for this paper and outlines the deficiencies in this learning environment. Section 4 forms the theoretical component of this paper, where the necessary functionalities for effective OSD projects are evaluated and areas to be strengthened with additional tools are identified. In Section 5, the missing functionalities are mapped to new tools that are reviewed and their deployment in the classroom described in Section 6. Finally, the paper closes with a review and description of necessary future work to evaluate the success of the deployments.

2 Offshore Software Development: Issues and Requirements

Within the field of SE, literature on OSD heavily relies on the findings within the fields of distributed software development (DSD) and global software development (GSD) respectively. Besides issues of physical distribution, OSD also takes people's different mindsets and cultures into account when analyzing methodology and improvements in project management.

Herbsleb and Moitra [17] classify the problem classes most often encountered in GSD and OSD projects as follows: (a) strategic issues, (b) cultural issues, (c) inadequate communication, (d) knowledge management issues, (e) project and process management issues, and (f) technical issues (for complementary analyses see also [5, 15]).

Each one of these problem fields demands different approaches and tools. This paper will not be primarily concerned with strategic and cultural issues due to the fact that these problems may better be solved in business administration and social science respectively. Problem classes (c) to (e) however require tool supported solutions and are therefore our main focus – (f) in our opinion characterizes a cross-cutting concern and is hence not analyzed separately. Each of the three areas described below overlap somewhat. For example there is no project management without communication and visualization of meta-data is important for all three categories. However, the categories can be broadly separated as follows: Project and process management issues correspond to coordination problems: e.g. synchronization and mutual awareness in concurrent globally distributed processes [17]. Communication issues pertain to a broader range of SE tasks, whereas knowledge management is the most abstract problem class as regards the scope of activities affected.

2.1 Project and Process Management Issues

Process management is highly critical in distributed scenarios. Software process coordination is mostly about the division of labor between distributed sites and developers: Tasks can either be divided according to the code structure or different development disciplines [29]. Either way, parallel concurrent processes have to be managed carefully [17], while still guaranteeing process flexibility and integration of different methods from the various sites [18].

As Requirements Engineering (RE) is the most critical phase in OSD [25], a systematic proceeding will be needed to provide efficient client integration and decision support for requirements selection even though physical meetings might not always be possible [12].

Especially in OSD, roles are highly important to help the coordination of a large number of developers [20]. A team member can take on one or more roles within a single project and consequently can be a developer and later a tester, with duties varying accordingly.

Empirical studies suggest that informal communication is a very important aspect of coordinating teams in uncertain tasks such as software development [6, 20]. The physical distance between sites makes it harder for distributed team members to spontaneously and informally communicate with other team members in order to coordinate their work [14]. This limitation within OSD implies fewer coordinating interactions since developers find it more difficult to discern people's current activity and whether it is appropriate to interrupt them at a certain time [1]. It can also mean that such developers encounter greater difficulties in coordinating OSD projects as a result. Therefore, team awareness and process transparency are crucial for OSD.

Moreover, change management and impact analysis are particularly critical coordination tasks in OSD. Distributed developers with different processes and tools make it even more difficult to coordinate changes to the code base and prevent conflicts [24]. Impact analysis, i.e. seeing the consequences of your changes in advance, is also significantly harder in distributed settings such as OSD projects since related artifacts are also most likely distributed over multiple sites [1].

Visualization and understanding of complex contexts, e.g. processes or artifact dependencies, greatly support the project and process management by providing a better view of the information.

2.2 Communication Issues

Software development is a very communication-intensive activity and issues raised of an inadequate communication are even more complex in OSD [17]. As had been mentioned before, distance introduces barriers to informal communication which leads not only to coordination issues [5, 14]. It also makes it difficult to establish trust and form relationships among distributed stakeholders [8].

Comparable to the problem of process integration, the integration of different communication tools – synchronous and asynchronous – must also be seen as a major issue in OSD. These tools need a well-defined interface because fuzzy interfaces will mostly lead to inefficiencies and other technical problems [17].

Moreover, visualization and understanding of complex contexts, e.g. processes, artifact dependencies, and social networks of developers, are often problematic as well. However, these visualizations are critical to support formal, project-related communication in order to make it more efficient. This issue is even more critical in OSD arrangements since visualizations can help overcome language barriers [11].

2.3 Knowledge Management Issues

In addition to coordination and communication issues, general knowledge management is vital to fully exploit the OSD potential [17]. In distributed projects, the physical location of information artifacts such as source code, task descriptions, or comments on changes, and the lack of "global knowledge" about their existence make traceability and rationale management an especially hard task in OSD [7].

Moreover, poor knowledge management leads to many missed reuse opportunities that otherwise would have potentially saved lots of time and money [17]. Global knowledge management (through visualization) is also critical in order to determine the overall status of the project at any given time, e.g. critical paths of activity flows and buffers among subsequent tasks [17].

In GSD, in addition to documenting the various artifacts, updating and revising the documentation is especially important since team-members are not all collocated. The usage of visualization tools is only as useful as the information within the tools is correctly updated. Automating such updates becomes particularly important. To prevent assumptions and ambiguity and to support maintainability, documentation must be current and reflect what various teams are using and working on [17].

3 Offshore Software Development in the Classroom

At Polytechnic University of Puerto Rico a recently established track in SE focuses on student learning in OSD. The students participate in a series of related classes including Software Engineering I (SE1: Foundations in Software Engineering Management and Methodology), Software Engineering II (SE2: Requirements Management with offshore component), and Software Engineering III (SE3: Offshore Software Development). In all cases, the emphasis is placed both on the project management and development process as well as the effective use of supportive technology and less on the quantity of project that was completed. This section describes the course setup followed by the learning objectives that are aligned with the issues identified in Section 2.

3.1 Classroom Scenarios

For the purpose of defining three types of classroom OSD scenarios, the division of labor splits according to SE workflows based on the Rational Unified Process (RUP) [21] into three tiers: Client (Business Idea), Intermediary (Requirements Specification, Analysis, Design, Implementation at the prototype level, Configuration and Change Management, Project Management), and Supplier (Implementation, Environment, Testing). Client, Intermediary and Supplier are each situated in a different location and time zone. The Client, in our case, is a single person from industry who has a project idea and has to agree with the final product. The Intermediary forms a buffer between client and supplier. This buffer has the function of alleviating the work load on the client side, dampen cultural differences and provide quality insurance. For the purpose of the classroom, the Intermediary takes on two functions in separate semesters.

In SE2, the class takes on the task of analyzing and specifying the requirements of the client in detail and building a prototype. In the second semester, the Intermediary is responsible for defining the technology, designing the software architecture, and overseeing the supplier class in building the entire project according to specifications. The Supplier provides the implementation according to specifications of the Intermediary. As a result of these high-level roles, two relationships can be emulated in the classroom: between Client and Intermediary, and between Intermediary and Supplier according to Figure 1. The split according to SE disciplines is described as follows for SE2 and SE3:

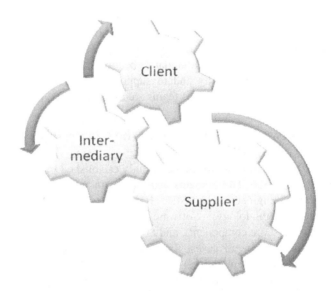

Fig. 1. Class roles include Client, Intermediary and Supplier. In SE1, these roles are collocated within the same classroom to teach the fundamentals of SE projects. In SE2 (Offshore Requirements Engineering) Client and Intermediary are located in different time zones. In SE3 (Offshore Implementation) Intermediary and Supplier are residing in different locations.

a) Requirements Engineering (between Client and Intermediary) in SE2

A client in a distant location poses the project idea in form of a short description of one to two pages. Usually an official or unofficial industry partner plays the role of a client. A typical profile of a client can be:

-   Someone who does not have the resources to define and follow up on a project but has a strong interest in seeing it developed further in order to have a detailed specification and a prototype.
-   A client who is training to become a manager for a global team and is supported by the company in participating with the class as part of a training.
    The class defines the project but additionally has to ensure that the client agrees with the specifications.

b) Implementation (between Intermediary and Supplier) in SE3

The Intermediary and Supplier class pair takes on a project resulting from collaboration between Client and Intermediary in order to specify the technology in more detail. The Intermediary supervises the development in accordance with the Client, where now all three (Client, Intermediary and Supplier) are situated in different locations – but not all in different time zones. E.g. Puerto Rico and Chile are in the same time and language zone which is exactly what makes this setup so attractive. The supplier codes the project assignment according to the specification of the intermediary and interacts with the intermediary only. A variation on this scenario is a role reversal between the participating classes in order to emphasize understanding of the entire process.

The course SE2 corresponds to scenario (a); it heavily emphasizes RE and is the focus of our attention in this paper. Scenario (b) emphasizes Software Architecture, Design and Implementation and is the subject of Software Engineering Special Topics course following SE2. While the focus of this paper is on SE2, it is important to ensure that the requirements for SE3 are met when choosing collaboration platforms.

3.2   The Collaborative Software Development Platform CodeBeamer

In the past, collaboration software has been in use for the SE2 class. Collaborative software development platforms (CSDP) allow the creation of project workspaces and can thus be used as central communication and coordination platforms. They generally include access control mechanisms and some standard tools like document management systems, different issue trackers, forums, and integration with different revision control systems [28]. Moreover they usually offer integration with other synchronous communication tools for audio- and videoconferences. CodeBeamer from Intland Software[1], VA Software and CollabNet[2] are examples of such CSDP's. CodeBeamer was chosen for our work because it offers the most balanced and integrated support in project management, requirements management and code management [29]. CodBeamer additionally possesses a seamless integration of a wiki system that allows linking asynchronous communication with artifacts. Wiki systems are collaborative page-editing tools in which users may add or edit pages directly through their web browser [28]. Relationships among pages and other resources are particularly easy to establish by means of wiki links. Thus they cannot only be used for knowledge management but also for requirements engineering purposes [12]. Flexible workflow and role configurations support customizing project management methodologies (such as standardized or company internal methods), with support for process management reporting.

CodeBeamer is complemented with the freely available tools Eclipse, Subversion, and Skype. Interfaces to all of these tools are already integrated in CodeBeamer CSDP, which will therefore serve as central point of integration. CodeBeamer has been provided to us for academic usage.

3.3   Learning Objectives and Evaluation

In accordance with the areas identified in Section 2, the learning objectives in SE2 are focused and evaluated with respect to project and process management, communication and knowledge management. For each of the issues identified in Section 2, the tools that are employed in the classroom can be evaluated with respect to their effectiveness of capturing and engaging the students in mastering the learning objectives as shown in Table 1.

Students who took part in the class of the case study have been evaluated through questionnaires according to their roles in the project [3] on each of the three categories (Project and Process Management, Communication and Knowledge Management) using a subset of the Bloom [4] taxonomy for stages of learning:

---

[1] http://www.intland.com/products/codebeamer.html (09/30/2006)
[2] www.vasoftware.com, www.collab.net (09/30/2006)

Table 1. Learning Objectives

Project and process management	Communication	Knowledge Management
• Role assignment • Process adaptation to chosen methodology • Efficient client integration • Decision support for requirements selection and prioritization • Team awareness • Change Management • Impact Analysis (consequences of change)	• Integration of informal networking into overall communication (socializing, trust) • Integration of various communication tools • Visualization and understanding of complex context	• Traceability • Understanding status of project • Updating of documentation

Knowledge. Knowledge of specific facts, terminology, methods, memorized facts, like what Function Points are.

Comprehension. Demonstrative understanding of facts and ideas by organizing material, ideas, making choices, designing. Knowing why something is important. For example Function Points – understanding their meaning by calculating them for actual use cases.

Application. Using new knowledge. Solve problems to new situations by applying acquired knowledge, facts, techniques and rules in a different way. For example, applying Function Points for project estimation and realizing that they have some limitations.

For each of the learning objectives in the three categories, students that passed SE2 were asked to rate their learning level from 0-3 (with 0: none, 1: basic 2:good and 3: high at three different times), before taking SE1, after SE1 and after SE2. The average result is shown below for six students and presents learning trends only, as the number of data points here is of course very low. However, each of the students' responses is similar to the average with exception to the Project Manger who is an outlier and not included in the average. The Project Manager has a much higher learning than the other students [3]. The result is depicted in Figure 2.

Figure 2 indicates that while students clearly feel that SE2 adds value beyond SE1, the learning impact can be significantly improved. The graph also shows that the highest perceived deficiency in learning is at the level of applying knowledge where the area of process and project management is in need of the most substantial improvement. These same findings hold for the Project Manager. The next sections of this paper deal with understanding how additional tools may support the learning in each of the deficient areas by analyzing the challenges for OSD projects in each of the three areas.

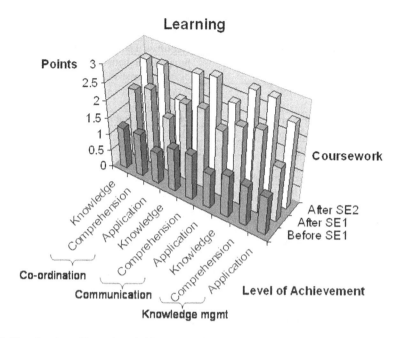

Fig. 2. Self-evaluation of Learning-Achievements in terms of Blooms taxonomy and Herbslebs identified key areas of project success

4 Functional Support for Problem Areas

This section presents the most essential functionalities to support OSD projects in each of the areas identified in Section 2 in order to identify how the learning deficiencies identified in Section 3 can be alleviated.

As for **Project and Process Management** issues, the OSD tools should support both architecture-based and discipline-based division of labor (DoL). In addition, asynchronous collaboration features are required to allow parallel and concurrent work even across different time zones. In order to support different development processes flexibly, methodological independence of the tools is important. Thus they should allow for "agile collaboration", i.e. flexibly supports different development processes. As mentioned before, RE is particularly important in OSD. To facilitate efficient client integration in the elicitation phase of RE, discussion forums are a promising option [12]. In order to obtain decision support for requirements selection, functionalities for both cost and value estimation of the requirements are needed. Furthermore the OSD tools should have implemented a role concept, which allows fine-grained rights and access management. As has been said, team awareness and process transparency are highly critical to OSD success. Therefore, tools must support both the visualization of team structures and processes as well as triggered notifications. Distributed change management in OSD requires traceability [15]. This in turn allows for better impact analyses, which is essential for coordinating changes to related artifacts. Table 2 lists the required functionalities to support project and process management.

Table 2. Tool Functionalities Required for Solving Project and process management Issues

Project and Process Management Issues	Required Tool Features
Division of labor	Support for both architecture-based DoL and discipline-based DoL
Parallel and concurrent work	Asynchronous collaboration (e.g. forums and comments)
Process flexibility within projects	Methodological independence, agility
Efficient client integration in RE	Discussion forum, Wikis, or similar
Decision support for requirements selection	Cost and value estimation for requirements
Role support	Role concept, rights/access management
Team awareness & process transparency	Visualizations and notifications
Change management & impact analysis	Traceability of dependencies among artifacts, process steps, and people

With regard to **communication** problems, OSD tools require features that allow for informal and spontaneous communication. We will entitle this concept "virtual water cooler", denoting synchronous virtual brainstorming session and general discussions spontaneously involving two or more people. In order to establish trust and substitute the lack of physical interpersonal relationships, OSD tools should include support for long-term virtual socializing, community building, and social networking [18].

Furthermore well-defined interfaces and central integration architecture are essential to seamlessly integrate those communication tools already in use in different organizations. Finally, visualization capabilities, based on integrated information from all distributed sites, are also needed in order to allow a visualization-supported communication in general and thus enhance mutual understanding of complex contexts. Table 3 lists the functionalities required for supporting communication.

Table 3. Tool Functionalities Required for Solving Communication Issues

Communication Issues	Required Tool Features
Informal/spontaneous communication	Synchronous virtual brainstorming and discussion
Establishment of trust	Virtual socializing, community building, and social networking
Integration of communication tools	Well-defined interfaces, central integration architecture
Visualization and understanding of complex contexts	Visualization capabilities, based on integrated information from all sites

As concerns **knowledge management** in OSD projects, traceability and rationale capturing must be covered for the whole SE process. For this reason, artifacts, processes, and users need to be represented as entities. Establishing a global traceability network including rationale information requires linking mechanisms, such as typed associations. Indexing, advanced search mechanisms, and cross references between projects foster reuse on a global scale. Process modeling and status capturing allow for detailed project status reporting.

Altogether, the most important feature of OSD tools is information integration on a global level which shall ensure an always up to date documentation of the overall process. Table 4 lists the functionalities required for knowledge management.

Table 4. Tool Functionalities Required for Solving Knowledge Management Issues

Knowledge Management Issues	Required Tool Features
Traceability and rationale management	Artifact, process, and user representations, linking mechanisms
Missed reuse opportunities	Artifact indexing and retrieval, cross references
Project status reporting	Process modeling, status capturing
Documentation of overall process	Information integration

5 Mapping Tools to Functionalities

Table 5 indicates how well the functionalities that were proposed in Section 2 are covered by Codebeamer and which additional functionalities are still required to improve the learning process in all areas. All areas are improved by adding additional tools and functionalities. Interestingly, a large number of identified missing functionalities fall into the area of project and process management, which correspond to the most deficient areas of learning in SE2 class, as indicated by Figure 2. In order to cover the missing functionalities listed in Table 5, this paper proposes two additional tools that are to be integrated with CodeBeamer for use in OSD projects and deployed in the classroom.

Table 5. Functional Analysis

Tool	Project and Process Mgmt.	Communication	Knowledge Mgmt
CodeBeamer (incl. Skype, Eclipse, and Subversion)	* Supports architecture-based and discipline-based DoL * Asynchronous collaboration * Methodological independence * Discussion forum and Wiki for spontaneous, agile coordination	* Virtual water cooler * Synchronous brainstorming * Virtual socializing * Central integration platform	* Project status reporting * Missed reuse opportunities * Documentation of overall process
Missing Functionalities	* Cost and value estimation for requirements * Traceability * Awareness * Support for change management and impact analysis	* Visualization capabilities	* Traceability and rationale capturing * Documentation of overall process

5.1 The Ibere Tool for Supporting Requirements Selection in OSD Projects

In order to support the requirements selection process in OSD projects, Internet-based cost and value estimation for requirements has to be conducted. For this purpose, the Ibere (Internet-based empirical requirements evaluation) tool, which guides distributed participants through the requirements estimation procedure, can be used. Ibere is also able to visualize interdependent requirements as a result of the requirements evaluation process in the form of a cost-value diagram (cp. Figure 3) by utilizing the analytical hierarchy process as algorithm for calculating the utility value for each requirement [12]. The units for utility and costs are given in percent, which means that e.g. a value of 0,04 represents 4 percent of the total value. Due to its import and export modules, a seamless integration to CodeBeamer is guaranteed: the requirements, which have to be evaluated, can be imported from CodeBeamer's Wiki tool and the selected requirements can be exported to the requirements tracker in CodeBeamer.

Based on this objectified foundation, it is possible to decide which requirements will have to be implemented immediately, totally discarded, or preserved for upcoming releases. In order to provide additional decision support, the diagram contains two straight lines (cp. Figure 3): combinations of requirements with at least two times more relative value than relative cost should be implemented in any case, whereas those with twice the relative costs should not be considered for implementation at all. These equations have been empirically tested and proven suitable to distinguish preferable requirements with high value-cost ratios from those with a low ratio [19].

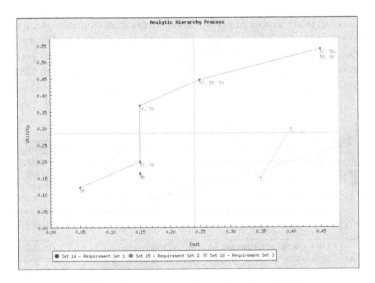

Fig. 3. Requirements cost-value estimation with Ibere

5.2 Trace Visualization and Analysis with TraVis

CSDP comprise and unify not only source code management, but multiple software development and knowledge management tools. These include build management systems, issue trackers, wikis, and discussion forums – tools that often have been successfully used in distributed open source software development projects and OSD scenarios [28].

The TraVis (**Tra**ce **Vis**ualization) tool leverages the use of dependencies among those different assets and their users by allowing the visualization and analysis of the different dependencies among various artifacts within CSDP. The traceability and rationale information from a CSDP is captured as distributed users develop and document their processes in OSD projects. These artifacts are annotated and connected with their respective descriptions, discussions (e.g. design-related ones), and process steps are represented as issue tracker items. Thus they form a heterogeneous network of information which can be extracted by TraVis. Managing all this information on one single CSDP allows linking all the artifacts, activity descriptions, and responsible users, consequently establishing the actual "traceability network" [22]. A traceability network combines information about the different software artifacts (requirements, architectural models, source code, test cases, etc.) and the user involved. Topology and semantics of these networks are therefore determined by the OSD projects' structure represented in the CSDP. Figure 4 shows an example of a traceability network with information on depending tasks and requirements as well as platform users and related documents. The screenshot displays TraVis' value-based view, i.e. the artifacts node size is determined by their importance based on the underlying evaluation of requirements conducted with Ibere (see above). The figure also depicts the rationale information for task 1195, e.g. comments made by users when committing changes.

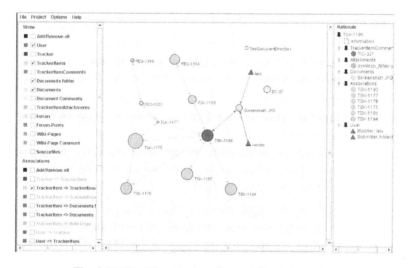

Fig. 4. TraVis: Visualization of traceability information

Technologically, TraVis extracts traceability information from CSDP over their remote API, e.g. via Web Services. The current prototype provides several filters for displaying certain aspects of the traceability network, e.g. particular artifact types, process categories, or user groups (Figure 2). Thus different role-based views, e.g. for source code developers, designers, project managers, etc., can be defined. Moreover, TraVis is able to display networks originating from particular artifacts, activities, and users (see also Figure 4). This, for example, supports impact analysis in OSD settings.

Table 6. Functional overview of the tools

Tool	Project and Process Management	Communication	Knowledge Mgmt
CodeBeamer (incl. Skype, Eclipse, and Subversion)	* Supports architecture-based and discipline-based DoL * Asynchronous collaboration * Methodological independence * Discussion forum and Wiki for spontaneous, agile coordination	* Virtual water cooler * Synchronous brainstorming * Virtual socializing * Central integration platform	* Project status reporting * Missed reuse opportunities * Documentation of overall process
Ibere	* Cost and value estimation for requirements * Role concept	* Well-defined interfaces	
TraVis	* Traceability * Awareness * Support for change management and impact analysis	* Visualization capabilities	* Traceability and rationale capturing * Documentation of overall process

Therefore, TraVis provides increased awareness within OSD projects based on a broad range of information from CSDP. TraVis allows for graphical representations and analyses at any time during a project through synchronization its data with the CSDP. Thus, collaboration among developers as well as with other stakeholder can improve, and the increased process transparency facilitates project management tasks and knowledge management in general. In our concrete set of tools TraVis operates on the data from the CodeBeamer CSDP described above. Table 6 summarizes the functionalities that each of the tools to be used in the classroom provides in each of the three areas of project and process management, communication and knowledge management. It can be seen that the two additional proposed tools cover the identified missing functionalities (see Table 5).

6   Utilization and Evaluation of Tools in Educational Projects

While CodeBeamer has been used for SE2 in the past, no special emphasis has been placed on using the tool with respect to the identified problem areas. The additional tools, Ibere and TraVis will be employed in the areas of project and process management, communication and knowledge management in order to increase the learning at the level where a student uses the new knowledge to solve problems in new situations or in a different way. Therefore, CodeBeamer serves as a basic platform providing most features that are required for OSD. The tools Ibere and TraVis complement this central platform for specific tasks which are particularly important in OSD: requirements engineering, visualization capabilities as well as traceability and rationale management as shown in Figure 5.

While no particular development process is prescribed, some methodological guidelines need to be followed when using these tools. The integrated Wiki system will be used for gathering and discussing the requirements together with the customer. Then the requirements are specified using use case templates in the requirements tracker of CodeBeamer. In the next step the most important requirements will be selected using Ibere. These requirements will then be prototypically implemented and

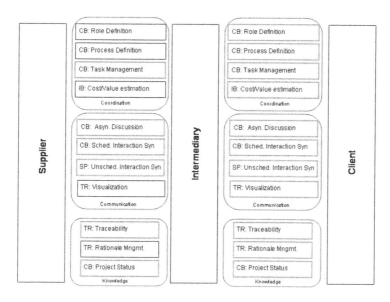

Fig. 5. Application of Tools to Improve Learning in Identified Problem Areas. (Functions are ascribed to tools. CB (CodeBeamer), IB (Ibere), TR (TraVis) and SP (Skype).

subsequently reviewed by the client. Finally, the prototypes will be constructed with regards to the comments of the client. Together they form the first version of the desired software.

Traceability and rationale management is also based on CodeBeamer. The association-mechanism as well as Wiki links are utilized in order to establish and maintain relationships among artifacts and users. Wiki and SVN comments reproduce rationale information, especially pertaining to changes and discussions about artifacts. During the whole development lifecycle, TraVis provides the visualization means in order to display this information in different contexts and according to various role-based views. In OSD projects, the whole process of capturing traceability and rationale information (Wiki-based traceability and rationale management, *Wiki-TRaM*) is covered by our three tools: CodeBeamer, Ibere, and TraVis. CodeBeamer stores the requirements evaluated by Ibere and their interrelations. Moreover, users link subsequent artifacts to these requirements by means of Wiki links and CodeBeamer's association mechanism. This information accounts for the topology and the semantics of the traceability network described in section 5.2 (cp. Figure 4).

Based on our argumentation in Section 4 and Section 5, we expect to see improvements in the self-evaluations of students showing a higher learning achievement due to SE2, with an increased ability to apply what was learned because of the off-shoring experience in combination with the proposed tools when compared to students that have not used the full spectrum of tools.

7 Summarizing Discussion and Future Work

This paper addresses the transfer of knowledge from the research community to education. Previous research has shown that certain skills are necessary for successful OSD projects. However, these issues have not been particularly and fully addressed by university curriculums so far. In this paper the authors have proposed a framework for defining and evaluating learning objectives in OSD projects that relate to the three most important identified problem areas of project and process management, communication and knowledge management. Previous evaluations of the learning environment in a SE course have indicated the need for improved learning in several of the identified areas. Based on identified functionalities of supporting tools that were not employed during this previous class, a set of innovative tools is proposed to expand on CodeBeamer as a platform in order to support students further. Based on the proposed combination of tools, all areas of learning in a SE or RE course are covered. As a result, students will be able to evaluate their learning specifically with respect to identified problem areas of OSD. Care has been taken to ensure that the factors that help students learn how to deal with the three problem areas are function specific to maintain generality before mapping these to specific tools. This way, transferability of this study provides a framework to evaluate other tools with proper coverage. The combination of real-world projects in the classroom (Section 3), with emphasis on three identified off-shoring problem areas (Section 2) combined with the usage of targeted supporting functionalities (Section 4,5) therefore supports the aim of proposing both short-term and long-term improvements for OSD practices and education.

In future work, the evaluation of students' learning using the larger spectrum of supporting tools will be used to track students' learning in OSD-related classroom projects along with the usefulness of the proposed set of tools to support this. As a result of data collected from this study over time, specific functionalities in tools can be measured for various stages within an OSD industry project. It is expected that the knowledge gained from classroom experience will eventually be transferable to industry.

Acknowledgments. Parts of this work are a result of the project CollaBaWue supported by the German state of Baden-Wuerttemberg and part of the research association PRIMIUM. Thanks for the students in the Master of Computer Science program at Polytechnic University of Puerto Rico and to Intland for providing the academic setting with the usage and hosting of CodeBeamer projects.

References

1. Bendeck, F., Goldmann, S., Holz, H., Koetting, B.: Coordinating Management Activities in Distributed Software Development Projects. In: Proceedings of the Seventh International Workshop on Enabling Technologies: Infrastructure for Collaborative Enterprises, pp. 33–38. IEEE Computer Society Press, Los Alamitos (1998)
2. Bellotti, V., Bly, S.: Walking Away from the Desktop Computer: Distributed Collaboration and Mobility in a Product Design Team. In: Proceedings of the 1996 ACM Conference on Computer Supported Cooperative Work, pp. 209–218. ACM Press, New York (1996)

3. Berkling, K., Zundel, A., Rodrigues, F., Rivera, E., Bentine, N.: Experience Report: Offshore Software Development in the Classroom. Knowledge Sharing and Collaborative Engineering. In: Proceedings of KSCE, Acta Press, Virgin Islands (2006)
4. Bloom, B.S.: Taxonomy of educational objectives. Published by Allyn and Bacon, Boston, MA. Copyright (c) 1984 by Pearson Education
5. Carmel, E., Agarwal, R.: Tactical Approaches for Alleviating Distance in Global Software Development. IEEE Software 18, 22–29 (2001)
6. Curtis, B., Krasner, H., Iscoe, N.: A Field Study of the Software Design Process for Large Systems Communications of the ACM, vol. 31, pp. 1268–1287. ACM Press, New York, USA (1988)
7. Damian, D., Chisan, J., Allen, P., Corrie, B.: Awareness Meets Requirements Management: Awareness Needs in Global Software Development. In: Proceedings of the International Workshop on Global Software Development (2003)
8. Damian, D., Zowghi, D.: Requirements Engineering challenges in multi-site software development organizations. Requirements Engineering Journal 8, 149–160 (2003)
9. Dourish, P., Bellotti, V.: Awareness and Coordination in Shared Workspaces. In: Proceedings of the 1992 ACM Conference on Computer-Supported Cooperative Work, pp. 107–114. ACM Press, New York (1992)
10. ETH: Chair of Software Engineering. Software engineering for outsourced and offshore development (30.09.2006) URL: http://se.ethz.ch/teaching/ws2005/0273/index.html
11. Froehlich, J., Dourish, P.: Unifying Artifacts and Activities in a Visual Tool for Distributed Software Development Teams. In: Proceedings of the 26th International Conference on Software Engineering, pp. 387–396 (2004)
12. Geisser, M., Hildenbrand, T.: A Method for Collaborative Requirements Elicitation and Decision-Supported Requirements Analysis. In: Ochoa, S.F., Roman, G.-C. (eds.) International Federation for Information Processing. Advanced Software Engineering: Expanding the Frontiers of Software Technology, vol. 219, pp. 108–122. Springer, Heidelberg (2006)
13. Heeks, R., Krishna, S., Nicholson, B., Sahay, S.: Synching or Sinking: Global Software Outsourcing Relationships. IEEE Software 18, 54–60 (2001)
14. Herbsleb, J.D., Grinter, R.E.: Architectures, Coordination, and Distance: Conway's Law and Beyond. IEEE Software 16, 63–70 (1999)
15. Herbsleb, J., Mockus, A.: An Empirical Study of Speed and Communication in Globally-Distributed Software Development. IEEE Transactions on Software Engineering 29, 481–494 (2003)
16. Herbsleb, J.D., Mockus, A., Finholt, T.A., Grinter, R.E.: Distance, dependencies, and delay in a global collaboration. In: Proceedings of the 2000 ACM Conference on Computer Supported Cooperative Work, pp. 319–328. ACM Press, New York (2000)
17. Herbsleb, J., Moitra, D.: Global Software Development. IEEE Software 18, 16–20 (2001)
18. Jarvenpaa, S.L., Leidner, D.E.: Communication and Trust in Global Virtual Teams. Organization Science 10, 791–815 (1999)
19. Karlsson, J., Ryan, K.: A Cost-Value Approach for Prioritizing Requirements. IEEE Software 14, 67–74 (1997)
20. Kraut, R., Streeter, L.: Coordination in Software Development. Communications of the ACM 38, 69–81 (1995)
21. Kruchten, P.: The Rational Unified Process - An Introduction. Addison-Wesley, London, UK (2003)

22. Lindvall, M., Sandahl, K.: Practical Implications of Traceability Software - Practice & Expererience, vol. 26, pp. 1161–1180. John Wiley & Sons, Inc, West Sussex, England (1996)
23. McDougall, P.: Gartner Predits Huge Increase in Offshore Outsourcing By, Informationweek (March 2005), URL (30.09.2006) (2015), http://informationweek.com/story/showArticle.jhtml?articleID=160400498
24. Perry, D.E., Siy, H.P., Votta, L.G.: Parallel Changes in Large-Scale Software Development: An Observational Case Study. In: Proceedings of the 20th International Conference on Software Engineering (1998)
25. Prikladnicki, R., Audy, J.L.N., Evaristo, R.: Global Software Development in Practice Lessons Learned. Software Process: Improvement and Practice 8, 267–281 (2003)
26. Polytechnical University of Puerto Rico (30.09.2006), (2006), URL http://www.pupr.edu/cs/cssite2.asp?id=171
27. PUPR: Caribbean Artificial Intelligence Group. Software Engineering - Part II. URL (30.09, (2006), http://ai.pupr.net/classes/softwareengineering2.htm
28. Robbins, J.: Adopting Open Source Software Engineering (OSSE) Practices by Adopting OSSE Tools. In: Feller, J., Fitzgerald, B., Hissam, S.A, Lakhani, K.R. (eds.) Free/Open Source Processes and Tools, pp. 245–264. MIT Press, Redmond, Washington (2005)
29. Rodriguez, F., Geisser, M., Berkling, K., Hildenbrand, T.: Evaluating Collaboration Platforms for Offshore Software Development Scenarios. In: Meyer, B., Joseph, M. (eds.) SEAFOOD 2007. LNCS, vol. 4716. Springer, Heidelberg (2007)
30. de Souza, C.R.B., Redmiles, D., Cheng, L., Patterson, D.J.: Sometimes You Need to See Through Walls - A Field Study of Application Programming Interfaces. In: Proceedings of the ACM International Conference on Computer-Supported Collaborative Work, ACM Press, New York (2004)
31. The Standish Group International: Extreme Chaos (2001)

Meeting the Challenge of Communication in Offshore Software Development

Henrik Munkebo Christiansen

NNIT A/S, Lottenborgvej 24, 2800 Lyngby, Denmark

Abstract. This paper will focus on what could be one of the biggest challenges in offshore development, communication. Communication is of such importance, that if it is not taken seriously in the offshore project, all the advantages of offshore development, such as access to talent, greater flexibility in access to resources and cheaper resources will be lost in the informational overhead. The paper will argue that communication channels and infrastructure are often not well established in offshore projects, which in worst cases results in project failures. The paper will focus on factors which have an impact on communication and on how to meet these challenges.

Keywords: Offshore software development, outsourcing, communication.

1 Introduction

When managers wish to integrate offshore development in their IT strategy, it is often project managers and developers who have to face the challenges and complications of integrating offshore development in their processes. Software development is already a very complicated discipline [1], and going offshore adds new factors to development, such as distance in culture, time and space. These factors will complicate development further. Team members may not only be located in different parts of the world, making different time zones a serious issue and face to face communication impossible. They may also be from completely different cultures, with different ways of expression and communication. As software development relies heavily on quick information flows, this makes communication a huge challenge in an offshore framework. Offshore software projects therefore become much more difficult to manage than collocated projects [7] and often operate at a sub-optimal performance level [8, 10].

This paper will focus on communication in offshore development and look at the different factors that have an impact on communication. The paper will investigate 'why' communication is such a huge challenge in offshore development and 'how' to meet these challenges. It condenses the lessons learned on communication from an investigation [2] of more than 22 different offshore cases. The cases are built upon interviews with managers and developers from China, India, the US, Russia and Europe, all of whom work with offshore software development (see appendix for research methodology).

B. Meyer and M. Joseph (Eds.): SEAFOOD 2007, LNCS 4716, pp. 19–26, 2007.

2 Factors That Have an Impact on Communication

This section will present factors that can have an impact on communication. Many of those factors are already present in traditional collocated forms of software development. But they tend to be amplified when offshore development is integrated in the IT strategy. To some offshore 'bystanders' [6] these factors can be a reason not to engage in offshore development. Others face these challenges boldly in order to get access to cheaper resources, talent and flexibility.

2.1 Different Time Zones

Different time zones place a burden on communicative relationships when the difference is more than 4 or 5 hours. I have found that having less than 3-4 hours of synchronous communication during a work day often makes communication hard and unnatural. Others have found that even one hour of difference in time zones can be an issue [13]. At all events, a significant difference in time zones means that communication has to be carefully planned. The time zone difference often means that the window for synchronous cooperation between onsite and offshore team members is very short. This goes especially for overseas relations, such as relationships between the US and India/China, where onsite team members in the US have to work at odd hours if they want to communicate directly with team members offshore – and vice versa. Direct communication becomes something that demands an extra effort, something one has to do either very early in the morning or very late in the evening. In consequence, direct communication is something one does only for very important things. The rest of the information is communicated via e-mail or other asynchronous communication tools. Nevertheless, the more asynchronously one has to work, the smaller is the possibility for direct feedback. For any knowledge intensive discipline, this poses a problem. Misunderstandings or questions which it would take a few minutes to sort out via direct communication, can take days to sort out via indirect communication. This means that time zones can delay the communicative process and thereby the ability to make informed decisions. It has also been suggested that difference in time zones increases coordination costs between 'shores' [11].

2.2 Different Cultures

Embracing offshore development in one's IT strategy often implies that one has to work with different cultures and organizations. Both can be very different from what one is used to and may demand adjustments in work patterns for onshore team members. Not only may the offshore organization have a different way to do things, but due to the different cultural setup the way things are communicated may also be very different. Getting used to these differences may take longer than one expects, not only for onshore team members, but also for offshore team members. However, offshore team members may be much more accustomed to work with different cultures than their onshore peers. At all events, if differences are not discussed and made clear to begin with this may cause problems later in the project.

2.3 Language

Heavy accents can be a burden for the communicative setup between onshore and offshore team members. This problem may not be so explicit when the team is together at kick-offs, etc. But on a noisy Indian telephone landline with delays and echoes, trying to communicate project critical information to a person with a very heavy accent may be a serious challenge, and one may very quickly rethink one's communicational strategy. This happened in most cases in the research material, no matter whether project members were Russians, Chinese, or Indians. In this scenario the only chance of proper communication will be simple communicational tools such as chat and e-mail. These communicative forms are widely used as many offshore developers' written language skills often are much better than their spoken language skills.

2.4 Thin Communication Channels

Heavy accents and time zones may force one to use electronic communication channels. If synchronous communication is possible and one needs quick feedback, one may prefer to use chat as the most important communicative tool. If synchronous communication is difficult or impossible one may prefer to use e-mail. Nevertheless, any step one takes from face to face communication will be a step down in communicational richness [3]. With chat one gets instant feedback but looses some of the richness of tonal expression one gets from a phone call. With e-mail one looses the chance of instant feedback and feedback circles will slow down. Every time one waits for feedback via e-mail, one delays the project and slows down the learning process in the project. Fast feedback cycles are of pivot importance for the project members' ability to learn. Compare this to the difference between learning from a teacher in a class room and learning from a teacher living 10 time zones away by e-mail exchange.

2.5 Different Platforms

Using different platforms in the project, whether it is operation systems, e-mail programs, developer tools or other important tools in the project, often leads to an incompatibility, which causes problems that could easily have been avoided by standardizing the IT infrastructure in the project. An unstandardized IT infrastructure can lead to smaller problems such as e-mails shown in different ways on- and offshore, or bigger problems such as programs that compile offshore, but do not compile onshore. Unstandardized platforms can make it very hard and time consuming to fix even smaller problems.

3   How to Meet the Challenges of Communication

This section describes how developers and managers in the research material have tried to meet the challenges of communication. Many, new to offshore development, have the naive belief that human interaction can be replaced by e-mail exchange and other internet-based communication tools. Research [4, 9] shows that these communication tools can be helpful, but that they cannot replace face to face interaction The following contains the lessons learned on how to improve communication in offshore projects.

3.1 Put Stress on Synchronous Communication

The faster the feedback cycles are in projects, the faster the project can learn and advance. If project communication is based on exchange of e-mails between dislocated team members, communication will suffer, misunderstandings will occur and the project will slow down. Putting stress on synchronous communication will mean much faster feedback cycles and much improved project understanding. Synchronous communication can take many forms, but the most common are chat, telephone and face to face communication. Most often, face to face communication is impossible, due to the added distance. Traveling between 'shores' can be expensive [10] and inconvenient for many [9]. However, in 'nearshore' projects where offshore members are no more than 2 or 3 hours away by plane, face to face meetings is an easier and important option to offshore development. Face to face communication is an informational very rich form of communication. The transfer of information is much higher than via other communicational means. If face to face communication is not possible, the telephone is an underestimated tool counteracting slow communication. Videoconferences are another option for synchronous communication. However, many people are reluctant to use this tool as they feel uncomfortable with it and prefer to use the phone or chat. Due to language problems (heavy accents etc.) many people prefer chat to telephone although chat by many is considered one of the least informative forms of synchronous communication [3].

Personal barriers such as shyness can also cause delays in the communication. Instead of making a telephone call, team members who do not know their recipient very well often feel more comfortable sending an e-mail. Such barriers are resolved when personal relationships cross 'shores' are built. Information flows faster and easier in a friendly atmosphere where one can talk informally. Therefore, bringing people together for kick-offs or conferences is an important step in improving communication between team members.

As we have learned from the previous section, synchronous communication is also impeded by time zones. If rich communicative feedback cycles are important for project success, then people have to change their work routines and work odd hours. This goes for both on- and offshore team members. The alternative is to place one's offshore center in a nearby time zone. For US companies, this could be Mexico or the Caribbean nations. For Europeans, it could be Russia or the Ukraine [12]. The alternative to odd work hours or 'near shore' development centers, is transferring knowledge via e-mail and documents. For knowledge intensive and complex projects this form of asynchronous communication means a slowdown in project progress.

3.2 Adapt to and Understand Other Cultures

Communication is a very important part of any culture, whether organizational or national. In large organizations with team members spread on different locations, e-mail may already be the main communicative tool. In this kind of communicative culture it may not be difficult to adapt to the traditional offshore scenario. Communication is already slow and feedback circles delayed. However, when a well-tuned organization with a high flow of information among collocated team members engages in offshore development, it is important to make sure that offshore members can absorb the same amount of information as onshore members can. Very often this is not possible, not because of the offshore members, but because of the communication channels used. If an onshore organization starts working with an offshore organization with a different communicative emphasis, cooperation will be made difficult. Therefore, it is very important in initial phases of cooperation to make sure that both organizations implement the same communication strategies.

Great differences in national culture may either disperse or connect on- and offshore members. Often, team members are enriched by working together and learn from each other. But different ways of solving things or working may also come as a bitter surprise. This can even be the case for cultures that are geographically close. If these differences are not either embraced or aligned, they can end up becoming an irritating and frustrating part of working in offshore projects, especially if the project members have a heavy work burden.

A way to embrace cultural differences is to celebrate the diversity. One example is developers in Russia having Swiss evenings where they made cheese fondues. Others had maps or flags in their offices representing the country of their customer [2]. Creating an open mind towards the people one is working with is vital for a good relationship between on- and offshore developers. If one can remove the idea of an on- and offshore team and work as one global team, barriers are limited and communication will certainly become easier.

Organizational differences may also turn out to impede offshore projects. Often problems will arise in the beginning of the project, delaying the offshore project in the long term. Some companies have taken the consequence of this and made their own offshore development center. These companies had less problems communicating as both their formal and informal communication channels were much more aligned, compared to projects where different organizations worked together. Working in the same organization, on- or offshore, gives one the same organizational pivot from where communication can be accelerated. This has also been indicated by other research [6].

3.3 Put Emphasis on Spoken Language Skills

The decision to bring a project offshore is often made from economical considerations. Onshore management simply expects to save money on their projects. However, the money saved on using developers offshore without proper language skills is lost on the communicational overhead. If one wishes to succeed with this strategy one has to make sure that the informational hubs in the project (often the project manager or the lead developer) have very good spoken language skills. To counteract this problem some companies offer English courses to team members [2, 12].

3.4 Rotate People Between Shores

In a traditional onshore-offshore relationship, the customer is onshore and the developers offshore. Often this setup is improved by bringing offshore members onshore and onshore members offshore. These persons are called straddlers [4], ambassadors [5], enablers [2] or cultural liaisons [12]. The research material show that the onshore organization often did not provide sufficient resources onshore ready to answer the questions of the offshore developers and help them move on. Most often the onshore organizations were the bottleneck in the organizational setup. Therefore, it helps the project having someone who can easily navigate in the onshore organization, making sure that things are happening and that the right persons are contacted. Team members traveling offshore with business knowledge can be a tremendous help for offshore developers. They can simply boost and accelerate the offshore developers' ability to understand what the customer wants. It has been indicated that for every 20 offshore team members, there should be one onshore member offshore [10]. If this is not possible, having an offshore developer onshore absorbing the business understanding and transferring it offshore is also helpful. Generally, it is much easier for offshore developers to ask questions directly to one of their own team members onshore. This person can then find the answers face to face with the customer. Every time the onsite offshore developer solves a problem for the offshore team, 2 or 4 hours are easily saved compared to when the offshore team has to solve the problem by themselves.

3.5 Use Artefacts Properly

All projects have some artefacts around which the projects evolve, in plan-driven projects it is often the requirement specification, in agile project it is often the code base or the user stories. Whatever methodology one chooses for the projects, it is important to continuously talk about the artefacts in the projects. These are the objects around which the learning processes in the project evolve. Review documents, prototypes, screen shots, test documents, whatever can help the project move forward is positive. These artefacts serve as tools which give birth to understanding in the project.

3.6 Aligning IT Infrastructure

Communication channels are often supported electronically. A lot of problems are avoided if both teams, onshore as well as offshore, work on the same platforms. This applies to all levels of communication, from operation system, e-mail program to compiler. The more standardized the IT infrastructure is, the less is the hassle with incompatibility and errors due to differences in IT infrastructure. This is often discovered too late in the project. Once standardized, it is also important to make sure that IT infrastructure works properly on both shores. If one chooses a strategy relying on interaction via telephone, it is extremely important that one makes sure that the phones really work. A lot of cases from the research material [2] report non- or malfunctioning telephone lines. Some solved this by using their own telecommunication infrastructure. Most used chat instead.

3.7 Use Requirement Specifications with Care

Very often it is believed that projects can be specified and then sent offshore. This is a serious misunderstanding which can end up in delays and, in worst cases, project failure. Requirement specifications contain a huge amount of implicit knowledge. And it often takes time to make implicit knowledge explicit and to transfer it. One onshore developer explained that specifying requirement to a level that was useable for offshore developers, was so time consuming that he could develop the software himself within the same timeframe [2]. This means that one should be ready to invest time and money in transferring the implicit knowledge. Once this knowledge is transferred requirement specifications will be easier to understand for offshore developers. Even for small well-specified projects it can take more time to transfer this knowledge than one expects. The transfer of implicit knowledge can be even more difficult in projects with a high attrition rate. In such projects it can be very hard to keep a critical mass.

4 Conclusion

When distance in time, space and culture is present between team members in software development, communication starts to suffer tremendously. This paper has presented factors which can have an impact on communication. Ways to meet these factors and ways to improve the communication have been suggested. Awareness of this challenge and how to meet it will help team members on both 'shores'.

If communication channels are used wrongly project delays and, in worst cases, failures will happen. It takes time to communicate the details and implicit knowledge which is an integrated part of software development. As the relationship between 'shores' develops and more project knowledge is sent offshore, more complex projects can be carried out. For many organizations it has taken years to build up knowledge and communicational forms in order to handle semi-complex projects.

With team members dispersed, software development will meet more challenges than with traditional collocated members. The research material show that companies which emphasized communication in their software processes ran into fewer problems, whether technical or organizational. Good communication in offshore projects is not without a cost, however. Software teams may have to work at odd hours. Team members may have to travel much more than they would in a traditional software project. 'Kick-offs' gathering all project members from both shores can be very expensive. Standardizing IT infrastructure is not free of cost either. All these factors do cost, but they also lower the informational overhead normally found in traditional offshore development. But offshore development is not a silver bullet. Nevertheless, if one wishes to take advantage of offshoring in ones IT strategy, one has to integrate good communication practices in the offshore projects and use them with care and attention.

References

1. Brooks, F.P.: The mythical man-month: essays on software engineering. Addison-Wesley Longman, anniversary edition (1995)
2. Christiansen, H.M.: An Empirical Study on the Challenges of Offshore Software Development - their resolution and some agile suggestions. MSc Thesis, IT University of Copenhagen (2005)
3. Cockburn, A.: Agile Software Development. Addison-Wesley, Boston (2002)
4. Heeks, R., Krishna, S., Nicholson, B., Sahay, S.: Synching or sinking: Trajectories and strategies in global software outsourcing relationships. Working Paper Series, vol. 9 (July 2000)
5. Martin Fowler. Using an Agile Software Process with Offshore Development. ThoughtWorks (accessed July 26, 2004) (2004),
   http://www.martinfowler.com/articles/agileOffshore.html
6. Carmel, E., Agarwal, R.: The Maturation of Offshore Sourcing of Technology Works, MIS Quarterly Executive, vol. 1(2) (June 2002)
7. Carmel, E.: Global Software Teams: Collaborating Across Borders and Time Zones. Prentice Hall PTR, Upper Saddle River, NJ (1999)
8. La Ferla, B.: Offshore Outsourcing: Out of Favour? IEEE Review (March 2004)
9. Kobitzsch, W., Rombach, D., Feldmann, R.L.: Outsourcing in India. IEEE Software (March/April 2001)
10. Laplante, P.A., Costello, T., Singh, P., Bindiganavile, S., Landon, M.: The Who, What, Why, Where, and When of Outsourcing, January | February 2004 IT Pro. IEEE Computer Society Press, Los Alamitos
11. Espinosa, J.A., Carmel, E.: Modeling Coordination Costs Due to Time Separation in Global Software Teams. In: International Workshop on Global Software Development, part of the International Conference on Software Engineering Work in Portland, Oregon, USA (May 2003)
12. Carmel, E., Agarwal, R.: Tactical Approaches for Alleviating Distance in Global Software Development. IEEE Software (March/ April 2001)
13. Herbsleb, J.D., Grinter, R.E.: Splitting the Organization and Integrating the Code: Conway's Law Revisited. In: Proc. 21st Int'l Conf. Software Engineering (ICSE 1999), pp. 85–95. ACM Press, New York (1999)

Appendix: Research Methodology

The approach for this research was primarily qualitative, as the project progressed more and more cases were added to the research material. In the end of the project, the number of cases added a quantitative aspect to the research methodology. The interviews were recorded and written down and reviewed with participants in order to avoid misunderstanding. The interviews were conducted iteratively. As the number of interviews progressed new questions arose, which meant that managers and developers were interviewed several times in order to clarify new angles on offshore development. Most interviews were conducted face to face in Russia or Europe. If face to face interviews were not possible they were conducted by phone. The cases varied in size and form. Some projects were smaller 20,000 US$ projects, while other were projects of 40 million US$.

Testable Requirements for Offshore Outsourcing

Jean-Pierre Corriveau

Carleton University, Canada
jeanpier@scs.carleton.ca

Abstract. Given that software offshore outsourcing is a business relationship, we assume that a contract is required in order to define what
services are requested from a contracted entity and how these services are
to be delivered to the satisfaction of the contractor. We first argue that,
at the heart of the quality assurance facets of such a contract, we must
find a single testable model of both the functional and non-functional
requirements of the system to be delivered. We present the key properties that such a model must exhibit: testability, executability, scenarios
as grammars of responsibilities, and support for abstraction. We then
observe that, typically, existing approaches to requirements engineering
do not offer such characteristics. We conclude by briefly discussing a prototype conformance testing environment that supports these properties.

1 Introduction

In the context of software offshore outsourcing, Meyer [1] observes that "quality
is indeed the central issue". It is commonly accepted in software engineering
that 'quality' "is the degree to which a system meets specified requirements" [2].
Furthermore, it is widely acknowledged that requirements of software systems
include both functional and non-functional aspects. Quality requires a comprehensive approach to validation and verification (hereafter V & V) (see [2]), that
is, one that addresses both functional and non-functional requirements. Investigating such an approach to V & V in the context of software offshore outsourcing
constitutes the central theme of this paper. For software development, outsourcing is a business relationship whereby one organization (hereafter the contractor)
contracts another (hereafter the contracted) for the realization of one or more
phases of the software development lifecycle. What exactly is outsourced can
vary considerably [3]: some contractors may delegate the complete development
effort, whereas others may hand over a more or less detailed design and request
its completion and implementation. Here, we are not concerned with process and
method but with the semantic vehicle used to capture quality and its V & V.
Given outsourcing is a business relationship, we assume a *contract* is required
in order to define a) what services are requested from the contracted entity and
b) how these services are to be delivered to the satisfaction of the contractor.
Because outsourcing is often motivated by cost reduction considerations, eventual legal battles are obviously to be avoided. This is particularly important in
the context of offshore outsourcing where internationalization can quickly and

B. Meyer and M. Joseph (Eds.): SEAFOOD 2007, LNCS 4716, pp. 27–43, 2007.

dramatically complicate such battles. Consequently, a software offshore outsourcing contract will clearly gain in including, among its quality assurance facets, the specification of a systematic approach to the objective V & V (and more specifically to the conformance testing [2]) of the functional and non-functional requirements of the system to be delivered (hereafter STBD). This approach must rest, first and foremost, on the ability of the relevant parties to capture the requirements of the STBD in a model that not only acts as a communication vehicle between these parties, but also as a means to determine conformance of an implementation to its requirements. The use of the singular when referring to the desired model is important. In the context of software offshore outsourcing, regardless of what models are used by the contracted company during the development lifecycle, we believe it is essential that a single model be used for capturing requirements. This belief proceeds from the fact that it is this model that defines quality, as well as how to verify it. In our opinion, introducing a multitude of models for the purpose of capturing requirements in fact is likely to open a corresponding multitude of doors for misinterpretation. Let us briefly elaborate. Before being tested for conformance, requirements must be agreed upon, which entails the contractor and the contracted must use some communication vehicle to discuss and ultimately document the requirements that are relevant to the verification of their common business contract. Minimally, what is at issue is the *conformance* of an implementation submitted by the contracted to the requirements etched in a contract. There are some disadvantages to using several models for this task of conformance testing:

- With respect to communication: the more models, the more semantics and consequently the likelier the occurrence of misinterpretations and misunderstandings. Also, the more models, the more syntax and semantics to learn (by both parties) and thus the higher the costs associated with learning curves.
- With respect to conformance testing: the more models, the likelier the task gets more complicated (as Binder [2] explains at length in his discussion of the testability of UML models).

More specifically, the more models, the more complicated it is

1. to verify that these models are semantically consistent between themselves, and
2. to semantically combine them to extract tests.

We believe advocating a single model for requirements capture and conformance testing is desirable in the context of offshore outsourcing. We elaborate on this standpoint throughout the next section in which we explore the key properties we require of this model.

2 Properties for Conformance Testing

There exists a large body of work on requirements engineering (e.g., see [4]), an activity that Meyer [1] sees as central to the success of software offshore outsourcing. Our goal in this section is to motivate the essential properties we require of the semantic vehicle used to capture and test the requirements of the STBD.

2.1 Strong Testability

Most importantly, we contend that requirements must be captured in what Binder [2] calls a *testable* model, that is, a model from which tests (intuitively, as queries on the structure and behavior of a system) can be extracted in a systematic way. If this is not the case, then we necessarily suffer from the so-called 'correspondence problem': we cannot rule out that a semantic gap (that is a lack of traceability [2,5]) may exist between the specification of the requirements of the STBD and the actual tests used for the conformance testing. In other words, if tests are not traceable back to requirements, then we cannot be certain that these tests *do* address the requirements of the STBD. Conversely, we want to adopt a strong interpretation of testability as the automated generation of tests from a model. 'Weaker' definitions do not demand this automation of the production of tests. Our motivation is obvious: if the production of tests is automated from a model of the requirements of the STBD, then such tests are expected to systematically correspond to this model, which is part of the legal document between the contractor and the contracted. Put another way, automated generation of tests from model considerably reduces the risk of a lack of correspondence between requirements and tests. Similarly, automatic generation of code from models, which lies at the heart of a model-driven approach [6] to software development, reduces considerably the possibility of a lack of correspondence between models and implementation. Please note however that the correspondence problem never completely disappears unless the correctness of this generation process can be demonstrated.

2.2 Executable Tests

Demanding that the production of tests from a requirements model be automated is not sufficient: If such generated tests are disconnected from an actual implementation, then we still have a *traceability* problem. In other words, it is still possible that the actual tests to be run against the implementation do not correspond to the tests produced from the requirements model. Consequently, we espouse an even stronger interpretation of testability, one that insists that tests obtained from a requirements model be *executable*. This standpoint has two important repercussions: First, the automated generation of executable tests from a single requirements model provides, in our opinion, a mechanism for the *objective* assessment of the conformance of an implementation against such requirements. Objectivity here stems directly from the ability to execute the generated tests. In other words, success or failure of a test is not a rhetorical exercise open to debate. Instead it consists in the outcome of the execution of a test on the target implementation. From a legal viewpoint this is important: both contractor and contracted will thus share a straightforward way of establishing conformance. Second, the previous point entails the existence of a conformance testing environment (hereafter CTE) capable of inputting the tests generated from a requirements model, executing them on the target implementation, and reporting on their outcome. At this point in the paper, what matters is that the contractor and the contracted must agree to both use such a CTE to capture requirements and to carry out and report on conformance testing.

2.3   Responsibilities and Scenarios

We must now address a concrete difficulty with the notion of executable tests: As previously mentioned, we are not committing to any particular process or method. More specifically, we do not presuppose how much or how little the contractor is involved in the development of the required implementation. Minimally, however, this contractor must approve the requirements captured in the testable model of a contract and then eventually must scrutinize the evaluation report produced by the CTE from the execution of tests obtained from this model. A question emerges from such an approach: how can a requirements model, which is to be specified completely independently of any implementation, generate executable tests? We suggest that a solution lies in the separation of the specification of tests from their context of use. Let us consider these two notions. Tests are to be produced from a testable model and are indeed to be independent of any implementation. They ought to be thought of as instructions for the CTE. Intuitively, as previously mentioned, tests can be thought of as queries on the structure and on the behavior of an implementation. In order to dissociate them from this implementation, tests, and their originating testable model, are taken to refer to the *responsibilities* of an implementation. Responsibilities act as placeholders for procedures of an actual implementation. For example, a testable requirements model for a sequential container [7] may refer to the responsibility *insertFirst*. A dynamic test [2], that is, a test on the behavior of this responsibility could then define pre- and post-conditions [8,9] for *insertFirst* (ensuring respectively that the container is not full before insertion, and that, after insertion, the size has been increased by 1). The precondition, for example, could be written as: *!is-Full*. The responsibilities *insertFirst* and *isFull* being placeholders, they would need to be subsequently bound to actual procedures of the implementation. The specifics of this binding task (e.g., binding to procedures with names different than those of the responsibilities) depend on the specifics of the testable model and of the CTE. They are not relevant here. At this point of our presentation, what matters is the idea of separating responsibilities from actual procedures. The binding of a responsibility to an actual procedure constitutes one aspect of a solution allowing tests to become executable. We also require what we call a context of use for each test. Continuing with our sequential container example, it is obvious that there is limited gain in testing the procedure corresponding to *insertFirst* in isolation, that is, in a minimal context of use. The conformance testing of the requirements of a STBD against an implementation dictates that responsibilities be tested in context, that is, as part of *scenarios* [10]. Indeed, scenarios are often taken as the semantic foundation for the modeling of the requirements of a system (e.g., [10,11]). Without committing to any particular formalism for the representation and exact semantics of scenarios, we can still adopt the position that scenarios are to be conceptualized as temporal flows of responsibilities [Ibid.]. Put another way, scenarios aim at capturing *paths of execution* each scenario corresponding to a multitude of paths of execution. And each such path constitutes one specific context of execution. In our simple example, it is possible to describe the use of a container via a scenario that captures the following flow of responsibilities:

1. the container is allocated and possibly initialized
2. an initial insertion occurs
3. a series of insertions, deletions and other operations (e.g., display) occur
4. the container is possibly deallocated.

A specific path through this scenario would explicit an exact sequence of responsibilities, that is, an exact sequence of operations on a container. Tests (e.g., the pre- and post-conditions mentioned earlier) would be associated with the responsibilities of a path. In order for such tests to be executable:

– Clearly, responsibilities would have to be eventually bound to actual procedures (as previously suggested) since procedures, not responsibilities, are executable.
– A *path generation and selection* algorithm would be required to generate (out of each originating scenario) a set of specific paths to use as contexts of use, and then select which ones to run. This task involves selection because it is not usually the case that we want to run all the possible paths out of a scenario. In fact, typically, applying the technique of equivalence partitioning [2], we will want to avoid selecting paths that, from a testing viewpoint, are equivalent.
– After eventually binding responsibilities to actual procedures, a path will consist of a specific sequence of actual procedures. In order for these procedures to be executable, each actual procedure of each path will need to be supplied with the parameters it requires. In particular, each procedure will need to obtain its receiver, that is, the instance on which it executes. We refer to this task as *path instantiation.* (Typically, such a task is greatly complicated by the fact that the receiver of each procedure may have to be put in a specific state [2].)

For example, we can obtain the path {*allocate, insertFirst, insertFirst, display, insertLast, deleteFirst, deleteLast, deallocate*} out of the previous scenario. Once each of these responsibilities would have been bound to a corresponding actual procedure (e.g., *insertFirst* could be bound to pushFront()), it would then be necessary to associate to each such procedure the parameters it requires (a cumbersome task faced by any tester using scenarios). Then, and only then, would the CTE be able to run the tests associated with the procedures of this path. In our simplistic example, all actual procedures would be performed on a same instance of a container. Thus, all the assertions associated with these procedures would pertain to the same instance. Generally, however, a path will involve procedures pertaining to several instances of different classes. Consequently, the task of path instantiation (or equivalently path sensitization [2]) will be obviously more difficult than in the case of a single instance. For example, consider customers waiting in distinct queues at a grocery store. Furthermore, assume such queues are monitored by a manager who decides when to open or close them. Here, there is a multitude of instances, some belonging to the same class (e.g., customers, queues), some being singletons (e.g., the manager). As there may be different types of queues (e.g., 'express' versus 'normal'), it may also be necessary to associate a number of items-to-purchase with each customer (see below). Does the manager contain a set of queues or is it each queue that has a pointer to this manager? Does each customer need to contain a reference to the queue that contains it? The point to be grasped is that path instantiation is intimately tied to an actual implementation and thus will very likely be carried out by the contracted company. In the same vein, we remark that, once responsibilities are bound to actual procedures, a path comes to constitute in itself a dynamic test: it is an expected sequence of procedure calls to be matched by actual behavior of the system. Consequently, a CTE must be able to perform such matches. However, intuitively, the feasibility of such matches is inversely proportional to the semantic richness of the formalism used to capture scenarios. For example, the use of an *abort* in a use case map[1], or of a *coregion* in a message sequence chart[2] offers significant semantic advantages, but also considerably complicates the task of matching the scenario in which such operators appear to an actual sequence of procedure calls. Understanding how complex path instantiation and path matching can be leads to a fundamental issue on which the contractor and the contracted must agree, namely, how much coverage [2] of the testable model is required. We now briefly elaborate on this topic.

2.4   Coverage

In practice, it is commonly accepted that testing may be an endless task [2]. In particular, a scenario-based approach to testing generally suffers from having a path generation/selection algorithm that possibly generates an intractable number of paths. Also, both path instantiation and path matching may be extremely difficult to achieve depending on the complexity of the semantics of the scenarios. Consequently, it is unrealistic to demand that all possible paths from all scenarios be selected, instantiated, tested and matched [2]. Instead, the contractor and contracted must agree and document in the contract how much *coverage* will be required. Let us elaborate. First, both parties must agree on a path generation and selection algorithm. Given that each selected path will have to be instantiated, matched and reported on (in particular, with respect to the tests associated

---

[1] Use Case Maps,
   http://jucmnav.softwareengineering.ca/twiki/bin/view/UCM/WebHom
[2] Message Sequence Charts, www.sdl-forum.org/MSC/

with the procedures of this path), this decision is crucial in defining how much actual testing will need to be performed. The key observation is that paths are generated from scenarios, and scenarios are in the testable model. Thus, coverage (as a set of selected paths) can be enshrined in the contract. Furthermore, two alternatives exist for path selection. Option 1: both parties agree to restrict testing to a specific set of scenarios and/or paths selected jointly according to a common documented (albeit somewhat subjective) criterion. Or, option 2, both parties instead adopt some commonly-accepted selection algorithm, in which case the selected paths will be systematically derived from the testable model (as opposed to being selected possibly subjectively by the two parties). Binder [2] presents in detail a hierarchy of coverage strategies for state machines and observes: the more coverage, clearly the more work required for path instantiation. More importantly, we remark that an algorithmic approach to selection and coverage (i.e., option 2) may be more objective than option 1 but it is knowledge-free. In particular, such algorithms typically minimize equivalence partitioning (which requires a deep understanding of the problem addressed by the STBD). Consequently, despite a possible loss of objectivity and systematicity, it is likely the contractor and the contracted will draw on their common understanding of the requirements of the STBD (as documented in the testable model) to select a set of paths to test (which also ends up in the contract). Second, because path instantiation is intimately linked to an actual implementation, assessing how much work is involved in the instantiation of a set of selected paths can likely only be performed by the contracted once an implementation is available. Therefore both parties must be ready to deal with the possibility that the contracted reports to the contractor that the set of selected paths to test requires too much effort in terms of path instantiation (with respect to a budget and/or timetable). Third, noticing Binder's insistence that a testable model be complete [2], that is essentially, that it document the handling of both valid and invalid paths, we stress that the complexity of path selection and of path instantiation indeed increases (possibly dramatically) when one does not limit these tasks to only valid paths. Ultimately, it is up to contractor and contracted to agree on how many invalid paths must be tested. (It is possible however that the use of assertions on scenarios may reduce the number of invalid paths to consider. This topic lies beyond the scope of this paper.) Fourth, as is widely the case in the software industry when developing large software systems (such as the millions of line of code of a telephone switch), achieving 100% success for a very large number of scenarios and tests is likely unrealistic. (Here 'success' consists in having actual behavior match expected one, as well as having the assertions of the relevant responsibilities of the selected paths be satisfied). Consequently, the parties may agree that only a certain percentage of the tests have to succeed at the time of 'official' V & V. In such a situation, it becomes crucial for both parties to agree on a) the prioritization (through subjective selection) of scenarios, b) the use of a problem tracking system, and c) the legal ramifications of working with a system that contains known errors and defects. Point a) emphasizes that ultimately the concept of *importance*, central to Boehm's [12] notion of convergence in incremental software development, directly pertains to V & V. In other words, parties involved in conformance testing must acknowledge that deep understanding of the 'domain' (or 'problem space') is required in order to carry out such prioritization (which also likely draws on equivalence partitioning). Point c) stems from point b): once parties accept that not all tests will be successful (or even attempted) by the agreed date for the delivery of the STBD, then parties must decide on the interpretation of this first V & V milestone. More precisely, the question is two-fold: i) what will constitute satisfaction of the legal obligations of the outsourcing contract and ii) will establishing contractual satisfaction be a one-time or an on-going process. Clearly, the latter option complicates the legal language to be used in the outsourcing contract. Finally, it must be emphasized once more that despite the numerous challenges presented by path generation, selection, instantiation and testing, the existence of a testable model ensures that path generation/selection, which is based on the scenarios of this model, need not wait for the implementation to become available in order to start.

2.5   Modeling a Continuum of Levels of Abstraction

Pinpointing how much coverage is to be achieved (at a particular point in time) does not solely depend on path generation/selection/instantiation from scenarios. In particular, how abstract a scenario is or is not will indirectly affect coverage. To illustrate this, let us consider an elevator system (often studied as, for example, in chapter 18 of Gomaa's book [13]). Gomaa suggests two highly abstract scenarios for this system (in the form of use cases [11]):

– user requests elevator
– user selects destination

If the elevator system is viewed as a black-box, then the paths obtainable from each of these two scenarios number few and are extremely simple (because the scenarios cannot refer to events internal to the system). Consequently, apparent complete coverage can be envisioned. Even if the system is broken down in a few objects, the possible paths for each scenario consist of a few messages (see figures 18.5 and 18.6 in [13]) and coverage remains unproblematic. However, as detailed design unfolds, more objects and more interactions are introduced, leading to far more complexity (see figures 18.34 and 18.35 in [13]!). In particular, the number of paths that can be generated from the scenarios increases dramatically (especially in light of concurrency)! It follows that supplying binding and path instantiation information becomes more work. Thus parties may likely agree to decrease coverage. Clearly, as previously mentioned, as there are more possible paths, there is less chance to achieve 'close-to-complete' coverage of this space of paths. Intuitively, coverage appears to be inversely proportional to the number of possible paths. The observation we want to emphasize is that the number of paths possibly generated from the scenarios of a testable model is directly correlated to the level of abstraction of this model. And because this level of abstraction typically evolves over time, it has repercussions on the verification of quality in the context of an offshore outsourcing contract. Let us elaborate. First, we remark that both scenarios and responsibilities are typically subject to refinements over the course of developing a software system [11,14]. More precisely, as a system is decomposed into finer-grained responsibilities, these responsibilities are associated to i) finer-grained scenarios (which capture more complex interactions) and to ii) fine-grained components (where a component, or class, is viewed first and foremost as a cluster of responsibilities [11]). The elevator case study of Gomaa [13], for example, constitutes an excellent full-length (approximately 70 page) illustration of this process of refinement. Second, and most relevant to this paper, the refinement of scenarios and responsibilities enables the refinement of tests captured in a testable model. Consider, for example, Gomaa's previously mentioned 'User requests elevator' scenario. If the elevator system is viewed as a black box, with only up/down 'floor buttons' (switched on or off) as its interface, then dynamic tests will be mostly limited to checking whether such buttons are correctly switched on or off at the correct time, and whether an elevator eventually services the requested floor. The point to be grasped is that such tests will be quite 'coarse-grained'. But as soon as the system is decomposed into the four components suggested by Gomaa (namely a Manager, a Control, a Scheduler, and a Plan & Monitor object), new responsibilities will appear and require testing. For example, in this scenario, the Scheduler is responsible for serializing floor requests, choosing an elevator to service each floor request, informing this elevator of this assignment, and obtaining a commitment from this chosen elevator. As this scenario is instantiated into specific paths (e.g., passenger X on floor 5 requests an elevator to go up), obviously the dynamic test corresponding to this path will be more complex to match if it involves these four finer grained components than if it only involves buttons and a single ElevatorSystem component. Also, the previously mentioned coarse grained tests associated with a single ElevatorSystem component will be replaced by a set of tests associated with each of the four finer-grained components. For example, for the Scheduler, a pre-condition to receiving a new floor request could test that the queue used to serialize such asynchronous requests is not full. The point to be grasped is that, as the conceptualization of a system is refined, so can its corresponding testable model. And this is directly relevant to the objective verification of the quality of an outsourced system. Parties must acknowledge that the higher the level of abstraction in scenarios, the more difficult path generation/selection is (due to the excessive abstraction of these paths).If, despite this observation, a contractor chooses to finalize a contract based only on high-level scenarios, then the contractor should have the contract require that the detailed scenarios as well as the set of actual paths selected by the contracted for testing be available for scrutinizing by the contractor. In other words, the contractor should insist on traceability information that allows this contractor to observe how much the system has been tested. (But this likely entails extra work for the contracted and may, in practice, not be that useful: despite traceability, the contractor may simply be overwhelmed by design details and not be in a position to evaluate how much coverage has in fact been done.) Otherwise, the contractor has to trust that the contracted will sufficiently test the system. In our opinion, this does open the door to legal battles. Conversely, the contractor may insist on the availability of detailed understandable scenarios before formalizing path selection into a contract. This is also problematic inasmuch as such an approach delays the finalization of a contract until considerable effort has been invested by the contracted in refining the initial requirements (and by the contractor in understanding these details). Ultimately, the issue of abstraction epitomizes the legal difficulties in dealing with deliverables whose verification (as well as themselves) evolves over time. It appears that contractor and contracted are faced with a tradeoff: either the contractor has the contract refer to a highly abstract testable model, in which case objective V & V is hard to formally define, or the contracted must invest in refining requirements without knowing how much testing will be requested. In our opinion, the solution to this tradeoff lies in thinking of abstraction as a continuum. As in most legal matters, a workable solution does not lie at the extreme but more towards the middle. In other words, the contractor and the contracted must reach a compromise as to when it is opportune to 'freeze' a testable model into a contract. Two observations help in deciding on the timeliness of this decision. First, Briand [14] observes that in the case of assertions (e.g., pre- and post-conditions), there is indeed generally a point after which the investment in refining such assertions becomes hard to justify. Second, we believe that observations like the one of Briand proceed from a more fundamental reality that is often forgotten: a testable model should not be conceived to test a specific system but rather a space of solutions. Adopting the terminology of system family engineering [15], we want a testable model to define a domain, that is, a set of requirements that will hold across a space of possible solution systems. We must never illusion ourselves in thinking that, given a set of requirements, only one correct and optimal system can be built. Consequently, it is crucial that a testable model capture variability across a space of solutions. And over-refinement eliminates variability. Thus, on the continuum of abstraction associated with the development of a software system, a testable model becomes too refined to be included in an outsourcing contract when it fails to capture variability across a space of solutions and instead becomes specific to a particular solution.

3   On Existing Modeling Approaches

We now briefly consider how some of the currently dominant approaches to software development accommodate the issues raised in the previous section. To do so, let us start by recapitulating these issues. We have argued for:

1. unified semantics for functional and non-functional requirements,
2. testability of a requirements model,
3. executability of tests,
4. semantics rooted in the notions of responsibilities and scenarios,
5. formalization of test coverage, and
6. abstraction of the testable model over a space of possible implementations.

It is important to understand that all of the previous discussion rests on the assumption that the contactor and the contracted will agree to formalize the

V & V of the quality of the STBD in a *contract*. In addressing current approaches to software development, we choose to first consider one that contests the need for contracts altogether. Indeed, several so-called *agile* [16] methods argue that contractual disputes may be avoided by placing much less emphasis on contracts per se and instead promoting intensive interactions between customer and supplier. Such a viewpoint is at the heart of the "Manifesto for Agile Software Development"[3] and its corresponding methods (e.g., [17]). Ultimately, the business relationship can take the form of a risk-sharing endeavor, that is, of some sort of commercial alliance. Regardless of the advantages and disadvantages of such approaches, let us simply observe that they do not readily fit, in our opinion, the context of offshore outsourcing. The reasons are quite obvious:

- Intensive intercontinental communications across different time zones may entail logistical problems (and their associated costs), and potentially, by sheer accumulation, communication costs.
- Human communication is inherently imprecise, if not ambiguous, and thus subject to misinterpretation (as proved by the existence of lawyers and judges). As Meyer [1] notices, this problem can be compounded by cultural differences.

The point to be grasped is that offshore outsourcing and risk-sharing alliances constitute, in our opinion, two fundamentally distinct types of business relationship. As the word suggests, outsourcing is about off-loading work, not highly interactive risk-sharing, quite on the contrary. Also, agile literature first and foremost focuses on process and method, not on testability. Consequently, agile development ultimately does not seem very relevant to a discussion of quality assurance for offshore outsourcing. However it does lead us to consider code-oriented methods, quite amenable to the agile philosophy of development, and still frequently used in industry. Stating the obvious, code per se is not a model. But, following the philosophy of test-driven development (TDD) [17], could we not express requirements as test procedures whose body needs to be filled in subsequently? The short answer is no. The reason is simple: reading carefully a TDD example, one quickly realizes that there is no testable model in it. More precisely, there is code to test code, nothing else; in particular, no abstraction, no coverage, no testability (inasmuch as there is no systematic production of tests from a model). In fact, there is an upfront commitment to avoiding models [Ibid.] and instead relying on constant evolution of code (including of the test procedures!). Put another way, the requirements are very indirectly (if at all) captured in test procedures highly coupled to the code they purport to test, both constantly changing. (This is particularly true for non-functional requirements: they are typically ignored.) Also, contrary to approaches relying on refinement of abstract models, in TDD there is no guarantee of incremental convergence [12] for there is no explicit requirements capture. Consequently, such an approach appears to be completely inappropriate in the context of outsourcing: as Meyer [1] observes, offshore outsourcing requires more engineering, not less. Code-oriented

---

[3] Manifesto for Agile Software Development, www.agilemanifesto.org

software development approaches do warn us against 'diagrammatic over-design' [16]: that is, that models can introduce notions quite distant from implementation, if at all realizable. We must keep this in mind as we now turn to requirement modeling approaches relying on comprehensive notations such as UML 1.x [18] and UML 2.0 [19]. Consider, for example, the specification for a software radio[4] (which, in essence, has been outsourced to several competing companies). Beyond text, the bulk of this specification consists in package and class diagrams, with some abstract descriptions of scenarios. Binder [2] explains at length why UML models are not readily testable. Yet we feel it is useful to look at the actual specification of a standard to summarize the type of information it contains:

- Package and class diagrams capture the structure of a system. Class diagrams are the entry point for refining attributes and procedures of a class (adding, for example, OCL [19] constraints as well as pre- and post-conditions [8,9], all of which are typically not executable in existing CASE tools).
- A statechart is used to capture the behavior of a class. With little effort (in making it a complete state machine [2]), it can be used as a testable model. Indeed, there is a vast body of work on the generation of tests from state machines (e.g., [2,10]).
- Scenario models such as use-cases, collaboration and sequence diagrams, (but also, beyond UML, use case maps (UCMs) and message sequence charts (MSCs)) capture flows of events at different levels of abstraction: from flows of user-observable events in use cases, to flows of responsibilities in UCMs, to flows of procedure calls in MSCs.

There are several points to be made here: First, the semantic richness of UML eloquently demonstrates the futility of attempting to model a system from a single viewpoint. For example, considering exclusively data flow diagrams or state machines simply does not work in terms of addressing the requirements of system. Indeed, both SCENT [10] and Binder's approach to testing [2] combine scenarios with state machines (the latter acting as the testable model). UML can be seen as a scenario-driven approach but it never tackles directly the testability of the models it advocates. For example, for scenario modeling, variables necessary to enable path sensitization [2] are missing. UML also lacks the temporal relationships proposed in SCENT [10] for inter-scenario relationships. Second, the impressive semantic richness of a modeling language such as UML may covertly introduce a semantic gap (that is, a lack of correspondence or traceability) between some complex concepts and their corresponding (to-be-generated) code. For example, in UML 2.0, the notions of ports and protocols (let alone the notions of optional and replicated capsules found in ObjecTime[5]) are semantically pivotal but difficult to tackle from a testability viewpoint. This reinforces the previous observation that UML models are not readily testable. In fact, work on the automated production of tests from UML model is in its infancy [20]. In particular, we are still far from the automated production of

---

[4] OMG Specification for PIM and PSM for SWRadio Components,
   www.omg.org/docs/swradio/04-01-01.pdf

executable tests. Furthermore, the existence of ATAM [21], GRL[6] and similar modeling methods for non-functional requirements emphasize the paucity of support offered in UML for modeling such requirements. In summary, the point to be grasped is that, despite current practice for the specification of some standards, UML models are not meant to address requirements capture per se and do not address testability.

4   A Prototype

In this paper, we have argued that offshore outsourcing requires that a testable model at the heart of the quality assurance facets of a legal agreement between the contractor and the contracted. We have emphasized that this model must offer

1. unified semantics for functional and non-functional requirements,
2. testability of a requirements model,
3. executability of tests,
4. semantics rooted in the notions of responsibilities and scenarios,
5. formalization of test coverage, and
6. abstraction of the testable model over a space of possible implementations.

Current industrial approaches to requirements engineering typically do not offer such characteristics. Consequently, we have built a prototype of a conformance testing environment (CTE) that addresses these issues and supports a simple form of static and dynamic tests [22].

At the heart of this environment is the ability of the test evaluation engine (TEE) to evaluate static and dynamic tests generated from a testable model, against a .NET managed executable. Such an executable allows the TEE to:

- reverse engineer the source code if it is not available,
- carry out static tests on the source code and
- instrument the dynamic tests of the testable model into the executable and then run them and create an evaluation report.

Due to space limitations, we will discuss here only some of the key modeling features of this prototype.

First, as suggested in Section 2, the pivotal semantic unit of the testable model is the responsibility. Each responsibility has a set of bindings associated with it: several components can share a same responsibility. Each binding is a pointer to the source code of a procedure of the actual implementation. While we will not discuss further the task of binding (whose technical issues lie out of the

---

[5] ROSE RealTime Developer,
   http://www-306.ibm.com/software/awdtools/developer/technical
[6] Goal-Oriented Requirements Language, http://www.cs.toronto.edu/km/GRL

scope of this paper), we will remark that such bindings allow the (static and/or dynamic) tests associated with a responsibility to be instrumented in each of its bindings. In essence, the tests specified in a responsibility (thus independently of implementation) are adapted and integrated in the code associated (through a binding) with this responsibility. This is how tests become executable.

Second, scenarios are implemented as regular expressions over substitutable testable tokens (STTs). An STT can either be another scenario (thus allowing for scenario refinement) or a responsibility. At the highest level of abstraction, we find a 'system grammar', which consists of a (likely partial) grammar of scenarios. This corresponds to the concept of 'interaction overview diagrams' in UML 2.0 [19], and high-level message sequence charts. In the grocery store example introduced in 2.3, the top level grammar could be written as:

{ *OpenStore , (ProcessACustomer*||ManageQueues*), CloseStore* }

Here we take the comma operator as indicating temporal ordering (viz., (a, b) means a is followed in time by b), the * operator as indicating unknown multiciplicity, and the || operator as denoting asynchronous concurrency. If, and only if, an STT corresponds to a unique responsibility (to be bound to actual procedure(s)), will this STT be of type RESPONSIBILITY. Otherwise the STT may be of one of two other types: B-TOKEN (for a token that can be bound to a scenario at path generation time) or D-TOKEN (for a token that is to be decomposed). In our example, OpenStore and CloseStore could possibly be modeled as responsibilities. In this case the tests (e.g., assertions) associated with these two responsibilities would have to 'apply' (that is, to be semantically relevant) across all procedures to which these responsibilities are eventually bound. Conversely, ProcessACustomer and ManageQueues could be of type D-TOKEN if they are taken to be decomposable. For example, ProcessACustomer could be decomposed in the following regular expression:

{ *CustomerEntersNShops, CustomerSelectsQueue, CustomerWaitsInQueue, CustomerIsServed, CustomerLeavesStore* }

Similarly, for ManageQueues: { *(OpenQueue , CloseQueue)** }

to capture that it is the manager who opens and eventually closes queues, each queue needing to be open before it can be closed. (Please note that the 'correctness' of such modeling and its underlying assumptions and decisions is not the issue here. In fact, we remark that the idea of the 'correctness' of a design is quite problematic. In this paper, we are instead concerned with conformance.) Now consider that a customer may use one of a multitude of different strategies to select a queue (e.g., pick the queue with the fewest number of customers, pick the queue with the fewest number of items across its waiting customers, etc.). If one adopts this conceptualization, then CustomerSelectsQueue will be of type B-TOKEN (which is semantically equivalent to the notion of a *stub* in use-case maps (UCMs))). Similarly, OpenQueue and CloseQueue each may have a multitude of strategies associated with them (e.g., based on the number of waiting customers, or the idle time of the cashier, etc.). They would also be modeled as B-TOKENs. B-TOKENs introduce variability in the grammar of scenarios (which, we insist, is to abstract over a space of possible STBDs). In order to enable path generation and selection, clearly all B-TOKENS must eventually be bound to specific scenarios. We allow a B-TOKEN to have either a static set of variants (in the form of a fixed set of references to other scenarios) associated with it, or to be bound to a specific scenario at the start of path generation. (Similarly, UCM supports both static and dynamic stubs.) The details do not import here. What matters is that the testable model allows variability, and that this variability be resolved in order to proceed with path generation/selection. The resolution of variability here follows the same conceptual approach as in generative programming [15]: our grammar of scenarios must be configured (via the binding of B-TOKENs) before paths can be generated and selected from it. This configuration step is the bridge between the problem space and the solution space [Ibid.]. Third, assuming that we have a grammar of scenarios in which all B-TOKENs are bound, we can now hope to generate and select paths. Making this task operational led to a key observation: the capabilities of the profiler of the CTE restrict the semantics of the temporal operators that can be used in the regular expressions capturing scenarios. Let us explain. Recall that SCENT [10] advocates a grammar of scenarios that relies on a rich set of temporal inter-scenario relationships. Also recall that a path constitutes in itself a dynamic test to be matched by some actual behavior of the STBD. In our current prototype, the profiler is able to instantiate a path, run it and then see if the actual sequence of procedure calls matches or not the corresponding regular expression. In other words, the profiler acts in this task as a parser able to recognize paths at execution time. (How this parser is built from the paths is explained elsewhere [22].) This is only possible if we restrict our regular expressions to use operators that the profiler can handle. Returning to our example, at the top level we introduce the , * and || operators. The comma operator is simple to parse. The * operator, whether placed on a responsibility or a scenario is also straightforward to parse. Conversely the || operator is hopeless to parse (see [20]) if concurrency is approached as corresponding to all possible permutations of its operands. Instead, we handle the || operator as a 'don't care' [2] temporal relationship. In our example, this means that we do not care about the ordering of the many instances of ProcessACustomer and of ManageQueues. (Syntactically, the () are essential in delimiting the scope of this don't care during parsing.) At this stage in the development of our prototype, we have been able to model our grocery store without introducing more complex temporal operators than those presented above. But it is certainly premature to claim this set of operators to be sufficient. Having paths that can be matched to actual execution constitutes one facet of dynamic testing. It presupposes the ability to generate paths (of procedures) from scenarios. We observe that, with the current set of simple temporal operators we use, the 'flattening' of a grammar of scenarios into a set of regular expressions on responsibilities is possible once all B-TOKENs have been bound. Then, once each responsibility has been bound to actual procedure(s), we can obtain regular expressions in which the tokens are names of actual procedures. Path generation then consists in producing a set of sequences of procedures to test out of these regular expressions. Given the semantic closeness of regular expressions to state machines, this task reuses the extensive body of work on generating paths from such state machines (see chapter 7 of [2]) Further details with respect to path generation, selection and instantiation, as well as details of static and dynamic tests on functional and non-functional requirements are given elsewhere [22].

Acknowledgements

Support from the Natural Sciences and Engineering Research Council of Canada (NSERC) is gratefully acknowledged.

References

1. Meyer, B.: The unspoken revolution in software engineering. IEEE Computer (January 2006)
2. Binder, R.: Testing, Object-Oriented Systems. Addison-Wesley, London, UK (2000)
3. Gold, T.: Outsourcing Development Offshore: Making it Work. Auerbach Publications (2004)
4. Kotonya, G., Sommerville, I.: Requirements Engineering. John Wiley & Sons, West Sussex, England (1998)
5. Davies, A.: Software Requirements: Objects, Functions and States. Prentice-Hall, Englewood Cliffs (1993)
6. Czarnecki, K., Stahl, T., Voelter, M.: Model-Driven Software Development: Technology, Engineering, Management. John Wiley & Sons, West Sussex, England (2006)
7. Corriveau, J.P., Bashardoust-Tajali, S.: Generative hierarchical contracts for conformance testing of sequential containers. In: Proceedings of IASTED's Conference on Software Engineering (2007)
8. Meyer, B.: Reusable Software: The Base Object-Oriented Component Libraries. Prentice-Hall, Englewood Cliffs (1994)
9. Meyer, B.: Object-Oriented Software Construction. Prentice-Hall, Englewood Cliffs (1994)
10. Ryser, J., Glinz, M.: Using dependency charts to improve scenario-based testing - management of inter-scenario relationships. In: Watanabe, O., Hagiya, M., Ito, T., van Leeuwen, J., Mosses, P.D. (eds.) TCS 2000. LNCS, vol. 1872, Springer, Heidelberg (2000)
11. Jacobson, I.: Object-Oriented Software Engineering. Addison-Wesley, London, UK (1992)
12. Boehm, B.: A spiral model of software development and enhancement (1988)
13. Gomaa, H.: Designing Concurrent, Distributed and Real-Time Applications with UML. In: Evans, A., Kent, S., Selic, B. (eds.) UML 2000. LNCS, vol. 1939, Springer, Heidelberg (2000)
14. Briand, L., Labiche, Y., Sun, H.: Investigating the use of Analysis Contracts to Improve the Testability of Object-Oriented Code, vol. 33(7), pp. 637–672. John Wiley & Sons, Inc, West Sussex, England (2003)
15. Czarnecki, K., Eiseinecker, U.: Generative Programming: Methods, Tools and Applications. Addison-Wesley, London, UK (2000)

16. Ambler, S.: Agile Modeling. John Wiley & Sons, West Sussex, England (2002)
17. Beck, K.: Test-Driven Development By Example. Addison-Wesley, London, UK (2002)
18. Rumbaugh, J., Jacobson, I., Booch, G.: The Unified Modeling Language Reference Manual. Addison-Wesley (1998)
19. Miles, R., Hamilton, K.: Learning UML 2.0. O'Reilly (2006)
20. Briand, L., Labiche, Y.: A uml-based approach to system testing. In: Gogolla, M., Kobryn, C. (eds.) UML 2001 – The Unified Modeling Language. Modeling Languages, Concepts, and Tools. LNCS, vol. 2185, Springer, Heidelberg (2001)
21. Kazman, R., Klein, M., Clements, P.: Atam: Method for architecture evaluating the quality attributes of a software architecture. Technical Report CMU/SEI-200-TR004, Software Engineering Institute, Carnegie Mellon University (2000)
22. Arnold, D.: Supporting Generative Contracts in.NET. PhD thesis (2007)

Introducing Global Supply Chains into Software Engineering Education

Olly Gotel[1], Vidya Kulkarni[2], Long Chrea Neak[3], Christelle Scharff[1], and Sopheap Seng[3]

[1] Pace University, Seidenberg School of Computer Science and Information Systems, Department of Computer Science, New York, NY, USA
{ogotel,cscharff}@pace.edu
[2] University of Delhi, Computer Science Department, New Delhi, India
vkulkarni@cs.du.ac.in
[3] Institute of Technology of Cambodia, Computer Science Department, Phnom Penh, Cambodia
{longchrea.neak,sopheap.seng}@itc.edu.kh

Abstract. This paper describes lessons from running software development projects across three globally distributed educational institutions. What was innovative about this study was that two of the institutions were located in service providing countries, conventional onshore/offshore roles were reversed, and students were exposed to the realities of global supply chain management. Three teams of US students were tasked to develop three different software products for Cambodian clients, while sub-contracting the database component to third-party teams of Indian students. This paper details the role of the three institutions, the prerequisites for planning and logistics for running such educational projects, and summarises the findings, while drawing broader parallels with the commercial world of offshore and outsourced development. It ends with recommendations for software engineering education to better reflect the needs and skills demanded of right sourcing in the global marketplace. These extend more generally to global software engineering.

Keywords: Global Software Development, Software Engineering Education, Supply Chain.

1 Introduction and Background

With the need to reduce development cost and improve quality, software products are increasingly developed via collaborations across people, organizations and countries. The challenges facing such globally distributed software development projects have been studied and reported in the literature, generally focusing on the economic, technical, organizational and cultural issues [4,15,16]. The September 2006 issue of IEEE Computer: *Global Software Development: How Far Have We Come?* explicitly captures the state of the practice in global software development.

B. Meyer and M. Joseph (Eds.): SEAFOOD 2007, LNCS 4716, pp. 44–58, 2007.

A global provisioning model often implies the existence of a prime (or lead) contractor and a chain of sub-contractors. Increasingly, it is likely that software houses will outsource well-defined components of their contracts to smaller companies, and even to cheaper service providing countries. The motivation is not always about sourcing software development in the cheapest place, but about sourcing it where there are the requisite skills and continuous coverage [19].

This model has an obvious implication for computer science and software engineering education around the world [1,2,9,10,21,22]. In these disciplines, students need to be exposed to the realities if they are to develop the differentiating 'softer' skills they will need [14]. The supply chain model of software development requires students to learn how to divide up a project into component parts for different parties to work on, these parties possibly being distributed across time zones and cultures. This obviously relies on a shared and systematic process. In addition, it requires students to learn about scoping and delineating boundaries, eliciting requirements from remote clients, communicating an understanding of requirements back to clients and then on to third-parties (not the same skill sets), and learning about the testing and integration needed to assemble a working whole product when the component aspects are not under their total control. A number of courses are now beginning to reflect some of these realities, focusing on requirements engineering [3,6], the development of software in a global context [17,18] and the provision of global projects from within corporations [20]. However, few pioneering courses appear to involve service providing countries, such as India and China and, to our knowledge, do not simulate supply chain development.

Since 2005, the focus of the US and Cambodian partners' undergraduate capstone software engineering courses has been global software development [11]. In 2005, teams of Pace University and Institute of Technology of Cambodia (ITC) students worked together to develop software products for the Cambodian market. The student projects were organized so that: (a) the Cambodian students acted as clients and end-users - they knew the problem the proposed system was to tackle, the environment it was to operate in and had the authority to accept the work of the providers (or not); and (b) the Pace University students acted as providers - it was their responsibility to 'capture' the requirements for the system, propose design options, develop the selected design and test the eventual system, while also handling requirements changes. In 2006, this model[1] was extended to include students from the University of Delhi. These students had expertise in database design, so the concept of a prime contractor and third-party supplier (sub-contractor) was introduced to reflect these skills. While the Cambodian students remained as clients, the provisioning of the solution was changed. The Pace University students sub-contracted part of the system design and development to the students from India, while also managing the end-to-end contract. This paper describes our 2006 study which examined the following questions:

---

[1] The web page dedicated to this study can be found at
  http://www.csis.pace.edu/~scharff/cs3892006

a) What is required to set up and run a global distributed project of this chained nature in an educational context?

b) How does the use of a supply chain impact the requirements engineering process, notably the handling of change and the assumptions made by the various parties?

c) What are the perceived communication and coordination issues along the supply chain, and do they differ?

d) Is there the perception of a 'global' team across a distributed supply chain and, if so, what social activities can foster this unity?

e) What are the main differences in interaction between prime contractors and sub-contractors and between prime contractors and clients?

f) How does the nature of this interaction impact project quality? 'Quality' here refers to the conformance of the end product to the clients' specified and perceived requirements [5], ascertained by final acceptance or rejection.

The remainder of the paper is organized as follows. Section 2 establishes the context of the study and Section 3 describes the preparation that is required to set up multi-institution collaborations of this nature (addressing question a above). The key findings from the study, with respect to questions b-f, are summarized and discussed in Section 4. Section 5 provides conclusions and recommendations to assist other institutions in reflecting the realities of the global marketplace in the curriculum.

2   Context

In this section, we describe the three institutions this study is based on, their roles in the global supply chain, the courses targeted by the study, the software that were developed, the composition of the global teams, and the process and technology that was used to enable collaboration in this global setting.

2.1   The Institutions

The Institute of Technology of Cambodia (ITC) (*http://www.itc.edu.kh*) is a leading semi-public higher education school in Phnom Penh accepting students on a competitive exam. The educational system is organized by trimesters. Cohorts of five-year engineering students go through the programs with about thirty hours of core science classes a week during the first two years, then specialize and attend about thirty hours of classes a week in their speciality.

Pace University (*http://www.pace.edu*) is a private university strategically located in New York offering programs at the undergraduate and graduate level. The educational system is organized by two main semesters. Undergraduate students go through the programs with a load of about nine to fifteen hours of computer science and liberal arts classes a week. The concept of a yearly cohort is less prevalent since students can take courses at their own pace, though most complete within four years.

The University of Delhi (*http://www.du.ac.in/*) is one of the prestigious public institutions in India granting Bachelors, Masters and Ph.D. degrees. Admission to all programs is through entrance examination and limited to thirty students in each program. Like the ITC system, students enrolled in these programs attend classes for about thirty hours a week and the educational system is organized by trimesters.

2.2   Institutional Roles and Targeted Courses

The study described in this paper involved a capstone undergraduate 'Software Engineering' course taken by junior (third year) and senior (fourth year) Pace University computer science students, a 'Software Engineering' course for fourth year ITC computer science undergraduate students and a 'Database System Implementation' course for first year M.Sc. in computer science students at the University of Delhi. The intention behind this effort was to provide students with a realistic co-production experience where software products have to be engineered by global partners with disparate skills and expertise. Note that the study ran from January through May 2006, so was aligned with the US spring semester.

ITC Students are Clients, Testers and Translators. Their responsibilities were to describe the software they wanted to be built and the context in which it was to operate. They also had to review and give feedback on the requirements, design and testing documents, test the software and submit bug reports, and ultimately deliver the software in French and Khmer for a Cambodian audience[2]. Their responsibilities also included reporting on the problems arising from working with the US students. At the end of the semester, the Cambodian students had to assess the software developed by the US students (with Indian sub-contracting) and to compare this with the software developed solely by the Indian students (see Indian roles later in this section).

US Students are Developers and Lead Contactors. Their responsibilities were to capture the requirements from the clients and produce an agreed specification, propose design options that subcontract part of the system design and development to Indian students, implement the software and test it, while concurrently handling requirements changes, integrating feedback and managing the end-to-end contract. At the end of the semester, the US students had to deliver the software to their clients. Additionally, the US students were required to maintain a web page for the project, report on the problems arising when working with the Cambodian and Indian students, answer a weekly questionnaire concerning communications and requirements changes, archive all emails and chat sessions, and document their experience with the software engineering process and communication protocols they followed.

---

[2] Due to time constraints the software was only delivered in English.

Indian Students are Third-party Suppliers. Their responsibilities were to provide the US students with a database design and the corresponding SQL code to be integrated in the overall system design. Their responsibilities also included reporting on the problems arising from working with the US students[3].

Global Supply Chain Scenario. This study was set up such that there were no contacts between India and Cambodia, as initially the Indian students were intended to act as pure suppliers in the project and joined the project one month after the Cambodian students. The Indian students had database expertise that was lacking in some of the US students' repertoire. The study was also explicitly designed to promote a reversal of conventional onshore/offshore roles for a number of reasons. Firstly, to give the US students the opportunity to find out what it would be like to be on the development side of the onshore/offshore scenario, and because the US students do not always have enough programming opportunities that demand version control and large scale integration. Secondly, to give Cambodian students exposure to the empowering position of being a customer and hopefully cultivating entrepreneurship. Lastly, to give Indian students a realistic experience of working with pre-specified requirements and learning how to work smoothly as part of a chain. All the students were to experience working with others from a different culture.

2.3 Teams

In the spring of 2006, the class at Pace University comprised eleven students, the class at ITC comprised sixteen students, and the class at the University of Delhi comprised thirty students. Of the Indian students, only six were part of the study - the six students who had obtained the highest score on the first midterm exam of the class. The study thereby consisted of three global teams each composed of ten to twelve students distributed amongst the three locations: three to four students from the US acting as prime contractors; five to six Cambodian students acting as clients; and two Indian students acting as sub-contractors. The term local team was used to refer to co-located team members. The students were free to choose their own local teams. The US and Indian students chose their global team partners in Cambodia and the US respectively based on project preferences. Students were assigned roles in the teams (e.g. team, communication and quality assurance leaders).

2.4 Projects

Three Cambodia-specific projects were proposed:

---

[3] Though the initial intent was for the Indian students to act as sub-contractors, they wanted to gain further experience in web-based software development. They consequently developed the whole software product in parallel with the software that was developed by the US students. One of the reasons why they were eager to do this was that they thought it would improve their resumes; reflecting their seriousness, they asked for certificates to present to future employers.

- **ITC Library Management System.** This project was to design and develop a system to replace the mainly paper-based activities of the ITC Library. The system had to support administrators, librarians and patrons, and provide the standard functionality of the existing system. An interesting aspect was to be uncovering the unique policies of the Cambodian library (i.e. the business logic). For example, there are no fees for the late return of books, as an honour system (preventing graduation) is in place.
- **Cambodian Crafts On-Line Store.** This project was to design and develop a system that would sell uniquely Cambodian crafts through the Internet.
- **Cambodian On-line Restaurant.** This project was to design and develop a virtual restaurant selling Cambodian dishes for home delivery via the Internet.

These last two E-Commerce projects were to manage the registration of customers, the placement of orders, and the fulfilment and control tasks of service staff.

2.5   Process, Technology and Communication Tools

Since this was a first software engineering class for the US students, they were exposed to a lightweight waterfall model with some iteration to help provide some overall shape and context. The software products developed by the US students were Java web-based applications (written using Servlets under Tomcat) with a back-end database implemented in MySQL or Oracle. Requirements mostly comprised textual documents and use cases, with some UML diagrams used for design. The development was all carried out within the Eclipse development environment. Students used the JUnit plug-in for unit testing and CVS for code sharing, and change and version management. Trac (*http://www.edgewall.com/trac*) open source wiki-based software was used for supply chain and project management. Clients used trac to report bugs, while developers used trac to fix and manage bugs. The Indian students produced Entity Relationship Diagrams for the database design; they did not use a particular tool. The Indian students developed their full software using JSP under Tomcat and Oracle. Students communicated using Yahoo! Groups mailing lists for asynchronous emails and using Yahoo! IM for synchronous chats. Local teams also communicated face-to-face. No specialized collaborative technology was used for distributed communication. Teams shared their work by posting document versions on their group websites.

3   Preparation

In this section, we describe the preparation that was necessary to set up a global supply chain management experience for students in terms of the project planning, communication coordination, faculty roles and continuous data gathering.

3.1   Project Planning

Many discussions on the countries, cultures, institutions, educational systems, academic calendars, students' background and Internet access had to take place to set up this project. Furthermore, the instructors had to design their syllabi (with grading policies) in collaboration and decide on the use of communication tools, CASE tools, and the software engineering process and communication protocols to be followed. Documents were exchanged between faculty and students, including country fact sheets, pictures of all students and faculty, and syllabi of individual courses. Instructors also needed to share all course materials (e.g. lecture notes, software engineering templates), exams, grades, feedback on the teams, video-taped presentations and software demonstrations for transparency. The milestones, schedules and deadlines of the projects for the three locations were designed in common and distributed as one document.

3.2   Communication and Coordination

The first important element that had to be taken into account in this study was the twelve hours time difference between Cambodia and the US, and the ten hours and thirty minutes time difference between India and the US. Another important element was Internet access. Cambodian students only had day-time access to the Internet from the ITC labs or from the widespread cyber-cafes for $1 an hour (an expensive proposition for Cambodians when the monthly average salary is around $60). Additionally, there were un-typically frequent power outages to work around due to the closure of an electricity power station in Phnom Penh. In one instance, this prevented the Cambodians from having access to the Internet for three days. By contrast, while Internet connectivity and power shortages were problematic at the university labs, most of the Indian students had reliable broadband high-speed access to the Internet from their homes. These factors meant that the US students and instructors had to coordinate and plan for communication. It was easier to contact the Cambodian students late at night and the Indian students early in the morning (US Eastern Standard Time).

3.3   Faculty and Their Roles

The faculty involved in this study have known each other for a long time. They have travelled intensively in Asia and in the US, and have a good understanding of US/India/Cambodia from a cultural, historical, educational, economical and political perspective, which is an advantageous foundation. Good relations and trust are crucial to the success of projects where there is a need for regular, open and transparent communication to plan, report, synchronize and solve problems in a timely manner. As part of the preparation, a site visit was made by one of the US professors to Cambodia and India for assessment of the infrastructure, coordination of the courses and syllabi, and to gauge the students' willingness and interest. The roles of the faculty had to be determined and agreed upon; faculty at one location had to oversee the three locations and play the role of project manager [17]. The US faculty carried out this role and the other faculty reported to the project manager. It was also deemed necessary that only one professor handled these activities on a daily basis. Had there been more than one 'manager', there could have been problems of misunderstanding and miscommunication.

3.4 Data Gathering

Blogs and surveys were used to monitor and control aspects of the project relating to cultural differences, time and space complications, project activities and assessment of quality. The US students were active in using blogs to describe their work; the Cambodian and Indian students did not make use of blogs – they are not so widely used in their societies and the potential value is thus less clear.

- An entry survey was taken by all the students and the results shared to permit students to understand each other's background.
- The US teams answered a weekly questionnaire about their communications: type (e.g. emails, chats), scope (e.g. local, global), main topic (e.g. planning, feedback) and usefulness (e.g. high, medium, low). This questionnaire also recorded the reasons for any requirements changes (e.g. ambiguity, inconsistency, assumptions) and the instigating actors (i.e. Cambodia, India, US).
- A mid-semester survey was administered to all students to determine any logistical problems and to inform the study. This was also conducted to see how students perceived their team functioning (e.g. leadership effectiveness, balance of workloads, alignment of motivation, local versus global team biases, etc.)
- Individually, all students submitted post project statements on the overall experience and answered a post project survey that focused on what the students learned from each other, the issues and problems encountered, and the perceived effectiveness and usefulness of the experience.

4   Findings

Students were all positive with respect to their overall participation in this experience. In this section, we address the study questions we originally posed in Section 1 and organize our findings on the requirements engineering process, communication and coordination, social and cultural aspects, and interaction and quality[4].

4.1 Requirements Engineering

Requirements Engineering Process. The Cambodian and US students learned important lessons about requirements engineering in this setting: the

---

[4] The results in this section are derived from the post project surveys.

necessity of careful elicitation; the need for negotiation; why requirements descriptions should be unambiguous and well written; and the role of requirements validation to check understanding. Requirements were captured predominantly using questionnaires and clarified using (large) chat discussions. Requirements validation was achieved through (small) chats in the first instance and re-validated using checkbox documents where each requirement could be accepted, accepted with modification or rejected.

Requirements Changes. As clients, the Cambodian students recognized that they changed their mind on requirements quite regularly (56% agreement). Not surprisingly, the US developers perceived that the clients changed their minds frequently on the requirements (64%). Students appreciate how important it is to have a shared and aligned awareness on others' actions and responsiveness to avoid tensions, and they also see the realities of frequent requirements changes.

Requirements Assumptions. The projects demanded innovative and creative thinking because many of the assumptions that the US students had about what would constitute a feasible solution needed to be radically altered for the Cambodian market. For instance, in a country where Internet connectivity is slow and intermittent, students had to re-think the everyday model of E-Commerce (e.g. the use of ubiquitous graphics). The virtual shopping carts that many take for granted are unheard of in Cambodia and the metaphors do not always transfer across cultures. This situation forced students to differentiate between facts, constraints and assumptions, critical issues that often underpin many failed software development projects [12]. The Indian students made more assumptions about the Cambodian domain. This seems logical given the US students had direct contact with the client and the Indian students only gained information via the US intermediaries. However, the US students still made assumptions concerning the need to enforce the policy rules of the ITC library, making their system unusable in the client's eyes. Interestingly, the Cambodian students did not reject this unusable software and we suggest it is related to social bonding (discussed in Section 4.3) [7,8,13]. In the Indian version of the software, they added an additional late fee penalty. This addition was due to the lack of transfer of supplementary domain knowledge from the US students; they didn't consider the need to document how the honour system worked in their requirements. Also, the Indian students developed the craft store software such that it was restricted to ordering products from addresses within the US; this was not stated in the requirements document and suggests the kind of assumptions that can arise when the needs are passed on through a proxy, in this case it reflected assumptions about an American market more so than a Cambodian one.

4.2   Communication and Coordination

67% of the Indian students and 44% of the Cambodian students perceived coordination as the largest problem they faced when working with the US students. 25% of the Cambodian students perceived communication (i.e. language barriers) and the limited availability of the US developers as problematic. From the

Indian and Cambodian perspective, the main issue here was aligning themselves with the US students across time zones and busy schedules, especially since these students had almost twice as many hours of classes than the US students. The Cambodian students had a high class load, coupled with Internet access problems. The Indian students experienced similar issues, though actually cancelled chat meetings in the belief that the requirements document was written well enough for them to be able to develop the required software, preferring to write emails if they needed any clarification.

From the US perspective, 45% of the students perceived communication as the largest difficulty they encountered on the project. They would be offended when questioned about whether they were on target for meeting the milestones by the other students as they perceived this as questioning their ability to deliver. This could be attributed to cultural and/or language differences and might have been interpreted differently in a face-to-face situation. The US students, even though they had logistical difficulties in scheduling meetings, needed to be reminded constantly by the professors to be proactive. There would then be some frustration at the lengthy time the non-US students would take to respond.

The Cambodian students ranked good communications as a crucial factor for the success of a global software development project (56%). The Indian students ranked good communications and clear project plans as equally important (each 50%), reflecting their position as service providers who need to fit into a wider context and process. The US students emphasized good communications more than the others (76%), probably due to their direct experience of playing a coordinating role. While collaborative tools were ranked third by US students, they were not considered crucial by the Indian and Cambodian students. This may be partially due to less prior exposure to such tools and the fact that the US students were taking on the bridging role. Interestingly, both the Cambodian and US students thought that 'softer' skills were more important to the success of a global project than technical skills; the Indian students were more divided on this matter. Direct experience of the client/prime contractor relation likely motivates this 'soft skill' appreciation.

4.3 Social and Cultural Aspects

Relations. The interaction between the US and Indian students (as prime contractor and sub-contractor) was remarkably different from the interaction between the US and Cambodian students (as prime contractor and client). The former was abrupt and impersonal, focusing mostly on project matters. The latter was more polite and social (e.g. they all wanted to agree and seek understanding before moving on to the next topic). The topics discussed between the Indian and US students mainly revolved around the educational systems, their universities and home cities. Neither side felt they had expanded their knowledge of the other culture. In contrast, the Cambodian and US students discussed history, jobs and salaries, family structures and entertainment. They both felt they had increased their knowledge of each other's culture. These differences in inter-personal relations may be explained by the fact that the Indian and US students already assumed they knew much about each other, whereas Cambodia is less well known. Also, the Indian students joined the project one month after the beginning of the project, so were really considered the 'hired help'. By contrast, the Cambodian students were the source of domain knowledge.

Learning from Each Other: US/India. The Indian students said they learned that US students "work according to the pre-specified plans and schedule and try to stick to those schedules. We in India don't go for the rigid plans." This seems in conflict with their reliance on good planning for successful projects, mentioned earlier in Section 4.2. When asked what they perceived the US students had learned about them, the Indian students said: "I think that would be determination and focus, which is a must for any successful professional." This emphasis on professionalism may be partially an explanation for expedience in communications. Further exemplifying this was the fact that once the US students had completed their final exams it was no longer possible to engage them further in the project. Their Indian counterparts, even after the end of their classes, still wanted to improve the software they had developed.

Learning from Each Other: Cambodia/US. The Cambodian students said that they had learned that US students "work until late at night". The US students said they learned that Cambodian students "do not have computers at home and go to school every day", "they are curious individuals who appreciate new technologies and educations", "they have much more school time than we do" and "they had no experience with credit cards and amazon.com". Credit cards and amazon.com usage may seem an integral part of life to US students, but they were not to the Cambodian students, and to some extent to the Indian students. The US students only discovered such realities during peripheral discussions with the Cambodians, not through project-specific questioning, and this was highly critical to the design of their E-Commerce systems. When asked what they believed was the most interesting thing the Cambodian students had learned from them, the US students said that they explained credit card usage and E-Commerce web site logic. They also added: "There seemed to be some assumption that all Americans are wealthy and opulent. I hope that our group served to dispel some of those myths."

Team Unity and Cohesion. Institution-specific gifts were exchanged between the US, Indian and Cambodian students at the beginning and end of the projects to create a community environment. In the mid-semester survey we found that the US students referred to the local team as 'the team', while the Cambodian and Indian students referred to the global team as 'the team'. When the Indian students discovered their names did not appear on the global team web site maintained by the US, this created some tension. Furthermore, the US students often referred to the Indian students as 'he', while five out of the six Indian students were female. The matter of gender amongst the Indian students is worthy of note and could be a possible reason for the nature of the terse communication outlined in Section 4.2. Indian girls may be more hesitant to instigate chat conversation beyond what is required to complete a project task with an all male US team, asynchronous email being a more acceptable route.

4.4   Interaction and Quality

No statistical correlation was found between the quantity of interaction and the quality of the final product. However, it appears that the project with the most chats was ranked last by both the US and Cambodian faculty and rejected by its clients, while the project with the most emails was ranked first by all parties. Notably, the US software that was rejected by the client also used an early throw-away prototyping model to understand the requirements and discuss GUI options with the client. The project with the most explicit synchronous interaction with the client about requirements seemed to have the most problems, which (on first sight) conflicts with recognized best practice. The reality was that this local US group did not function as a team. While some of the students worked on a prototype with the clients, others in the team built a system to the original requirements, not accounting for the requirements learning. When the clients saw the product it not what was expected. They also ran into scheduling issues since they were keen to exploit technologies and tools that they did not have previous knowledge of. They became overwhelmed.

On the whole, the Cambodian students were more positive about the US software (the software implemented by the US with the Indian database component) than the purely Indian-built final software. Though technically limited in scope, it was ranked higher because it met the needs of the clients and did not make as many assumptions. However, the Indian software was actually more reliable in operation, and more care had been taken in creating a professional-looking product. One hypothesis could be that the friendly contacts between the US and Cambodian students led to a better experience and hence perception of the end product [7,8,13]. Another is the fact that the Indian students designed and built to second-hand information, and had no opportunity to manage the end clients' expectations throughout. Per the post project survey, the Indian students would have liked contact with the Cambodian students (83% expressed desire) and 68% of the Cambodian students concurred. Both parties believed this would have led to fewer assumptions and better products on the Indian side. Projects such as this do serve to convince students of the criticality of stakeholder contact and communications.

With respect to the sub-contracted work, the Indian students' designs were all very well done. However, assumptions were made with regard library late fees as discussed in Section 4.1, an example of incorrect information being passed down the supply chain. When the US team realized their error, they requested a change. Since the Indian team did not respond promptly, the US team went ahead and designed the database component themselves (still with some assumptions). This team included the most technically competent US students. It can be difficult to teach such students to delegate part of their work as this requires trust. Both the restaurant and craft store projects did use the Indian students' work, which integrated quite seamlessly. This was perhaps more possible since this technical knowledge was more lacking across these two US teams.

5   Conclusions and Recommendations

Software engineering education needs to reflect the realities of changing professional practice. Students should be prepared and flexible to adapt to whatever role they find themselves in. It is intrinsically feasible and practical for students to learn how to identify, build and integrate component parts of a software project in a multi-cultural university setting, and educationally critical for them to experience all sides. A global supply chain model provides a way for students to learn about the long-term skills that will be needed to augment their technical skills. In this study, two of the three projects were able to leverage skills in the global team that were lacking in the local team. However, care must be taken not to alienate those students taking on a sub-contractor role. While the relationship between the US/Cambodian students was carefully planned for by the instructors, the US/Indian relationship was left more to the students. Consequently, student photos were not distributed in a timely fashion and incorrect first impressions were made. Social bonding, getting to know the team members and their wider interests, lies at the heart of relationship management and has repercussions for the health of a global supply chain. Instructors need to instigate this process at the onset of the project and ensure mechanisms to facilitate this are built in throughout.

Regular communications are essential to ensure momentum and to keep projects on track. With supply chains, transparency is desirable all the way through the chain when students are learning about subtle dependencies and trust. Coupled with this is the important role of a shared process and an up-to-date version controlled repository for information exchange. Attention needs to be paid to explicitly designing a simple process and a straightforward communication and change management strategy with the students, and to avoid overwhelming them with the latest tools and technologies.

In a project of this nature, it is easy for course instructors to become project managers. Such a situation can prevent students from experiencing milestone setting, planning and coordination tasks. Projects need to be designed to off-load more of this task on to the students so they understand its role in running a successful project and buy into it. One suggestion is to involve business or graduate software engineering students in this capacity. For a capstone course in software engineering, there is already much to cover.

The perception amongst the US students in the study was that they were doing the most work. An environment must be cultivated where the view is one of a shared venture in which all parties are contributing equally, albeit in different and equally valuable ways to prevent resentment. Issues of perception, along with trust, need as much attention as the technological and process skills that the course is teaching. More needs to be studied about the balance of competition and collaboration on global student projects of this kind. The Indian students wanted to create their own software and desired technological perfection. Relations were a little smoother between those students with whom the US students did not feel they were competing.

While some global team working skills can be learned on the job, others may need to be explicitly taught in the software engineering classroom. The global teams that operated the most effectively were the ones where the local teams (the ones playing the integrative role), functioned well internally and had the process in place to broaden out.

Acknowledgments. This project was undertaken under the auspices of a Pace University presidential grant. We would like to thank all the students who participated. We are grateful to Professors Sok and Chanthearith who helped guide the interactions between the Cambodian and US students. We thank Doug Tidwell, IBM cyber-evangelist, for the Eclipse training he provided to the US students. Finally, we thank Dean Susan Merritt for her support with this project.

References

1. Aspray, W., Mayadas, A.F., Vardi, M.Y: Educational Response to Offshore Outsourcing. In: Proceedings of the 37th SIGCSE Technical Symposium on Computer Science Education (2006), March 3-5, pp. 330–331. Houston, Texa, USA (2006)
2. Aspray, W., Mayadas, F., Vardi, M.Y: Globalization and Offshoring of Software. A Report of the ACM Job Migration Task Force (2006)
3. Audy, J., Evaristo, R., Watson-Manheim, M.B.: Distributed Analysis: The Last Frontier? In: Proceedings of the 37th Hawaii International Conference on System Sciences (HICSS'04), p. 10010. Big Island, Hawaii (2004)
4. Coar, K.: The Sun Never Sets on Distributed Development. ACM Queue 1(9), 32–39 (2004)
5. Crosby, P.B.: Quality Is Free: The Art of Making QualityvCertain. McGraw Hill, New York (1979)
6. Damian, D., Hadwin, A., Al-Ani, B.: Instructional Design and Assessment Strategies for Teaching Global Software Development: A Framework. In: Proceedings of the 28th International Conference on Software Engineering (ICSE'06), May 20-28, pp. 685–690. Shanghai, China (2006)
7. Damian, D., Zowghi, D.: Requirements Engineering Challenges in Multi-site Software Development Organizations. Requirements Engineering Journal 8(1), 149–160 (2003)
8. Favela, J., Pe-Mora, F.: An Experience in Collaborative Software Engineering Education. IEEE Software 18(2), 47–53 (2001)
9. Ferguson, E., Henderson, P., Huen, W., Kussmaul, C.: IT Offshore Outsourcing: Impact on CS/IS Curriculum. In: Proceedings of the 36th SIGCSE Technical Symposium on Computer Science Education, February 23-27, pp. 258–259. St. Louis, Missouri, USA (2005)
10. Ferguson, E., Kussmaul, C., McCracken, D., Robbert, M.A.: Offshore Outsourcing: Current Conditions and Diagnosis. In: Proceedings of the 35th SIGCSE Technical Symposium on Computer Science Education, March 3-7, pp. 330–331. Norfolk, Virginia, USA (2004)
11. Gotel, O., Scharff, C., Seng, S.: Preparing Computer Science Students for Global Software Development. In: Proceedings of the 36th ASEE/IEEE Frontiers in Education Conference (FIE'06), San Diego, California (2006)
12. Jackson, M.: Software Requirements and Specifications. Addison-Wesley Professional (1995)

13. Kobylinski, R., Creighton, O., Dutoit, A., Bruegge, B.: Building Awareness in Global Software Engineering: Using Issues as Context. In: Proceedings of the International Workshop on Distributed Software Development (GSD'02), Orlando, Florida, May 21 (2002)

14. McCracken, W.M.: Counter Point-SE Education: What Academia Can Do. IEEE Software 14(6), 27–29 (1997)

15. Meyer, B.: The Unspoken Revolution in Software Engineering. IEEE Computer 39(1), 121–123 (2006)

16. Olson, J.S., Olson, G.M.: Culture Surprises in Remote Software Development Teams. ACM Queue 1(9), 52–59 (2004)

17. Petkovic, D., Thompson, G., Todtenhoefer, R.: Teaching Practical Software Engineering and Global Software Engineering: Evaluation and Comparison. In: Proceedings of the 11th Annual SIGCSE Conference on Innovation and Technology in Computer Science Education (ITiCSE'06), June 26-28, pp. 294–298. Bologna, Italy (2006)

18. Purvis, M., Purvis, M., Cranefield, S.: Educational Experiences from a Global Software Engineering (GSE) Project. In: Proceedings of the 6th Conference on Australasian Computing Education (ACE'04), pp. 269–275. Dunedin, New Zealand (2004)

19. Ribeiro, J.: Indian Outsourcers Continue to Make Gains. Computerworld (August 14 2006)

20. Richardson, I., Milewski, A.E., Mullick, N., Keil, P.: Distributed Development: An Education Perspective on the Global Studio Project. In: Proceedings of the 28th International Conference on Software Engineering (ICSE'06), Shanghai, China, May 20 - 28, pp. 679–684 (2006)

21. Tromby, M., Marcus, B.: Bridging the Chinese Skills Gap. Computerworld (June 6 2006)

22. Xiaoqing, L.: Collaborative Global Software Development and Education. In: Proceedings of the 29th International Computer Software and Applications Conference (COMPSAC'05), p. 371. Edinburgh, Scotland (2005)

Turn on Lean Governance ...
for Return on Outsourcing

Mohan Kancharla

Tata Consultancy Services Ltd
mohan.kancharla@tcs.com
http://www.tcs.com

Abstract. This paper focuses on outsourcing IT and Business Processes, with the added dimension of the provider of the service being 'offshore' or in a different geography. Highlighting the unique characteristics of the Lean Governance model, the paper stresses the importance of moving outsourcing status from customer-vendor to being partners in attaining enterprise goals. Explaining the concept through case studies, the author demonstrates the importance of structures and processes, as organizations become more mature in the outsourcing process and as business imperatives change. The Lean Governance model encompasses these very elements, and is therefore a force multiplier for achieving the outsourcing objectives of both business and IT dimensions.

1 Outsourcing Definition

Outsourcing can be defined in simple terms to describe a situation where one organization gives work to other firms, which can execute this work more efficiently, usually for lower costs, and whose capabilities complement or supplement their own.

Outsourcing enables organizations to focus on their core business, and in addition, it usually reduces costs, provides access to skilled resources, improves process quality and takes advantage of difference in time zones. Organizations jumping on to the outsourcing bandwagon should have a realistic understanding of these factors. They need to objectively assess gains and risks associated with outsourcing decisions. Above all, organizations should be willing to invest in time and talent for creating long-term relationships.

Michael F. Corbett author of "The Outsourcing Revolution" (2004) says: "For success in outsourcing, organizations need to take long-term value of offshore outsourcing, building advantages that go beyond near-term cost-saving. Building long-term relationships and leveraging the same becomes integral part of organizations' strategic and tactical fabric".

The benefits can range from being strategic, operational or technological. The risks involved also are varied. At a macro level, risks can be classified as political, legal, regulatory and economic risks. At a micro level the risks can be further classified as risks arising out of decision making flaws and implementation flaws.

Conventional wisdom indicates much of the outsourcing model or outsourcing best practices are centered around cost arbitrage, supplier selection, risk diversification,

B. Meyer and M. Joseph (Eds.): SEAFOOD 2007, LNCS 4716, pp. 59–66, 2007.

knowledge dissemination between client and supplier and micromanagement of supplier by the client. But much less is addressed on the governance aspect of client-supplier relationship that not only supports current needs ("to keep the lights on"), but also addresses future business needs. Supplier's relationship, transformation and delivery capabilities are crucial for building a win-win customer-vendor relationship in outsourcing initiatives.

2 Lean Governance Model [1]

IT departments within a business are traditionally segregated by application areas or technology platforms each of which typically have a hierarchical structure for implementation and control of processes.

Though various business functions[1] are critical to the organization, changing business imperatives are forcing IT departments to be more accountable. With the increasing number of outsourcing initiatives[2], IT is forced to stream-line and structure its operations in order to create a "Governance" model that is "Lean" in nature. Womark and Jones in their seminal book "Lean Thinking" proposed following core concepts for defining "Lean" [2]:

- Specify value in the eyes of the customer
- Identify the value stream and eliminate waste
- Make value flow at the pull of the customer
- Involve and empower employees
- Continuously improve in the pursuit of perfection

"Lean" thinking in manufacturing, service or IT is based on simplicity and achievability of goals. The above concepts boil down to four basic principles of "add nothing but value, empower front line people, add value rapidly and eliminate organisation barriers".

We postulate that these principles are relevant for IT organizations in delivering business value to the business client, in an outsourcing arrangement.

Lean Governance extends to demonstrate the following characteristics in building cohesive customer-vendor relationship:

- Structure that supports the complete life cycle of enterprise's IT operations
- Ownership and accountability of the IT vendor's organization
- Incorporation of speedy roll-out of best practices
- Continuous value addition on an Incremental basis
- Flexibility in size of the IT organization.

Lean Governance is built on the Lifecycle Methodology that enables an organisation to create a structure that supports the complete cycle of an enterprise's IT operations from customer needs to business requirements to IT project definition/delivery to support and maintenance.

---

[1] Include, Strategy & Planning, Demand Management, Resource Management, Change Management etc.

[2] Rottan *et al.* (2006) research indicate that the clients micromanage the offshore suppliers. This practice can increase the cost and erode saving from outsourcing.

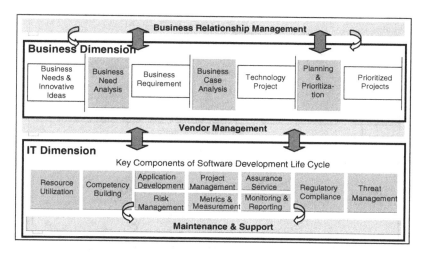

Exhibit 1. Lean Governance framework for relationship management between Client and Vendor

2.1 Application of Lean Governance

In conventional IT Organizations, the IT department is a combination of representation from 'in house' teams and Vendors, where the accountability to business lies with 'in house' IT managers. However, in Lean Governance these roles drop one level, the ownership for IT operations move to the Vendor with accountability to the residual 'in-house' Lean IT organization. In this process the two areas which gain increased importance for in-house IT are Business Relationship Management and Vendor Management.

The Business Dimension will comprise of series of Committees[3] to facilitate the functioning of the Business functions. The Committees mentioned are for guidance only.

The IT Dimension through the Vendor Management layer will provide directions on Application development, Architecture & Technology, Infrastructure, Support & Maintenance, Metrics & Measurement, Change management and Project Management Office (PMO) functions.

2.2 Results of Lean Governance

When applied to a real organizational scenario, lean governance will have various committees with representation from both the in-house teams and vendor teams. These committees are at multiple levels, namely strategic, tactical and operational levels. The communication between the customer and vendor is streamlined to address the business essential, progress, and relationship.

---

[3] Executive, Planning, Steering, Strategy & Planning Group and Strategic Initiatives Group, plus a Business Relationship Manager.

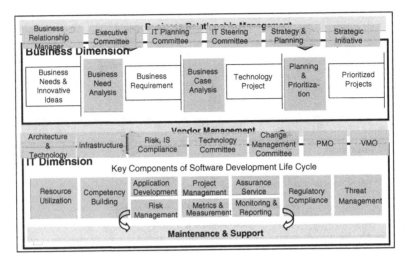

Exhibit 2. Demonstrates application of Lean Governance framework on Business and IT dimensions

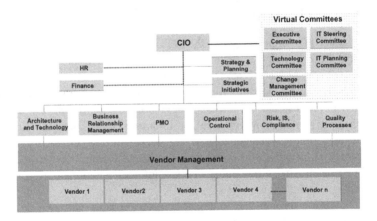

Exhibit 3. A typical Lean Governance structure. This structure is for guidance purpose only and can be further stream-lined based on the size & scale of the organization making sure that all the functions are assigned to a role.

Lean governance does not deal with only the governance structure. It also incorporates the best practices required to ensure value addition on a continuous and incremental basis for the client. The process improvements can vary from situation to situation depending upon the client's needs.

In general the following process elements have to be addressed for any outsourcing initiative to be successful – Establishing a strategic partnership, Sustaining the relationship, Delivering value and Enhancing the relationship into a partnership.

The power of Lean Governance is that it encapsulates all the elements of the enterprise lifecycle and is still flexible for right-sizing without compromising on any role /responsibility.

The following two case studies demonstrate how Lean Governance was implemented both at the structural level as well as process level to achieve the above advantages. This has enabled the 'customer' organizations to gain value over and above those derived from 'vanilla' outsourcing.

3 Case Studies on Lean Governance [1]

3.1 Case Study 1: Lean Governance for Value Enhancement in Outsourcing

3.1.1 Outsourcing Context

Often outsourcing contracts start as a one-off project and with time develop into a well knit relationship which requires proper governance to ensure mutually beneficial results to both the client and the Vendor. In a similar case an outsourcing relationship started between XYZ Ltd. (henceforth called the Customer) and Vendor in a single geography for a single project. With time the deal grew to be a multi-geography and multi-project outsourcing contract.

3.1.2 Lean Governance: Structure Standpoint

As the contract grew in scope the channel of communication became hazy with multiple sources of reporting and contact. This gave rise to a web structure of communication with no clear lines of responsibility and accountability at most parts and duplication of information reporting at other parts. A 'lean' governance structure, therefore was an immediate necessity.

Applying the principles of Lean Governance the Vendor appointed a Global Account Director (GAD) as a single point of contact between the Customer and the Vendor. All delivery and relationship managers would report to the GAD directly, thus removing multiple layers of reporting. Suitable relationship managers were appointed at the critical geographies and extra relationship managers were placed in geographies where it was felt there were greater opportunities.

A think-tank consisting of senior relationship managers was formed with the mandate of meeting once every week to discuss all matters related to the account. This resulted in proper collaboration with sharing and contribution at all levels. In addition a global PMO was formed with PMO from every delivery location with the responsibility of the governance of the global relationship.

All these Resulted in a streamlined communication channel on the vendor's side and a well defined set of contacts for the customer side.

3.1.3 Lean Governance: Process and Innovation Perspective

Application of Lean Governance is never complete by mere restructuring of work process but involves actual process changes and improvements to aid the restructuring. Thus the Vendor in this case to ensure proper implementation of Lean Governance modified processes to aid the change in structure. A system was put in place to document the benefits accrued by using the Vendor's tools and products.

More autonomy was given to the group managers to source people from wherever skills were available resulting in virtual groups. That is, the virtual group was independent of the constituents' geographical location. This resulted in a better collaboration and competency matching to the tasks at hand.

A near shore center was set up and mode of operation was shifted from a single center three shift delivery model to a two center two shift delivery model. This not only provided the client with the required 24/7 service but also reduced the burden of night shifts for the employees.

To keep improving the processes constantly, the innovation process was also formalized. All ideas were logged into a register with a review committee giving a go/no-go on the merit of the ideas. A selected idea was given incubation support and the solution idea was given implementation support. To give incentive to the flow of ideas the Customer at the end of the year gave awards to the top three ideas.

A three year strategy for the relationship with three horizon windows of twelve months each was created after rigorous brainstorming sessions amongst the senior managers of the relationship from the Vendor side. This was solicited by the managers from the Customer side. This ensured a long term and fruitful relationship between the Customer and the Vendor. Finally to ensure that overall strategy did not loose its path Key Performance Indicators (KPIs) were identified and rigorously tracked.

3.2 Case Study 2: Outsourcing Maturity Through Lean Governance

3.2.1 Outsourcing Context

Value delivery through innovation and improvement by the outsourcing vendor becomes a critical driver from the long-term perspective of the customer-vendor relationship. In a relationship between XYZ Ltd. (from now on referred as Customer) and Vendor that is a few year old, the Vendor helps the Customer both with its IT outsourcing as well as Business process outsourcing. For ensuring best results to the Customer, the Vendor implements best practices for outsourcing from day one of the relationship.

3.2.2 Lean Governance: Structure Standpoint

The Vendor finds that a well defined communication framework is essential a step ahead in the customer-vendor relationship. The Vendor ensures that there is regular interaction between the Customer and Vendor at multiple layers. For instance, the Customer's Strategic team and Vendor's strategic team comprising of the Executive Sponsors and Members of Advisory Committees need to open up direct channel of communication. Similar practices adopted at tactical and operational levels.

The Vendor realizes that for any relationship to flourish from being a customer-vendor status to being partners it is necessary to have a proper governance structure. The governance structure should not only be able to support the present functioning but also be flexible enough to take care of future demand. Keeping this in mind a multi layer governance structure was constituted. Committees with representations from Vendor and the Customer side were in place at various levels with distinct tasks to perform. For instance the higher level executive from the Vendor and Customer perform Governance Board review at a regular intervals. They involve in setting strategic directions, validate the business alignment, ensure corporate governance and assess relationship health-check. A portal was set-up to ensure communication, interaction and proper functioning of governance model on a real time basis.

3.2.3 Lean Governance: Process and Innovation Perspective

While structure and tools help to maintain steady relationship, the Vendor needs to be a cut above in adding value to the client, in terms of process improvements and innovations.

The Vendor institutionalized a Center of Excellence (CoE) for Testing. This was different from other testing centers as it not only looked at doing the testing but also at improving the process through automation thereby increasing the overall quality of work. To ensure that the endeavor was a success various KPIs were identified and tracked rigorously.

The Vendor also developed enhanced risk management tool called failure mode effect analysis (FMEA) which was evaluated on the parameters of severity, occurrence and detection score. This led to proper risk management enabling risk identification preemption and mitigation. Thus, reduced cost for the Customer.

Process improvement along with a robust governance model together laid the basis for Lean G3overnance. This led to a fruitful and rewarding continuing relationship for both Vendor and XYZ Ltd. The benefits were tracked on a balanced score card format.

Table 1. depects the XYZ relationship scorecard. The savings are purely due to process improvements and value generation and do not reflect the gains for the customer due to vanilla outsourcing.

Metrics	Measure
Financial Perspective	
Onsite/Offshore Ratio	30:70
No. of People on the relationship	637
*Savings due to Process Improvements and value generation only	1,340K GBP
Customer Perspective	
Number of customer appreciations	130
Number of customer concerns	19
Transformational initiatives [Factory Approach, Testing CoE, CMMi, HR Training, FMEA, Dedicated Portal, Architecture CoE, OD]	9
Customer Satisfaction Index	**86.7**

4 Conclusion

In conclusion, Lean Governance is an excellent governance framework for both the Outsourcer and the Outsourcee as their respective structures are aligned, with clearly defined span of operations and accountability built-in. The Relationship goals roll-up to the Business goals of the enterprise through measurable Key Performance Indicators guaranteeing better Returns on Outsourcing through Lean Governance.

References

1. The concept of Lean Governance is built on the TCS Lifecycle Methodology and best practices implementation. Case studies referred in this article are derived from the Tata Consultancy Services (TCS) experiences and on going relationships with its customers. For the purpose of confidentiality and the customer data security the names of the customers are being omitted, in place the authors have used a fictitious name XYZ Ltd. Vendor cited in the case studies refers to TCS
2. Womack, J.P., Jones, D.T.: Lean Thinking. Simon & Schuster, New York (1996)
3. WTO: Offshoring Service: Recent Development and Prospects - Exploring the Link between Trade, Standards and the WTO. World Trade Report (2005)
4. Corbett, M.F.: The Outsourcing Revolution. Published by Deorborn Trade (2004)
5. Rottman, J.W., Lacity, M.C.: Proven Practices for Effective Offshoring IT Works. MIT Sloan Management Review 47(3), 57–63 (2006)
6. Vertring, T., Rouse, T., Reinert, U.: Hedge your Offshoring Bets. MIT Sloan Management Review 46(3), 27–29 (2005)
7. Feeny, D., Lacity, M., Willcocks, L.P.: Taking the Measure of Outsourcing Providers. MIT Sloan Management Review 46(3), 41–48 (2005)

Making IT Offshoring Work for the Japanese Industries

Sakura Kojima and Makoto Kojima

Tsuda University, Tokyo, Japan
kojimasa@tsuda.ac.jp
Takushoku University, Tokyo, Japan
mkojima@ner.takushoku-u.ac.jp

Abstract. IT offshoring has now become imperative not only for the IT industry but also for the manufacturing industry in Japan. The Japanese hardware industry which has long been globally competitive now faces unexpected challenges, i.e. swelling volumes of programs embedded in electronic devices and systems. The impending serious shortages of IT engineers will soon erode the competitiveness of the industry. Increased global competition and serious manpower shortages are the major background for the IT offshoring. Japanese offshoring is yet at an immature stage, turning mainly to China due to cultural similarity, Japanese language proficiency, and geographical proximity. Through analyzing both failed and successful projects, the authors try to explore fundamental causes for the poor performance and provisionally determine critical factors contributing to the successful offshoring.

Keywords: IT Offshoring; Japanese Manufacturing; Embedded software; Globalization; Global Competitiveness.

1 Introduction

Major Purposes:

Japanese hardware industries have faced unexpected challenges, i.e. swelling volumes of program embedded in an electronics system. Rapid digitization and networking has resulted in an increased importance of "software" in the hardware products. Serious shortages of IT engineers, due to continuous lower-birth-rate, massive retirement of baby-boomer employees, and unpopularity of software industry among younger generation, have made IT offshoring imperative. Japanese IT offshoring is still at an immature stage, lagging far behind the U.S. in its maturity and scale. While most U.S. companies who are mature in IT offshoring are now benefiting from visible cost savings it provides[1], Japanese companies have not yet fully exploited its advantages.

---

[1] According to Gartner, cost savings from offshoring in the U.S. are roughly estimated in the range of 25-50% [5]. In Japanese offshoring, clients companies were reportedly struggling to take even 10% off [6].

B. Meyer and M. Joseph (Eds.): SEAFOOD 2007, LNCS 4716, pp. 67–82, 2007.

IT offshoring has proved to bring various visible benefits (savings in cost and delivery time, and securing IT manpower, etc.) to the outsourcers, apart from risks including security, privacy, and confidential information, but the authors also pay attention to the invisible but innovative aspect it provides: renovation of corporate culture and management to cope with globalization, and presupposes that IT offshoring profoundly affects the Japanese corporate culture and the peoples' mindsets. IT offshoring is far from a mere extension of domestic outsourcing.

The major purpose of this paper is to find out the critical factors for successful IT offshoring, based on the case studies and company interviews. The authors conducted company interviews in three countries: Japan; China; and India between 2004 and 2006 (see Appendix). Since the sample size (21 companies)[2] is too small to analyze the results quantifiably, and the information is patchy and partly subjective, methodology is qualitative (descriptive). The findings and conclusions are tentative. The authors will conduct company interview more and determine critical factors based on purposive sampling in the future. However, it may be meaningful to show the overall picture of Japanese IT offshoring, focusing on embedded software, as a starting point for further discussions.

2   Japanese IT Offshoring Trends

2.1   Size of the Japanese IT Offshoring

The global IT service (including BPO) market amounted to US$ 748 billion in 2003, of which North America accounted for 51%, 30% for the EU and 15% for Asia-Pacific region including Japan [1]. According to the Nasscom-Mckinsey Report, the extent of the global IT offshoring market was estimated to around US$ 30 billion in 2005 [2]. The figures for total Japanese IT offshoring value are not officially available. JISA (Japan Information Technology Services Industry Association) releases the figures annually based on a questionnaire sending to its 670 member companies[3] [3]. However, the figures (US$ 447 million in 2004) seem extremely undervalued and unreliable. Measuring the extent of offshoring is a difficult task even for the U.S. According to the ACM (Association for Computing Machinery), extent of the U.S. offshoring was estimated to be in a range of US$ 10 to 20 billion [4]. According to Gartner Japan, the total value of Japanese IT offshoring to China was estimated to be $750 million in 2004, compared to $250 million of offshoring to India [7]. China and India were the largest recipients of the Japanese offshoring. The authors also made its estimation mainly from the statistics of CSIA (China Software Industry Association) and NASSCOM (National Association of Software and Service Companies) of India. The Japanese offshoring to China in 2004 was estimated to US$ 1.6 billion[4] [8] while offshoring to India was almost US$ 500 million [9]. It seems, therefore, safe to say that the size of the Japanese offshoring is in a range of US$ 1 to 2 billion.

---

[2] The authors interviewed almost 10 Chinese IT vendors, five Japanese client companies, and six Indian IT vendor companies.

[3] Return rate was about only 30%. The number of member companies has increased to 736 in 2006.

[4] Chinese software and IT service exports amounted to almost US$ 2.6 billion in 2004 of which 60% were destined to Japan.

Table1. Software Exports Destined to Japan from China and India (US$ million)

	2003-04	2004-05
China	1,380	1,560
India	385	500

(Source: CSIA [8] and NASSCOM [9])

Table2. Japan's Share in Chinese and Indian IT Services Export

	2003-04	2004-05
China	69.0%	60.0%
India	3.0%	2.8%

(Source: same as Table 1)

2.2 Main Features

To some degree, a global division of labor in offshoring partnership is beginning to form: India serving the English-speaking world, former Eastern Europe and Russia serving Western Europe, and China serving Japan. India exported almost 70% of software products and services to the U.S, while China's export share towards Japan amounted to almost 60% in 2004 [9] [8].

A questionnaire done by JISA in 2003 clarified that only 18% of replied companies (N=32) were actually executing IT offshoring, of which 88% companies utilized China and 33% also utilized India [3]. China and India are the most popular offshore locations (see Fig.1).

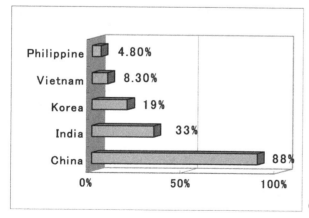

(Source: JISA [3])

Fig. 1. Top Five Offshore Locations

While the share of companies who were actually executing IT offshoring in 2000 was only 6 %, the share of the companies who have plan to start offshoring until 2006 was 49% [3]. This indicates Japanese IT offshoring will be greatly accelerating. The survey also clarified that offshoring accounted for only 10% of total outsourcing costs (as of 2003), reflecting Japan's immaturity.

Most Japanese companies tend to prioritize language proficiency and cultural similarity when they select an offshoring destination. There are significant numbers of Chinese students studying in Japan (63,000 in 2005) who will be candidates for high-level manpower bridging the gap between the two cultures. In this connection, Indian students studying in Japan amounted to only 364. The manpower with language proficiency plus multi-cultural comprehension, besides IT knowledge, is being called "Bridge Software Engineers (Bridge SE)." Regarding availability of Bridge SE, China is much more attractive for Japanese companies than is India.

The aims of IT offshoring to China are, first and foremost, cost reduction, followed by securing a certain amount of IT engineers (especially of Java language and web technology), reduction of development cycle time, and exploiting the Chinese domestic market (localization of Japanese software products)[10]. Wage rate of IT engineer in Shanghai (one of the most expensive areas), for example, was almost half of the Japanese average rate [10].

2.3 Background of Japanese IT Offshoring

Japan is a late starter of offshoring business which has accelerated on a full-scale since 2000, exclusively turning to China. Development of embedded software (like car navigation and mobile phone, for example) rather than business application software has constituted a major part of offhored products or services. In light of Japan's weak competitiveness in the field of business software products, especially package software, OS, middleware and tools, majority of which are imported from the U.S. [3], most promising sphere left for Japan must be in an embedded software. Japan's electronic industry has now confronted with mushrooming of the program size. In the case of mobile phone, for example, the size of embedded software in terms of LOC (line of code) has increased from 700k in 1996 to 2.2M in 2002, while required development periods have shortened from one year in the early 90s to half a year in 2002 [11].

In Japan, there are almost 380 thousands "embedded system engineers" in 2005, of which 46% or 175 thousands are classified as "embedded software engineers" [12]. A shortage of embedded software engineers was estimated to be around 75,000 in 2004 [12]. Shortages of manpower will be accelerating due to the continuous lower-birth-rate phenomenon, beginning of massive baby-boomer retirement from 2007, and the increasing unpopularity of demanding IT industry among younger generation.

Global competitive pressures, in addition to the serious shortages of IT engineers, have compelled Japanese companies to increasingly incline to IT offshoring since the end of the 1990s. Offshoring to China theoretically makes Japanese client companies save, on average, around 30 to 50% of development costs[5] except initial costs, if the

---

[5] Actually, though, cost saving ratio may be, on average, less than 10% at this point, according to one estimate [6]. 20% in cost savings was considered thresholds for dividing "success" and "failure." [14].

processes are properly managed. If the quality is assured, offshoring will provide them with merits in cost, securing skilled IT manpower, and precise delivery. IT offshoring becomes an unavoidable option, especially in the sphere of embedded software.

2.4 Immature Stage of IT Offshoring

According to the global experiences, probability of failure becomes higher for the case of initial projects or immature stage of offshoring. In the U.S., for example, most companies which become matured in offshoring have generally shifted their perception from negative and skeptical attitude to an appreciation of the savings it can provide for [5]. China was most popular destination due to the availability of a significant number of IT engineers with good Japanese language proficiency. In spite of the lower language barriers, not a few earlier projects in the 1990s were said to be failed or unsatisfactory. This may be partly because of the lesser accumulated experiences on both sides, and partly because "cost reduction" was top-prioritized without knowing necessity of initial costs and difficulty in quality management. Nowadays, achieving 70% of targeted quality and delivery for the case of the initial offshoring are considered as satisfactory [10].

Recently, various useful knowledge of IT offshoring have been accumulated within an individual company (especially larger-sized System Integrators) so that IT offshoring performance among these companies has become much better than in the past. However, this valuable knowledge are not commonly shared yet.

3 Problems of Japanese IT Offshoring

Not a few projects offshored to China have been unsatisfactory or even failed in spite of lower language barriers. Japanese companies complained that quality was not satisfactory, and the cost turned to be much more than they expected, and so forth [6]. Poor performance may be particularly observed at an earlier stage of offshoring universally. Nowadays, some lessons drawn from the earlier failed projects are available.

Major purpose in this section is to identify the root causes for poor performance based on an analysis of a few failed projects. But before that, the authors clarify how reasons for the failure were subjectively perceived by both parties, i.e. Japanese companies and Chinese (and Indian) IT vendors.

3.1 Lessons from the Earlier Projects

It has passed almost a decade since the Japanese companies started their earliest projects. Although very few cases[6] were successful, many of the earlier projects were reportedly failed. This was partly because the purpose of offshoring, at that time, was

---

[6] The case of Neusoft seems exceptionally successful. This company, now ranked as the second largest software vendor in China, used to be a very small venture when it had started software business at the Northeastern Univ. and formed a joint venture in 1991 with the Japanese car navigation maker, Alpine. Now the total employees were 6,000 in 2004.

exclusively "cost reduction" so that Chinese vendors were considered cheap subcontractors, and outsourced only downstream (or lower-value-added) processes like coding and testing without knowing the basic design and entire configuration. Chinese software engineers are, on average, paid a third of Japanese engineers. Even if the total cost when offshoring to China becomes half of Japanese domestic outsourcing, at least 20% to 30% of initial cost may accrue [10]. "Cost imperative" without fine-tuned communications and mutual understanding had resulted in an unexpected increase of cost and poor quality.

Most companies now think much of quality as well as cost element. In order to improve overall quality, they tend to ask Chinese engineers to participate in from the upstream processes and a joint review [17]. Other valuable lessons are also drawn from analyzing a few "successful projects" [7] offshored to China [17]:

First, enhancing language proficiency, mutual cultural understanding, fine-tuned communication, and frequent meeting are significantly critical at an early stage of IT offshoring. One successful company, for example, purposely tried to standardize terminology or jargon for decreasing bugs from the beginning.

Second, investment in knowledge transfer education for IT engineers, especially at an initial stage, must be critical.

Third, monitoring or joint reviews are to be executed regularly and as frequently as possible.

Fourth, long-term contract based on partnership rather than subcontractors, which may also improve motivations of Chinese vendors, is thought to be important [17].

Many Chinese IT vendors have established their subsidiary companies in Japan, serving Japanese client companies. Today, this pattern is most common in which a Japanese client company first contracts with a Japanese IT vendor who will in turn contract with a Japanese subsidiary of Chinese vendor to do programming work in China. Although this model is costly, it is said to enhance better and frequent communications, and allows Chinese engineers to join in the upstream software process.

3.2 Problems of IT Offshoring: Japanese Client Views

A questionnaire survey revealed the most serious problems recognized by Japanese companies (as of 2003) were as follows [14]:

First, language barriers and time-consuming translation work;
Second, reluctance to cope with specification changes and lack of earnestness to understand customers' requirements;
Third, cost-push factors including frequent overseas travel expenses, translation costs, and additional expenses for making documents;
Fourth, poor quality caused by low motivation and poorly managed quality control;

---

[7] Although "success or failure" should be technically evaluated from to what extent the original estimate in QCD is fulfilled, the author found that the definition of "successful project" seemed very vague and subjective. Each company has its own goals and metrics to gauge the performance, but principally they depended more on the subjective evaluation from longer perspective.

Fifth, low levels of overall technology including lack of domain knowledge and significant variance in skill-levels among team members.

Other problems were: reluctance for overtime work; high attrition rate; poor development infrastructure; and security lapses and leak of confidential information.

3.3 Problems of IT Offshoring: Overseas Vendors Views

The most formidable problem that the Chinese (and Indian) IT vendors felt when doing offshore business with Japanese customers was, first and foremost, the "frequent changes of requirements and specifications" [18]. Software development process commonly seen in Japan significantly differs from globally accepted norms. They usually start software development without clearly defined requirements, specifications and functions beforehand, and change specifications (and even requirements) frequently to meet the targeted quality and configuration at a later stage. This method presupposes frequent face-to-face communication and hard work including overnight work, which can function in a domestic outsourcing environment, but are quite hard for offshoring.

Second, "lack of mutual understanding (frequent occurrence of misunderstanding)" and "not listening to what vendors say or suggest." [18]

Third, ambiguous expressions in specifications, documents, and quality definitions [18]. Overseas vendors consider that this is mainly because of lack of writing skills on the side of Japanese engineers. This can be partly because of a homogeneous society, in which Japanese are unconsciously accustomed to ambiguous expressions and verbal communications based on a tacit understanding. "Visibility" or efforts to make everybody understand has long been undervalued.

Fourth, treating overseas vendors as subcontractors, not as business partners mainly from their cost saving purpose. Much of the offshored business is patchy, lacking in continuity and low-value added. For example, an installation-only job for ERP imported from the U.S. is the case [18].

The authors also interviewed with some Indian IT vendors[8] doing embedded software business in Japan. According to them, in spite of the huge potential in embedded software offshoring, Indian IT vendors face difficulty to get the jobs because hardware and software are interlinked in an embedded system, and it is not easy to separate software only for outsourcing [19]. This may be caused by the unique Japanese development process, largely based on "integral architecture," rather than "modular architecture."

3.4 Fundamental Causes for the Problems

If both Japanese companies and overseas vendors accumulate more experiences in IT offshoring, the performance will be eventually improved, depending on the interactive learning curve. Through various company interviews conducted, the authors tentatively concluded that Japanese companies (outsourcers) are primarily responsible for the performance:

---

[8] Currently, there are more than 70 Indian IT vendors in Japan (as of 2005), according to the IT Club.

First and foremost, unique Japanese software development process or technique bears the blame for the problems when it is applied to overseas outsourcing. They usually start software development with loosely defined requirements and specifications and change specifications frequently to meet the targeted quality levels and final configurations. This gradual improvement approach with continuous adjusting and changing is called "integral architecture," rather than "modular architecture" [20]. Because of the complexity and interdependence of subsystems in the integral architecture, collaboration with foreign engineers or slicing off software only for outsourcing is difficult.

This technique or approach has been recently recognized as inefficient and time-consuming even among Japanese companies [21]. A Software Engineering approach has not yet been well diffused to the Japanese IT industry, especially in the embedded software sphere [22]. Japanese companies should endeavor to adopt global standard techniques as much as possible if they want to succeed in getting benefits from IT offshoring.

Second, ambiguous expressions (based on a tacit understanding) observed in requirements, specifications, and documents have caused serious problems including fatal errors when it comes to transmitting business requirements or technological specifications which require strictness, were it done with foreign entities outside Japan. Ambiguity is the great bugaboo of requirements specifications. Many software problems arise from shortcomings in the ways that people gather, document, agree on, and modify product requirements [23]. Errors made during the requirements stage account for 40 to 60 % of all defects found in a software project [24]. Ambiguity should be reduced as much as possible, and the writing skills of technology specifications among engineers need to be improved through training. A Requirements Engineering approach is very much needed in Japan. A major consequence of requirements-related problems is rework which can consume 30 to 50 % of the total development cost, and requirements errors account for 70 to 85 % of the rework cost [25]. It costs far more to correct a defect that is found late in the project cycle than to fix it shortly after its creation [26]. Quality level to be required by clients should also be clearly defined beforehand.

Third, Japanese companies should have clearly-defined strategy for what to be outsourced and how to manage the divided process. Especially, nurturing the high-level manpower who is in charge of managing IT offshoring process is an urgent task [27]. Differentiating offshorable (suitable for offshore) from non-offshorable processes or business is a prerequisite for successful offshoring. The requirements that are unsuitable for offshoring are, for example, small development projects; short-term delivery business; the case where frequent change is being required; products requiring high quality and superior performance; and products containing critical technology. Modularized functions which are separable and not integrated with other functions could be preferable for offshoring.

Fourth, Japanese companies tend to treat overseas IT vendors as their subcontractors, rather than partners. The "client-subcontractor relationship" has long been the norm of the software industry in Japanese domestic outsourcing. IT vendors must learn the customers' unique and specific business terminology and development techniques, and adapt everything to the customer's business environment. It must be quite hard for foreign IT vendors to emulate. Problematic is that offshoring was still considered a mere extension of domestic IT outsourcing by many client companies. To maximize the benefits from IT offshoring, the client companies are advised to change their attitudes toward IT vendors, and build an partnership with them from a long term viewpoint.

Fifth, successful offshoring constitutes good communication and comprehension capability on different cultural background. Steeped in a monolithic culture, most Japanese are poor in understanding different cultural or multi-cultural context. To cope with globalization, English proficiency and comprehension capability on different cultures among IT engineers should be enhanced either through intensive training or increased exposure to the multi-cultural context.

4 Strategic IT Offshoring for Maintaining Competitiveness

The most promising and potentially competitive software sphere left for Japan must be embedded software. Until recently, Japanese software companies have exclusively supplied their custom-made products to the domestic market rather than supplying generic package products to the global market [13]. They have avoided competing outside Japan, and remained in a cozy domestic market. However, the Japanese domestic consumer market will soon start to get shrinking due to continuous lower-birth-rate. According to the Government estimate, one of the serious economic effects may be lowering her economic growth rate (from 2.6% in 2000 through 1.8% in 2010 to 0.8% in 2025) and reducing annual growth rate of per capita income (from 1.9% in 2000 to − 0.3% in 2025) [15]. It is also said that the software companies would not survive in the future unless they become dominant players in a global market.

If they would like to become global suppliers of embedded system, Japanese companies need to renovate their corporate culture and management drastically, including adoption of a globally accepted development methodology. The authors believe that IT offshoring, especially to India, may provide one effective route for them to transform their inward-looking corporate culture and mindsets.

4.1 Strategic Selection of Offshore Locations: Benchmarking Indian and Chinese Software Strength

China still remains most favored destination, while some companies turn their concerns to Vietnam, for example, for risk-spreading and avoiding a wage-hike in China. When supplying to the Chinese and Japanese domestic markets, it must be logical for the Japanese client companies to outsource to Chinese IT vendors. However, when supplying to the global market, Japanese companies likely turn to Indian IT vendors for collaboration because of their rich business experience with major U.S. and EU companies.

India and China have rapidly come to the forefront in a global IT services offshoring market, thanks to their rich reservoir of human resources. Given that offshoring to China and India is further accelerating, Japanese companies are increasingly keen to benchmark Indian and Chinese IT vendors and assess their weakness and strengths, which may be necessary and helpful for making effective sourcing strategy [29].

The 2002 annual Chinese software industry turnover reached US$ 13.3 billion, finally overtaking the Indian IT service industry (see Fig.2). However, the Chinese software industry significantly fallen behind India in global offshoring business. China has much less experience in IT offshoring, to say nothing of global business experience. At least, India's top five players like TCS, Infosys, Wipro. Satyam, and HCL have rich global business knowledge and experience, which Chinese IT companies are eager to learn from them [30]. Almost 90% of Chinese software industry turnover was from her domestic market, with majority of Chinese exports heading for Japan, while most of India's sales (80%) accrued from overseas: 70% from the U.S., 23% from the EU, and 3% from Japan [9]. India surpasses China significantly for IT services export (see Fig.3).

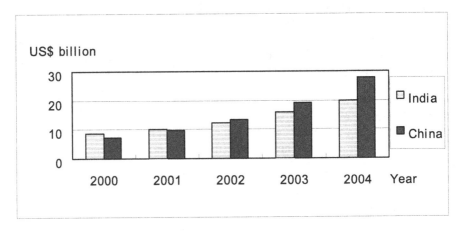

Fig. 2. Annual Turnovers of Software Industry in China and India

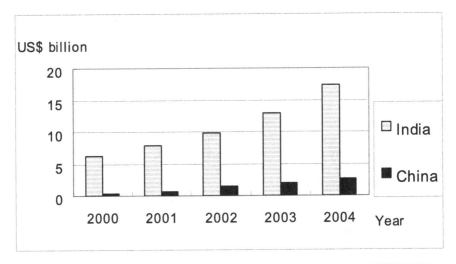

Fig. 3. Software Exports from China and India (Source: CSIA [8] and NASSCOM [9])

The authors tentatively found the strength and weakness of Chinese and Indian software industry as follows:

First, export-oriented Indian IT industry has much more experiences in global offshoring businesses, compared to China.

Second, the average IT worker wage levels in India are higher than those in China. NASSCOM admitted the recent Indian IT industry labor wage hike [9].

Third, Chinese IT industry has rich domain knowledge in manufacturing, which may become competitive in embedded software in future.

Fourth, India is superior to China in higher quality and adhering to global quality standards. By 2005, India had 85 companies at SEI-CMM Level 5 [9], while China has 17 companies only [8].

Fifth, one major difference between Indian and Chinese software industries is in the size of the companies and projects. India has many larger-sized companies among which top ranked TCS, for example, employs 45,000 (as of 2005), while China has mainly medium- and small-sized companies. Even 2nd ranked Neusoft had only about 6,000 employees (as of 2004).

Company size seems closely related to project size. Especially big Indian companies have had long offshore business history with major American MNCs (Multinational Corporations), and experienced numerous big projects. Through this, they have learned how to manage larger projects effectively, mastering the best practices in project management techniques. China, meanwhile, has generally lacked such experiences, consequently falling greatly short of project managers.

4.2 One Effective Way Leading to Successful Offshoring: Training in India

Although Indian IT industry is nowadays much more evaluated in terms of export-orientation, rich global experiences, higher quality levels, and higher capability of larger-sized project management, India had been psychologically and geographically remote and negatively-stereotyped for most Japanese companies. However, recently, a risk-spreading mentality and recent serious concerns over intellectual property have also made Japan's offshoring business swing from China to India. Although there are many more hurdles to overcome when they outsource to India than to China, major Japanese companies begin to recognize various advantages of utilizing Indian vendors.

The authors believe that deepening offshoring businesses with Indian IT vendors who have rich experiences and accumulated know-how in business with global players, will eventually bring benefits to the Japanese companies when they start to learn globally standardized development style or methods prevailing among major Western companies, to say nothing of tapping emerging market in India.

Recently, major Japanese electronics companies like NEC and Toshiba, for example, have begun to utilize India for their IT training.

Both Toshiba and NEC have dispatched their engineering employees to India where they would be given several-months intensive training. The person at Toshiba, told us that nurturing Japanese IT engineers with global mindsets is critical not only for future successful IT offshoring but also for the global competitiveness of the company, and India is most suitable place for training of Japanese engineers in various meanings:

First, training curricula are more sophisticated and comprehensive than those at Japanese training institutes, which provide only patchy and insufficient curricula.

Second, knowledge of state-of-the-art technology is available.

Third, accumulation of rich knowledge and experiences in global offshoring with major Western client companies could be learnt.

Fourth, the training menu is more practical and business-oriented.

Fifth, training fees are less expensive.

Training in India was expected to improve the weaknesses of Japanese software engineers, i.e. enhancing their cross-cultural communication skills, English proficiency, requirements and specifications writing skills, and project management capability [16].

Considering that there are much more hurdles to overcome when they outsource to India than to China, training Japanese IT engineers in India may indirectly contribute to the successful offshoring to India in the future.

5 Making Offshoring Work for the Japanese Industries

Generally speaking, there are, so far, very few success stories in offshoring business with India mainly because of language and cultural barriers. But the authors found one successful case (Firm JO) which has already started LSI design and embedded software offshoring to India since 1988. This case is exceptional but considered to provide many useful lessons for other Japanese companies.

In this section, through introducing and analyzing this case, the authors try to provisionally determine the critical factors making offshoring work for the Japanese industries. Before introducing the case study, the authors briefly describe the overview of the Japanese embedded software industry.

5.1 Overview of the Embedded Software Industry

According to the first comprehensive survey conducted by METI in 2004, the annual turnover of embedded software was estimated at more than 2 trillion yen (US$ 17 billion) in 2003[9] and the figures for embedded systems amounted to 5 trillion yen (US$ 43 billion) [12]. The total turnover of Japanese electronics industry was about 20 trillion yen (US$ 174 billion) in 2003, according to JEITA (Japan Electronics and Information Technology Industries Association), of which 10% was, therefore, produced by the embedded software [28]. The importance of software vis-à-vis hardware in a system has significantly increased.

The engineers who specialize in embedded system development are divided into two: embedded software engineer and embedded hardware engineer. A number of embedded system engineer was estimated at 380 thousands in 2004 of which 175 thousands were classified as embedded software engineer [12]. A large number of

---

[9] The Japanese IT services industry as a whole produced annual sales of 14 trillion yen in 2003 [3].

companies are suffering from dire shortages of embedded software engineers especially in such fields as factory automation and robotics, digital consumer electronics, wireless communication equipment (including mobile phones), automotive electronics and have plans to significantly increase their numbers within three years. According to a reliable estimate, the deficiency is in a range of 75,000 to 90,000.

5.2 Recent Trends in Embedded Software Offshoring

Especially, application and middleware layers of embedded software, of which program volume has been mushrooming, are said to be suitable for offshoring either to China or India, compared with other layers. Japanese companies have recently been more cautious about offshoring in this field to China, who is rapidly catching up to Japanese hardware industry and whose intellectual property regulations are unreliable and weak. In this regard, India or Vietnam (to a lesser extent) is considered appropriate alternative location. India is said to be rather weak in hardware manufacturing, but its chip design capability is highly evaluated and especially, since 2000, the number of chip designers and embedded software engineers has greatly increased [31]. Rapidly expanding Indian domestic market in consumer electronics also becomes attractive for them.

Recently, many Japanese electronics and semiconductor manufacturers have rushed to start offshoring to India. Renesas Technologies, Elpida Memory and NEC Electronics are the cases. However, it was only last year (in 2006) for them to begin offshoring to India, while global top players like Texas Instruments and STMicroelectronics had already started offshoring to India since the latter half of 1980s [32].

5.3 Successful Offshoring of VLSI Design and Embedded Software to India: The Case of Firm JO

The earliest successful offshoring projects in the embedded software to India can be found in the case of Firm JO which had started business with India since 1988. Firm JO has outsourced design and development of OS for 16 bit (recently 32 bit) microcomputer and various kinds of application software to medium-sized Indian IT vendor which is based in the U.S. There is no capital relationship. There is an offshore development center (ODC) in Noida where 75 Indian and 25 Japanese engineers work together.

According to the Executive Director of Firm JO, the firm could achieve the highest efficiency and performance that it had ever attained (20 to 30 % above the global levels) and the highest quality in addition to the enormous cost savings [33]. The firm has evaluated IT offshoring to India "successful" for almost 18 years. It has a clear-cut definition on what the "success" is. There are three criteria: "on-time rate," measuring to what extent each work being done according to the original schedule; "process compliance rate," assessing to what extent the work being done process by process in due order that was defined in the specifications; "function achievement rate," measuring to what extent the functions being fulfilled and achieved. [33].

The authors analyzed the case carefully, and tentatively drew some lessons:

First, IT vendor selection must be a key factor influencing the outcomes. The Indian vendor in this case has already proved sufficient high performance in offshoring business, and is furnished with excellent manpower and better development infrastructure. Quality control concept at the vendor could be shared with Firm JO since it fully implements and applies Japanese quality and production system (TQM) to its software development and maintenance processes, in addition to achieving the highest quality levels in terms of CMM and ISO.

Second, long-term relationship, based on "partnership," may bring benefits for the client company in terms of significant cost savings (since vendor is said to be willing to provide a service at discounted rate to Firm JO, presupposing their long-term contract); fine-tuned communications; and shared destiny.

Third, unlike other typical Japanese companies, Firm JO strictly defines requirements and various specifications, and excludes ambiguity in the Japanese language before translating into English. Specification itself is verified beforehand as much as possible. Some critical terminology is always defined beforehand to have same meaning to both Indian and Japanese engineers.

Fourth, concerning which processes are to be outsourced, Firm JO found that offshoring from the detailed specification design process proved to be more efficient.

Fifth, to cope with specification changes effectively, Indian vendor implements either feasibility studies or developing a prototype [33].

This case indicates that if software engineering approach is properly implemented, language barriers which constitute most formidable challenge could not be such a serious bottleneck for Japanese companies.

The authors attempt to collect and analyze the successful cases like Firm JO more, and will quantitatively determine the critical factors making Japanese offshoring work in the near future.

Acknowledgements

The authors are deeply grateful to the representatives of the 21 companies for their extensive cooperation in interviews and detailed answers to my many questions.

References

1. WISTA: Digital Planet 2004. Arlington (2004)
2. NASSCOM-McKinsey Report 2005. NASSCOM, New Delhi (2005)
3. JISA: White Paper on Information Technology Services Industry 2004. Computer Age, Tokyo (2004)
4. Aspray, W., Mayadas, F., Vardi, M.Y.: Globalization and Offshoring of Software. A Report of the ACM Job Migration Task Force. ACM (2006),
   http://www.acm.org/globalizationreport
5. Gold, T.: Outsourcing Software Development Offshore. Auerbach Publication, Washington, D.C (2005)

6. Jinnai, K.: Learn from Offhoring. Project Management Magazine (in Japanese), Shoeisha, Tokyo, vol. 1, pp. 83–103 (2005)
7. Gartner Japan: Offshoring to India and China: Competitors? Subcontractors? Partners?. In: IT Management (October 5, 2005)
8. CSIA: Annual Report of China Software Industry 2005. CSIA, Beijing (in Chinese) (2005)
9. NASSCOM: Strategic Review 2006. The IT Industry in India. NASSCOM, New Delhi (2006)
10. Study Group of Overseas Outsourcing: Overseas Outsourcing Guide Book of Software Development to China. Computer Age, Tokyo (in Japanese) (2005)
11. IPA (Information Technology Promotion Agency), SEC (Software Engineering Center): Embedded Technology Report, Shoeisha, Tokyo (2005) (in Japanese) (2005)
12. METI (Ministry of Economy, Trade and Industry), Commerce and Information Policy Bureau: Survey on the Current Embedded Software Industry, METI, Tokyo (2005) (in Japanese) (2005)
13. Cusumano, M.: The Puzzle of Japanese Software. In: Communications of the ACM, vol. 48(7), ACM Press, New York (2005)
14. S-open Offshoring Development Study Committee: Comprehensive Guide Book on Software Development Offshoring. Nikkei BP, Tokyo (in Japanese) (2004)
15. National Institute of Population and Social Security Research: Web Page on Problems of Population, http://www. Ipss.go.jp/syoushika/seisaku/html/121b1.htm
16. Interview with Toshiba (April 2006)
17. Interview with three Japanese clients companies (JI; JF; and JH) and three Chinese IT vendors (CS; CT; and CB)
18. Interview with four Indian IT vendors (II; IK; IN; IA) and five Chinese IT vendors (CY; CP; CB; CS; and CO)
19. Interview with Indian IT vendor (IK)
20. Cusumano, M.: The Business of Software. Free Press, New York (2004)
21. IPA SEC: Establishing the Software Engineering Approach in Japan. Nihon Keizai Shinbun (in Japanese) (April 28th 2005)
22. Interview with Japanese client company (JO and JT)
23. Wiegers, K.: Software Requirements, 2nd edn. Microsoft Press, Washington (2003)
24. Davis, A.: Software Requirements: Objects, Functions, and States. Englewood Cliffs, NJ (1993)
25. Leffingwell, D.: Calculating the Return on Investment from More Effective requirements Management. American Programmer 10(4), 13–16 (1997)
26. Grady, R.: An Economic Release Decision Model. Insights into Software Project Management. In: Proceedings of the Applications of Software Measuremnet Conference, pp. 227–239. Orange Park, FL (1999)
27. Interview with three Japanese Client Companies (JT; JH; and JF)
28. JEITA: Data Map for the Electronics and Information Technology Industries in Japan. JEITA, Tokyo (2003)
29. Kojima, M., Kojima, S.: The Catch-up Game between India and China. In: Asian Management Review (October- December, 2005)
30. Interview with vice director of Beijing City Software Industry Promotion Center, (September 7, 2005)
31. Indian Semiconductor Association-Frost & Sullivan Study on the Indian Semiconductor Industry: VLSI and Embedded Design Market and Its Impact on Indian Economy, http://www.isaonline.org/pub-mrreport.html

32. Kojima, Ikutaro: Indian Power in LSI Design. In: Nikkei Microdevices (In Japanese) (December 2006)
33. Interview with Company (JO) in (December, 2004 and January 2007)

Appendix: Abbreviation of 21 Companies Interviewed

The author avoids mentioning the names of the companies interviewed in order to protect their privacy.

Japanese Companies	Client	Indian Vendors	Chinese Vendors	
1. JT		1. II	1. CT	7. CW
2. JH		2. IT	2. CN	8. CO
3. JO		3. IK	3. CF	9. CH
4. JI		4. IJ	4. CH	10. CS
5. JF		5. IN	5. CB	
		6. IA	6. CP	

Mastering Dual-Shore Development – The Tools and Materials Approach Adapted to Agile Offshoring

Andreas Kornstädt and Joachim Sauer

Software Engineering Group, Department of Informatics, University of Hamburg
and C1 WPS GmbH, Vogt-Kölln-Str. 30, 22527 Hamburg, Germany
{ak,js}@c1-wps.de

Abstract. Software development in offshoring settings with distributed teams presents particular challenges for all participants. Process models that work well for conventional projects may have to be adapted. In this paper we present case-study-reinforced advice on how to extend the Tools & Materials approach – a well established communication-centered agile design and development approach – to the field of dual-shore development in offshoring projects. We show how communication challenges can be tackled with common guiding and design metaphors, architecture-centric development, task assignments with component tasks and extensive quality assurance measures.

Keywords: Offshoring, Tools & Materials approach, dual-shore, architecture-centric development, agile practices.

1 Motivation

Offshoring is a dominant trend in software development with annual growth rates of about 33% in markets such as India [1]. It promises benefits in the areas of costs, flexibility and concentration on core competencies. Empirical studies have shown, however, that offshoring also entails a considerable number of challenges. Offshoring projects are at the top of the complexity scale with diverse issues in areas of organization, management, communication and teamwork. This is especially true for projects that feature geographically separated onshore and offshore project teams [2]. When over 5000 executives across North America and Europe were asked about the success of their offshore strategy in 2004, 36% considered their offshore strategy failed and over one in three had to move work back from their offshore to their onshore team [3].

Given these figures, it is easy to see why looking at measures that help preventing project failure is worth the effort. In this paper we show how process models can be extended and adapted to the complex challenges of offshore projects. We have explored these issues based on the Tools & Materials approach (T&M) [4] which has been used successfully in many single-site agile development projects. The extensions have been validated in a first substantial case study with onshore and offshore teams.

After giving an overview of different offshoring approaches and limiting this paper's scope to the dual-shore approach we go on to demonstrate that communication is a core challenge in offshoring projects. We then present the T&M approach and

B. Meyer and M. Joseph (Eds.): SEAFOOD 2007, LNCS 4716, pp. 83–95, 2007.

show how it has helped us meeting communication challenges in single-site projects. We describe how this approach has been adapted to dual-shore development by augmenting it by four new elements. Then we present findings from the case study. Finally, in the concluding section, we will sum up the essence of the extended approach and give an outlook on future research.

2 Collaboration Models for Offshoring

Offshoring comes in many flavors, but not all of them are pertinent to solutions in the area of software architecture. The only – although highly relevant – two complications that classic offshoring projects introduce are those of cultural differences and split locations. While these problems are not to be underestimated, they can be seen as just an exacerbation of the classic problems between the business-side and the engineering-side of a "normal" single-site software project because the line between on-site and offshore is identical with the line between specification and implementation. These difficulties, however, aren't new and have been thoroughly dealt with in software engineering literature [4].

Experience reports have shown [5] that this classic offshoring setting works best with stable specifications and a minimal need for communication during implementation. To put it in an oversimplified way: The specification is sent to the offshore location and after a while the binaries are shipped back for testing. Many software development projects are too complex to be dealt with in such a fashion. They require frequent interaction between the business-side and the engineering-side due to complex and rapidly changing requirements on the business-side. The dual-shore model for offshoring caters to these needs: As trying to discuss these changes in requirement over huge distances with people from different cultural backgrounds appears to be too difficult, development is carried out on-site as well as offshore. The on-site team is staffed with local developers who deal with the business-side. As both sides are from the same cultural group and located at the same site, classic offshoring problems between business-side and engineering-side can be avoided completely. The divide between shores now runs right through the development team. But this location of the rift is still advantageous to the classic setting because now communication partners on both sides are engineers.

It is this dual-shore setting that we have in mind when dealing with offshoring in this paper. Before describing the specifics of our dual-shore approach in section 5, we will first establish the necessary basis by taking a closer look at the challenges that these projects are faced with (section 3) and by introducing the T&M approach which encompasses many helpful concepts in overcoming them (section 4).

3 Offshoring Benefits and Offshoring Challenges

Clearly, the dominant expectation of corporations that outsource (parts of) their IT is cost saving [6]. While there are other factors such as increased flexibility, none of these factors comes close to the 90% mark that is reached by cost benefits.

While past studies used to focus on benefits, recent studies have also examined challenges that offshoring entails. These include unexpectedly high costs for infrastructure, communications, travel and cultural training; lower productivity due to high staff turnover at the offshore site and low morale at the onshore site; management problems due to cultural differences and a poor spread of information; problems when communicating with customers; and technical mismatches of all sorts [2, 5, 7].

When faced with these problems in an unsorted and condensed form as above, they appear to be very hard to tackle. It helps, however, to examine how these problems interrelate. This leads to a distinction between problems on different levels where the problems at the higher levels are direct consequences of problems at the lower levels. We describe these levels here as introduced in [8].

Primary or *root challenges* stem directly from the decision to outsource to an offshore location:

- Morale at the onshore site is low.
- It is difficult to develop a team spirit that spans two sites. Sharing the goals of the project, expectations, and domain-specific as well as technical knowledge is not easy.
- Onshore and offshore staff comes from different cultural backgrounds. This entails various kinds of misunderstandings. Different views about how to deal with the role of authority make management an especially hard challenge. Direct communication between the customer and the offshore site can make these problems stand out in a very pronounced way.
- Transferring data to and exchanging data with an offshore site usually reveals technical incompatibilities of some sort.
- Serving as an offshore development center for many different distant corporations, there is often a high staff turnover at the offshore site which exacerbates all other primary challenges above.

When the following measures are taken, they constitute *secondary challenges* in their own right:

- travel to establish as much face-to-face contact as possible
- cultural training for onshore and offshore teams
- additional planning to accommodate the lack of direct communication
- technical harmonization

All of these measures eventually lead to *tertiary challenges* which directly affect balance sheets:

- unexpectedly high costs
- lower than expected productivity

With this distinction between primary, secondary and tertiary levels in place, it is obvious that it is advantageous to start tackling the five challenges at the root level before proceeding to derived ones.

Software related technologies cannot do anything to ameliorate problems in the area of morale and they cannot change inherent cultural characteristics. They can help only indirectly in establishing a better understanding between people from different cultural backgrounds. Of the remaining three challenges, technical incompatibilities pertain to infrastructure software exclusively and not to the software under development proper, so they are out of the scope of this paper. Both of the final two challenges (sharing knowledge of any kind, facilitating staff changes at the offshore site) are about communication about the software under development – in the first case between onshore and offshore locations, in the second case between staff members at the offshore site.

These challenges have to be dealt with in development processes. We chose the T&M approach that already incorporates measures to improve communication in development projects to give an example of how to evaluate and further enhance established development processes for dual-shore development. We will present its relevant basic concepts in the next section before we continue to describe necessary enhancements in the following section.

4 The Tools and Materials Approach

The Tools & Materials approach (T&M) facilitates application software development by providing guidance in matters of software architecture and the software development process. It is based upon object-oriented design and development and an evolutionary, agile proceeding.

4.1 Enhancing Communication

T&M focuses on two aspects of communication:

– *precise communication* between all stakeholders (customers-developers, developers-developers, customers-customers), and
– *frequent communication* between all stakeholders

Both aspects aim at reducing to a minimum the impact of unavoidable miscommunication – the core problem of software development in general and especially of offshore outsourcing.

Precise Communication
Based on the realization that communication works best on the basis of a common frame of reference, T&M provides several means of providing this very frame. To do this, it does not introduce new concepts, but recurs to culturally established concepts: metaphors, leitmotifs, and patterns:

Metaphors are at the core of the approach. They provide a very high level of abstraction which is ideally suited for a field that is governed by a high degree of complexity. Without reducing complexity to meaningless statements, metaphors are very compact ways of throwing light on specific aspects of an issue. The main metaphors of T&M are Tool, Material, Automaton, Container and Working Environment (see Fig. 1). These metaphors have the benefit that they are so basic that every customer and every developer has a precise of what a tool is like and – equally important – what a tool is not. By recurring to these five metaphors, there is a level playing field on which all stakeholders can move freely without one of them gaining the upper hand due to an advantage in communication. Developer organizations often unintentionally tend to have these advantages over customers by using UML diagrams that customers do not fully understand. While customers agree to what can be seen in the diagram out of insecurity about its precise semantics, they later complain about the software that has been developed based on this miscommunication.

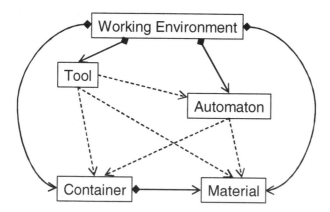

Fig. 1. Main Metaphors of the T&M approach and dependencies between them

As individual metaphors are not necessarily perfect fits, T&M makes use of *guiding metaphors* which establish a common framework into which individual metaphors fit. For generic office applications, the guiding metaphor "Expert Workplace" is a good fit: It is easy to envision Tools, Materials, Automatons (such as a calculator), Containers (such as folders) and a Working Environment (such as a desk with in and out boxes) at an Expert Workplace. Depending on the project in question, the individual set of (guiding) metaphors has to be determined. In many cases, however, only a few metaphors have to be exchanged.

Metaphors of any kind are great for communication between customers and developers (and customers and customers as well) but they are too imprecise when making the transition to executable code [9]. T&M uses two kinds of patterns to smooth that transition:

Conceptual patterns are based on one design metaphor and delineate what a software artifact based on that metaphor behaves like and what it does not behave like. For example, conceptual patterns for materials include "materials never change their state except when handled by a tool or an automaton" and "materials do not hold display code – it is the sole responsibility of tools to display the materials they let the users work on".

Design patterns describe the static and dynamic interaction of individual classes / objects. While some conceptual patterns can be broken down to at least some of the patterns introduced in [10] (Tools are *Observers* of Material), most T&M design patterns, are custom patterns that stem directly from T&M.

(Guiding) Metaphors and conceptual as well as design patterns are excellent means of establishing communications between all stakeholders and have been tested time and again since the 1990's in numerous projects of radically different application domains such as insurances, public utilities, oncology, logistics and oncology. Nevertheless, these means can only provide the elements that are discussed during business process analysis. As conventional UML diagrams have the inherent problems mentioned in the preceding paragraph on metaphors, T&M makes use of *exemplary business process modeling* (EBPM [11]). In contrast to UML diagrams, EBPM diagrams tell the story of a certain process in pictures complete with actors, materials, tools, automatons and containers as well as a different kinds of communication and a explicit thread (indicated by ordinals) along which the story unfolds. See Fig. 2 for an exemplary diagram.

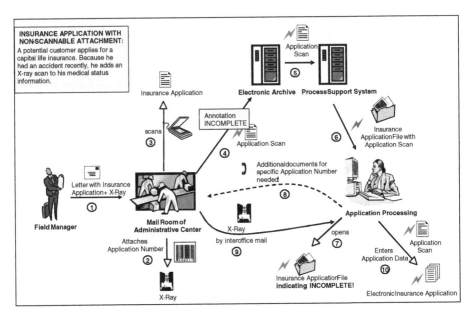

Fig. 2. Example of an EBPM cooperation scenario in the insurance sector

Frequent Communication

As has been shown in the beginning, large communication gaps will eventually lead to costly miscommunications. This is especially true in projects with complex application domains and / or complex team structures. To avoid this source of miscommunications, T&M employs an agile development process with numerous feedback loops ranging from months to seconds in length. For a full list see [9]. Important loops include:

Releases aim at developing new application functionality. The scope is negotiated by customers and developers in planning games about every 6 weeks. This allows for maximum flexibility and avoids the typical problems of formal "complete" specifications which are usually outdated the moment they have been completed (see [9] for benefits of agile development).

Daily *stand-up meetings* during which developers tell each other what they did since the last stand-up and what they intend to do until the next one. These meetings help to evenly spread knowledge about what goes on in every corner of the project.

Programming pair negotiations take place twice a day. By sharing a single computer, developers derive a common understanding about almost every part of the source code. During pair programming, developers are exposed to each others constructive criticism every second so that the software's architecture is constantly a matter of discussion.

Developers can request the presence of an *On-Demand-Customer* any time in case they have questions that cannot be answered by looking at the specification made during the planning game. The customer is obliged to help them within one day. [12]

4.2 Architecture-Based Development

For the implementation part, T&M encourages architecture-based development. According to Bass and Kazman [13], *architecture-based development* "differs from traditional development in that it concentrates on driving design and maintenance from the perspective of a software architecture. The motivation for this change of focus is that a software architecture is the placeholder for system qualities such as performance, modifiability, security, and reliability. The architecture not only allows designers to maintain intellectual control over a large, complex system but also affects the development process itself, suggesting (even dictating) the assignment of work to teams, integration plans, testing plans, configuration management, and documentation. In short, the architecture is a blueprint for all activities in the software development life-cycle."

Architecture-based development thus facilitates communication by improving comprehension through one common object of work that all project participants use and understand. The architecture description introduces terms and concepts that serve as a common language for all stakeholders. Hence it enables precise discussions and arrangements. It also constitutes the basis for verifiable architecture rules. Automatic rule checking improves implementation consistency and reduces the number of errors.

4.3 Summary

Fig. 3 brings together the most pertinent features of the T&M approach: (Guiding) Metaphors form the basis for communication between all stakeholders.

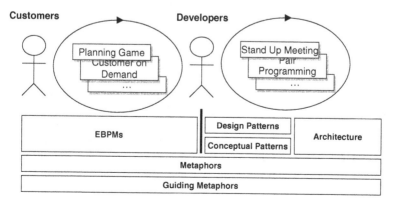

Fig. 3. Overview of the main features of the T&M approach

Customer-Customer and Customer-Developer communication also draws upon EBPMs while Developer-Developer communication uses Conceptual Patterns, Design Patterns and architecture on top of the Metaphors.

All stakeholders communicate on the basis of guiding metaphors and metaphors. On top of that, EBPMs are used between customers and developers. Among developers, architecture descriptions as well as conceptual and design patterns are employed.

5   Extending T and M for Offshore Projects

In section 3 we have discussed the basic problems affecting offshoring projects, leading to the conclusion that communication is of paramount importance. In section 4, we then continued to describe the (single-site) T&M approach which already puts a strong emphasis on communication by introducing metaphors and assigning much importance to architecture. In this section, we draw conclusions from our extensive experience with the application of the T&M approach in single-site projects and challenges and solutions we found in case studies with offshoring projects.

We will first present how single-site T&M should be extended to a dual-shore T&M which can facilitate dealing with offshore communication problems. After introducing our dual-shore model, we will discuss the importance of having a strong focus on architecture and assigning offshore-development tasks component-wise before validating our approach in section 6.

5.1   Dual-Shore Development with Adjusted Agile Practices

The geographical separation of teams in the dual-shore model prevents offshore developers from having an on-site customer at their disposal (*Customer-On-Demand*) and from participating in iteration *Planning Games*. To accommodate for these changed settings, roles are unequally distributed across the teams. The onshore team is made up of software architects and developers. Software architects are responsible for designing and maintaining the application's architecture and carrying out quality assurance. They also serve as business analysts that directly interact with the customer, elucidate the requirements, plan iterations and releases and design the application. The onshore developers train their offshore counterparts at the beginning of projects, perform the main implementation work during the first iterations and tackle difficult implementation work in later iterations. They may also directly interact with the customer to resolve questions.

The offshore team consists entirely of developers. They receive work assignments in the form of component tasks (see 5.3) which they implement in a largely independent fashion, possibly clarifying questions with onshore software architects or in exceptional circumstances with onshore developers.

If possible, the first iterations should be tackled in mixed teams so that the developers get to know each other and develop a common understanding of the domain and the development process. This phase of common development establishes a sound communication basis which can be drawn upon after the offshore team has moved to its offshore location.

5.2 Architecture-Centric Development in Offshoring Projects

While we use architecture-centric development in conventional projects following the T&M approach, it becomes even more valuable in offshoring settings. Communication between the teams benefits greatly from a uniform language and a common technical basis [8].

Architecture also helps in assigning tasks that are decoupled from each other and thus can be developed largely independent by teams at distant sites. So the organization can be split along the product structure [14], reducing the need for inter-site coordination. Additional communication can also be avoided when developers know how they can introduce new features to an application without asking for permission or detailed instructions, e.g. by providing hot spots for enhancements or an explicit plugin-concept.

Architecture rules are defined and regularly checked with automated tools. Onshore software architects design and maintain the application's architecture. The architecture description is regularly communicated to all developers. Changes to the architecture by the developers have to be arranged with the software architects. This way the architecture also evolves from the basis, not only top-down from a software architect's specification. It would be impractical if developers always had to consult a software architect regarding these changes. They should on the other hand be guided in their actions to ensure a reasonable evolution of the architecture.

In the extended T&M approach, the architecture is maintained by an onshore software architect. He verifies that changes and enhancements by the developers are valid and compliant with his architectural vision against the background of the overall application architecture and planned future requirements. He also maintains a master description of the project-specific architecture that is made available to all developers, e.g. through the common version control system. Controversial or comprehensive architectural changes should be discussed with the development team to ensure a common understanding.

This division of labor guarantees that developers can work without bottlenecks and that the evolution of the architecture is guided by an experienced architect. Our experience shows few cases where architectural changes by the developers had to be corrected by the software architect. With the guidance of a common architecture, explicit metaphors and good examples in the existing implementation, developers have a good basis for their design decisions.

With the importance of architecture validation and the complexity of today's applications, a software architect has to rely on software tools for quality assurance. Their help permits an automated comparison of the planned and the really implemented architecture. They also provide metrics and queries for an in-depth review of the implementation [15].

5.3 Component Tasks

The story cards of the widespread agile process model of Extreme Programming, that are also used in most current projects based on the T&M approach, capture only the essence of requirements in the form of informal stories. The details need to be discussed and clarified with the customer and the team. This is difficult in offshoring settings and increases the demand for communication. Therefore, we use component tasks in the adapted T&M approach.

The use of component-based development is well-suited for agile projects [16]. Components make it possible to divide along well-defined interfaces. The relationship between components has to be explicitly defined by architecture rules so that they can be developed and tested mutually independently to a large extent. The component descriptions can serve as a basis for coordination and discussion between teams.

Components can have different sizes and can be ordered hierarchically. This enables an incremental shift of more and more tasks from the onshore to the offshore team. Small initial components give offshore developers a manageable task to start with. They do not have to understand all of the domain and the business logic from the beginning. These components are assembled into more complex components and integrated into the application by an experienced onshore team. Over time, bigger and bigger components can be constructed and integrated offshore, leading to overall cost reduction.

Component tasks define not only components to be developed but also the required context of the application domain to minimize callbacks, the hot spots or extension points for this component and, if possible, tests that the component has to satisfy. Fig. 4 shows the adapted T&M approach.

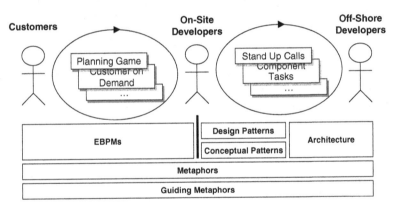

Fig. 4. The adapted T&M approach

As in the basic T&M approach, developers communicate on the basis of guiding metaphors, metaphors, conceptual patterns, design patterns and architecture descriptions. Single-site agile techniques which are incompatible with dual-shore development are replaced with suitable alternatives. The communication between customers and (on-site) developers remains unchanged.

6 Case Study

To validate the extensions for offshoring projects to the T&M approach, a case study was conducted. During four months (March to June 2005) two teams developed a prototype for an order entry and customer information system. The teams consisted of up to six onshore developers at Hamburg, Germany, and six offshore developers at Pune, India.

6.1 Setting and Process

The development was carried out following the dual-shore offshoring model. The elicitation of business requirements and the iteration planning was done by onshore analysts with the customer. Onshore developers built a core system during the first iteration while instructing two offshore colleagues on site. These returned to India after the first iteration and established a developer team there, consisting of about half a dozen members. In the following iterations, offshore and onshore developers worked in parallel, with the onshore developers concentrating on work that required customer interaction, architectural know how such as integrating components that were built offshore. These components were aligned with the application architecture. They were specified in fair detail with the necessary domain knowledge. Unit tests were developed together with the components. Quality assurance was carried out onshore before integrating the components.

A software architect was responsible for the initial design of the architecture and for quality assurance. Advancements of the architecture were done autonomously by the developers and checked weekly by the architect who also maintained the central architecture description. The architecture descriptions were shared with the offshore team after updates.

6.2 Findings

The results from the case study show that the described extensions to the T&M approach work well in practice. The following issues are worth noting:

Dual-Shore Development
The separation of tasks between onshore and offshore-teams worked very well. There was no need for direct communication between onshore and offshore developers. Coordination occurred solely between the onshore and offshore project leads. The offshore team also did not communicate directly with the customer. Tasks that demanded direct communication, e.g. set-up of the database connection, were handled onshore.

Architecture-Centric Development
Almost no architecture violations were committed by the onshore or offshore teams. The few ones that occurred could be detected and resolved very fast. Extending the architecture was solely the onshore teams' tasks. The learning curve for the offshore developers was quite steep. Comprehension could be significantly improved by providing good examples, e.g. similar components implemented by experienced onshore developers. A longer prior training and pair programming with experienced developers at the start of the project could help.

Our experience also shows that architecture violations are much easier to correct right after they are introduced rather than at later stages. This is especially true for cyclical dependencies. Small cycles are easy to comprehend and dissolve. As cycles

tend to grow rapidly, it usually does not take long before they embrace so many artifacts that it is not obvious where to cut them. The conclusion is to take architecture
validation seriously and to correct mistakes right away.

Component Tasks

We found that a stronger orientation on components can improve task sharing between onshore and offshore teams with a more strongly formalized approach on the
basis of a common architecture.

The concept of component tasks worked well. The structure of the task descriptions was refined throughout the project. Most of the time the tasks were defined clear
enough and only minor misunderstandings occurred. At first, only small tasks were
handled offshore. In later iterations of the project, bigger tasks, e.g. larger components, could be developed offshore. At the peak about a quarter of the overall work
was done offshore.

7 Conclusion – An Extended T and M Approach

In this paper we examined benefits and challenges of offshoring and described how
process models can be adapted to offshoring projects by the example of the Tools &
Material approach.

While the basic concepts, such as guiding and design metaphors, conceptual and
design patterns, architecture-centric development based on an explicit model architecture and agile, iterative development remain unchanged, the process model was
adapted to incorporate onshore and offshore teams with fixed assignments and responsibilities. Architecture-centric development plays an even more important role in
the extended T&M approach and helps in assigning tasks to teams, directing and formalizing communication between them and thus reducing the need for direct communication. We also presented results from a case study that we conducted to evaluate
the adapted approach and where we could validate the extensions for offshoring. In
the future, we plan to evaluate the approach in other projects and advance it further.

We hope that our results on how a single-site approach can be extended to offshoring settings will be transferable to other development approaches and that this helps to
decrease the rate of failed offshore projects in the medium term.

References

1. Ribeiro, J.: India's offshore outsourcing revenue grew 33%, Computerworld, 06/06 (2006),
   http://www.computerworld.com/action/artcle.do?command=printArticleBasic&articleId=
   9000877
2. Kalakota, R., Robinson, M.: Dual-shore project management: Seven techniques for coordinating onshore-offshore projects (2005),
   http://www.informit.com/articles/article.asp?p=409917
3. Hatch, P.J.: Offshore 2005 Research: Preliminary Findings and Conclusions, Vers.1.2.5
   Ventoro (2005), http://www.ventoro.com/Offshore2005ResearchFindings.pdf

4. Züllighoven, H.: Object-Oriented Construction Handbook: Developing Application-Oriented Software with the Tools & Materials Approach, dpunkt.verlag. Co-publication with Morgan-Kaufmann (2004)
5. Sauer, J.: Agile practices in offshore outsourcing – an analysis of published experiences. In: Proceedings of the 29th Information Systems Research Seminar in Scandinavia, IRIS 29 - Paradigms, Politics, Paradoxes, August 12-15, pp. 12–15. Helsingoer, Denmark (2006)
6. McCarthy, J.C.: Offshore Outsourcing: The Complete Guide. Forrester Research, Cambridge, MA (2004)
7. Huntley, H.: Five Reasons Why Offshore Deals Fail, Gartner, Stamford, CT (2005)
8. Kornstädt, A., Sauer, J.: Tackling Offshore Communication Challenges with Agile Architecture-Centric Development. In: Proc. of the Sixth Working IEEE/IFIP Conference on Software Architecture (WICSA 2007), Mumbai, India, January 6-9, pp. 6–9 (to appear, 2007)
9. Beck, K.: Extreme Programming Explained: Embrace Change. Addison-Wesley Longman Publishing Co., Inc, Boston, MA, USA (1999)
10. Gamma, E., et al.: Design-Patterns – Elements of Reusable Object-Oriented Software. Addison-Wesley, London, UK (1995)
11. Breitling, H., Kornstädt, A., Sauer, J.: Design Rationale in Exemplary Business Process Modeling. In: Dutoit, A.H., McCall, R., Mistrik, I., Paech, B. (eds.) Rationale Management in Software Engineering, pp. 191–208. Springer, Heidelberg (2006)
12. Lippert, M., Becker-Pechau, P., Breitling, H., Koch, J., Kornstädt, A., Roock, S., Schmolitzky, A., Wolf, H., Züllighoven, H.: Developing Complex Projects Using XP with Extensions. IEEE Computer Magazine 36, 06/03 (2003)
13. Bass, L., Kazman, R.: Architecture-Based Development, Technical Report CMU/SEI-99-TR-007, ESC-TR-99-007 (1999)
14. Grinter, R.E., Herbsleb, J.D., Perry, D.E.: The Geography of Coordination: Dealing with Distance in R&D Work. In: Proceedings of the international ACM SIGGROUP Conference on Supporting Group Work, November 14-17. GROUP '99, pp. 306–315. ACM Press, New York (1999)
15. Bischofberger, W.R., Kühl, J., Löffler, S.: Sotograph – a pragmatic approach to source code architecture conformance checking. In: Oquendo, F., Warboys, B.C., Morrison, R. (eds.) EWSA 2004. LNCS, vol. 3047, pp. 1–9. Springer, Heidelberg (2004)
16. Stojanovic, Z., Dahanayake, A.N.W., Sol, H.G.: Component-oriented agile software development. In: Marchesi, M., Succi, G. (eds.) XP 2003. LNCS, vol. 2675, pp. 315–318. Springer, Heidelberg (2003)

Evaluating Collaboration Platforms for Offshore Software Development Scenarios

Felix Rodriguez[1], Michael Geisser[2], Kay Berkling[1], and Tobias Hildenbrand[2]

[1] Caribbean Artificial Intelligence Group CAIG, Polytechnic University of Puerto Rico,
Electrical and Computer Engineering and Computer Science Department, 377 Ponce de Leon
Ave, Hato Rey, PR 00918, Puerto Rico
`felix.rodriguez@ieee.org, kay@berkling.com`
2 Lehrstuhl für ABWL und Wirtschaftsinformatik, Universität Mannheim,
D-68131 Mannheim, Germany
`{geisser,hildenbrand}@uni-mannheim.de`

Abstract. Offshore software development has become one of the prominent software engineering trends in recent years. Many software development projects are switching to offshore sites due to global and economic reasons. This trend has resulted in the need for new tools and platforms to provide support for the challenges that are faced by collaborators in global teams in distributed communication, coordination and knowledge management. Understanding and employing appropriate platforms presents one of the important factors in successful global software development projects. The purpose of this paper is to compare several market-leading tools that aim at assisting software development within an offshore scenario. In doing so, new and important aspects of evaluating these tools are taken into account that are specific to the distributed aspects of these projects.

Keywords: Collaboration Platform, Collaborative Software Development, Offshore Software Development Tools, Computer-Aided Software Engineering.

1 Introduction

Offshore software development (OSD) is a particular kind of outsourcing that deals with the enhanced challenges and complexity of developing software when the contracting parties reside in different countries [8, 15]. The additional complexity factor of OSD is due to the fact that the development team is spread out remotely and over several cultural environments. Our experience shows that special attention needs to be brought into place when offshoring a software development project [2]. We have analyzed the functionality of several tools that have shown to be helpful in managing an OSD project. Even though there are no definite answers for tool selection along with the tool's functionality there are influence factor's such as costs, ease of use and training time that support the final choice. However tradeoffs are always inevitable when selecting a tool.

The goal of this article is to provide a method for evaluating a set of available software development tools and their capabilities to facilitate managing the software

B. Meyer and M. Joseph (Eds.): SEAFOOD 2007, LNCS 4716, pp. 96–108, 2007.

development workflow or lifecycle for an OSD project – thus providing guidelines for the process of tool selection in these contexts.

This paper is structured as follows: Section 2 will provide some background information on OSD projects and the major problem areas for managing such projects. Section 3 explains the setup of the analysis to be performed on the selected tools, and Section 4 presents the results of the analysis performed. Finally, a conclusion of the tools analysis as well as future directions will be presented.

2   Offshore Software Development

To get a better understanding of the OSD requirements it is useful to understand its crucial activities. All OSD projects vary from one project to the other. Since this practice is still in development, some major challenges are still ahead. Some of these challenges [14] faced by OSD projects are listed in the following table:

Table 1. Major Offshore Development Challenges [14]

1	Communication Gap
2	Transfer Business Domain
3	Decreased Project Visibility
4	Configuration Management
5	Disconnection on Project Estimation
6	Client Business Security
7	Document Maintenance and Synchronization
8	Cultural Differences

The list of activities that usually takes place during an OSD project can be summarized in two groups. One group includes all activities that take place at the front office through the project management team. The other group denotes the activities that are usually outsourced or developed externally. Notice that in an OSD project these activities can be moved from one group to another depending on the needs of a specific project [14]. Table 2 gives a summary of these activities.

Table 2. Typical Offshore Activities Division [14]

Front Office Activities	Back Office Activities
- Project Inception	- Design
- Requirements Specifications	- Implementation
- Requirements Change Management	- Testing
- Analysis	- Maintenance
- Integration Testing	- Change Implementation
- Deployment	
- Project Monitoring	

Most of the typical OSD activities listed in Table 2 can be characterized into at least one of three functional groups of software development:

1. Project management,
2. requirements management, or
3. source code management.

In other words, a tool that can be characterized according to its capabilities in one or more of these functional groups would allow an OSD project to carry out some of the activities listed on Table 2. Many other available software development tools could be characterized a part of one of those three software functional groups as well. We will analyze the common functionalities found within each of these functional groups that could be used to support in OSD projects.

2.1 Project Management

The project management (PM) functionalities comprise the tool's capability to facilitate common management tasks within software projects. Such tools shall have capabilities that include project planning and control, project governance and team management [11]. It deals with functionalities such as assigning tasks as well as managing identified project risks. This also includes tracking changes. PM tools try to provide project visibility to the client and serve as well to provide time and cost estimates to the development organization. For an OSD scenario, it is very critical that the users' access to the platforms is controlled and information sharing can be managed effectively. Important features of these tools include project management activities such as task assignment, track requirements or tasks changes as well as task status view. For this purpose, the tools are also evaluated with respect to their ability to generate reports on tasks, deliverable status or time spent compared to time allocated. Other functions include user access controls, enforcement of a project workflow or support of different development methodologies. The tool should also provide the basis for communications and knowledge transfer; provide the means to inform remote members of project status and centralize the project's risk management. It must also provide the capabilities to support and enforce any standards adopted for the offshore development. In fact, it shall enable the management team to control the project as a whole.

2.2 Requirements Management

The requirements management (RM) functionalities of a tool have to support the organization of software requirements, the information gathered from customers' requests, encompassing the requirements engineering process in general [17]. The process of managing requirements is a systematic approach of organizing and storing relevant information about requirements, while ensuring their traceability in the subsequent process and managing changes to these requirements during the whole lifecycle of the development [12]. RM serves as a basis for the system under development and is one of the most important risk factors for successful project completion [9, 16]. A tool has to provide the capability to manage requirements in such a way that team members for all roles are aware of the underlying requirements despite the globally distributed nature of the project and its different artifacts [15]. Apart from effectively yielding an overview, the tool has to provide project analysts with the ability to review, iterate and update requirements, models, and project deliverable documents. Customers should receive a role enabling their review, approval or recommendations with respect to the requirements. The tool in fact should provide the basis for such iterations to occur [13]. The tools are therefore evaluated with respect to how well they manage required functionality, track their changes and deliver the functionality stated above [12].

2.3 Source Code Management

The code management capabilities of the tool must handle the development team workspaces where the developers build, test and debug source code. The tool should also handle a large amount of code, code branches, the propagation of code changes, and automated build [5, 22, 24]. A tool with code management capabilities should interface with common source code repositories such as CVS and or SVN. This allows all necessary personnel to access the repository to work or review information. It also enables developers and testers to work together with the intention of speeding up development and test time by providing concurrency. One of the most important features of an integrated code management system is the ability to relate code changes to feature and bug requests for the purpose of project tracking [5].

3   Evaluation Criteria for OSD Tools

This section presents the evaluation criteria that will serve as a guideline for the process of tool selection. Based on the three main management areas that require tool support (project, requirements and source code management), a set of functionalities will be defined and assigned a weight relating its importance in OSD. First, a defined list of all activities that are intended to be carried out in OSD environments is required. Once this list is compiled the activities can be sorted out between back office and front office activities. This activities list would vary from one OSD team to the other because it will depend on the actual location of the project team and the distribution of the activities over the different locations. Based on the activities list and particular project needs all weights are assigned according to the degree to which they allow more control, more project visibility and provide the means for better communication and information sharing in OSD [11, 21].

3.1   Criteria for Tool Comparison

A criteria set for comparing tools provides us with the ability to quantitatively reason about various tools. For this purpose, the following chart was developed. The chart in Table 3 below summarizes a set of important capabilities along with the corresponding weights. The selected functionalities per area were chosen and weighted by the project team based on what they identified as functions that would facilitate their software development project in a distributed collaboration environment, OSD, for instance.

Table 3. Tools Analysis Table

Tool Capability	Tool Functionality	Weight [%]	Overall [%]
Project Management	Collaborative User Access Control	6 %	35%
	Task Assignment	8 %	
	Changes Tracking	8 %	
	Automated Report Generation	5 %	
	Workflow Enforcement	5 %	
	Time Tracking Functions	3 %	
Requirements Management	Requirements Text	9 %	35%
	Requirements Modeling	8 %	
	Requirements Baseline	4 %	
	Requirements Traceability	5 %	
	Exporting/Importing Requirements	3 %	
	Requirement Docs Automation	6 %	
Code Management	Automated Code Builds	7 %	30%
	Check In / Check Out Code	9 %	
	Code Versioning	9 %	
	Code Testing	5 %	

3.2 Market Research

Preceding the actual comparison of tools, a market research was performed with the purpose of gathering the list of tools that would fit into the collaborative development scenario. This list served as a mechanism for selecting a subset of the most relevant tools for evaluation, and excluding others from the analysis as follows: Tools that did not have any capabilities in at least one of the areas were left out of the study. After this market research, 12 tools were selected as a subset to be evaluated. They are summarized in Table 4.

4 Evaluation Results

The process of evaluating the tools listed in Table 4 consisted of a complete analysis with respect to the criteria listed in Table 3. It is clear that not all tools have the same functionality but the evaluation chart for each tool was standardized and weighed in the same manner for all tools. Tools were given partial credit for their capability to integrate with other products within the same brand or external programs in order to comply with a given functionality. Tools were given full credit for having the specific functionality integrated and ready to use in a collaborative environment [21]. Table 5 was thus derived from Table 3 and it provides an example of the tool evaluation process. It demonstrates how the tool CodeBeamer was evaluated following the chosen criteria. As full credit was given only if the evaluated tool provided the

Table 4. Summary of the selected tools

Tool Name	Short Description	Website
CodeBeamer (version 4.2)	Delivers a J2EE-based, collaborative software development platform that provides software life cycle management capabilities and captures the invaluable intellectual capital generated and transferred in development related communications [3].	www.intland.com
CollabNet (version 4.0)	Delivers a fully integrated web-based collaborative environment specifically tailored to the needs of Open Source communities and public developer networks [4].	www.collab.net
Doors (version 8.1)	Delivers a Requirements Management and traceability tool for teams working from the same geographic (co-located) site [6].	www.telelogic.com
GForge (version 4.5)	Delivers tools to help your team collaborate, like message forums and mailing lists; tools to create and control access to Source Code Management repositories [10].	www.gforge.org
Rhapsody (version 7.0)	Delivers a Model-Driven Development (MDD) environment for systems, software, and test [20].	www.ilogix.com
Visual Paradigm Team Work Center (version 2.3)	Delivers a version control system for Visual Paradigm's products which helps you to carry out the Collaborative Software Development for your team. Allows to work within an integrated set of software development tools [26].	www.visual-paradigm.com
ArcStyler (version 5.5)	Provides the ability to create a dynamic link between business and technology. Application logic is captured in models which serve as the basis for automatic transformation to various technologies [1].	www.interactive-objects.com
Polarion (version 2.5)	Delivers Software Lifecycle Management solutions providing a collaboration environment and CM controls [18].	www.polarion.com
EProject (version PPM6)	Delivers On Demand project and portfolio management solutions [7].	www.eproject.com
Sun Java Studio Enterprise (version 8)	Java IDE that includes powerful features to speed development, such as UML modeling, instant collaboration, and application profiling [23].	www.sun.com
Twiki (version 4.0)	Flexible and powerful enterprise collaboration platform and knowledge management system [25].	www.twiki.org
Rational Suite (version 7)	Integrated set of software development tools [19].	www.ibm.com

specific functionality, CodeBeamer received full credit for its collaborative user access control because the tool provides this functionality. As partial credit was given to the tool if it provides partial capability itself or a means for integration with another tool, CodeBeamer received partial credit for the requirements modeling functionality. Even though CodeBeamer does not provide this capability directly, it provides version control for requirements modeling documents via its repository. This supports the requirements modeling functionality partially in an OSD project. All the selected tools where subject to the same evaluation process to produce objective and reproducible results for the tool evaluation.

Table 5. Tools Evaluation Example: CodeBeamer (overall score: 77%)

Tool Capability	Tool Functionality	Maximum Weight [%]	Functionality Weight [%]	Overall [%]
Project Management	Collaborative User Access Control	6 %	6 %	34 %
	Task Assignment	8 %	8 %	
	Changes Tracking	8 %	8 %	
	Automated Report Generation	5 %	4 %	
	Workflow Enforcement	5 %	5 %	
	Time Tracking Functions	3 %	3 %	
Requirements Management	Requirements Text	9 %	8 %	22 %
	Requirements Modeling	8 %	2 %	
	Requirements Baseline	4 %	3 %	
	Requirements Traceability	5 %	5 %	
	Exporting/Importing Requirements	3 %	3 %	
	Requirement Docs Automation	6 %	1 %	
Code Management	Automated Code Builds	7 %	6 %	21 %
	Check In / Check Out Code	9 %	8 %	
	Code Versioning	9 %	7 %	
	Code Testing	5 %	0 %	

4.1 Tool Comparison

All tools were analyzed following the three most important characteristics identified for collaboration in OSD projects with the resulting scores depicted in various figures in this section.

Figure 1 summarizes the results obtained from the evaluation in terms of the **project management** capabilities of the tool. The chart clearly identifies the tools with the strongest features. CodeBeamer, Polarion, EProject, and CollabNet show their strength in the project management capabilities according to the criteria outlined in Table 3 that were selected for this study.

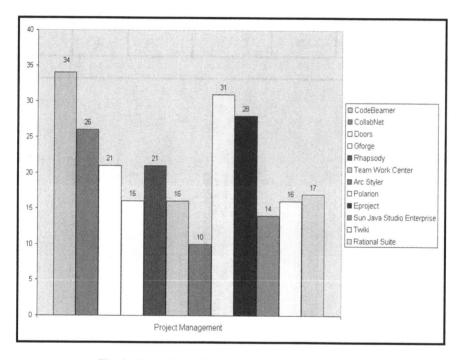

Fig. 1. Comparison of Project Management Capabilities

Table 6 provides a detailed summary of how the top scores under the Project Management capabilities were evaluated on the basis on the selected criteria presented in Table 3.

The chart in Figure 2 summarizes the results obtained from the evaluation in terms of the **requirement management** capabilities of the tool. As can be identified from the chart there are tools that show clear advantage over the rest. Tools such as Rhapsody, Doors, Rational Suite and ArcStyler show their strength in the requirement management capabilities via the selected functionality evaluated by this study as described in Table 3.

Table 6. Results Summary for Project Management Functionality

Tool Functionality	Max Weight [%]	CodeBeamer	Polarion	Eproject	CollabNet
Collaborative User Access Control	6 %	6 %	6 %	6 %	6 %
Task Assignment	8 %	8 %	7 %	7 %	6 %
Changes Tracking	8 %	8 %	7 %	7 %	6 %
Automated Report Generation	5 %	4 %	7 %	3 %	3 %
Workflow Enforcement	5 %	5 %	2 %	3 %	3 %
Time Tracking Functions	3 %	3 %	2 %	2 %	2 %

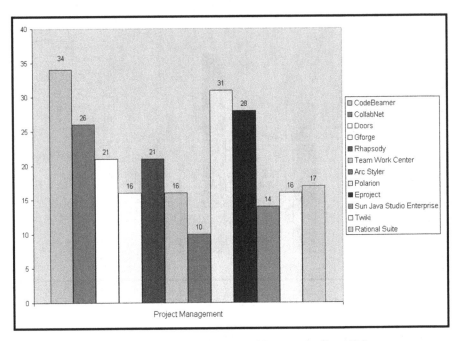

Fig. 2. Comparison of Requirement Management Capabilities

Table 7 provides a detailed summary of how the top scores under the requirements management capabilities were evaluated on the basis of the selected criteria presented in Table 3

The chart in Figure 3 summarizes the results obtained from the evaluation in terms of the **source code management** capabilities of the tool. As can be identified from the chart, there are tools that show clear advantage over the rest. Tools such as

Table 7. Results Summary for Requirements Management Functionality

Tool Functionality	Max Weight [%]	Rhapsody	Doors	Rational Suite	ArcStyler
Requirements Text	9 %	9 %	9 %	8 %	8 %
Requirements Modeling	8 %	8 %	5 %	5 %	8 %
Requirements Baseline	4 %	4 %	3 %	2 %	2 %
Requirements Traceability	5 %	5 %	5 %	3 %	3 %
Exporting/Importing Requirements	3 %	3 %	3 %	2 %	1 %
Requirement Docs Automation	6 %	6 %	4 %	6 %	3 %

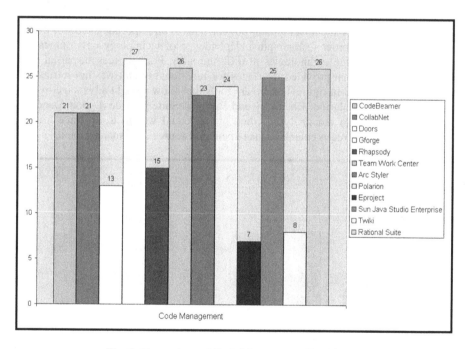

Fig. 3. Comparison of Code Management Capabilities

GForge, Team Work Center, Rational Suite, and Sun Java Studio demonstrate their strengths as regards the code management criteria in this study.

Table 8 provides a detailed summary of how the top scores under the project management capabilities were evaluated on the basis of the selected criteria presented in Table 3.

Table 8. Results Summary for Code Management Functionality

Tool Functionality	Max Weight [%]	GForge	Team Work Center	Rational Suite	Sun Java Studio
Automated Code Builds	7 %	7 %	7 %	5 %	6 %
Check In / Check Out Code	9 %	9 %	8 %	8 %	7 %
Code Versioning	9 %	9 %	9 %	8 %	8 %
Code Testing	5 %	2 %	2 %	5 %	4 %

4.2 Results of Tool Analysis

We can observe that there are certain tools that provide a good basis for OSD. Not all tools may have the entire set of features but they have a good foundation for controlling an OSD project. Most importantly, many tools have a basis for integration with other tools during the development project. This is an important aspect of the tool selection process in order to maintain independence of technology environment and include several existing technologies at different sites. For this reason, partial credit was given to a tool that provided interfaces for functionality that was not intrinsically provided. As depicted in figure 4, there are tools that show a slight advantage over the rest: CodeBeamer, Polarion, Rhapsody and Rational Suite provide a good foundation for OSD according to our analysis, when giving equal weight to all three areas of project management, requirements management and source code management.

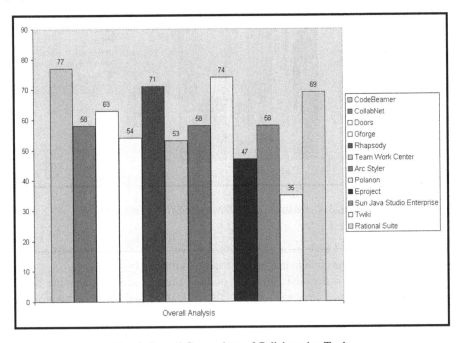

Fig. 4. Overall Comparison of Collaborative Tools

5 Conclusion

In this article we have listed a set of challenges that usually have to be faced by OSD stakeholders. A list of criteria was compiled to evaluate a set of available software development tools. During the tool selection and evaluation there were a few critical questions to be answered. Are the tools readily available? Can the tool be integrated with other tools? Does the tool supports the OSD team in mastering the challenges of global development? We developed and presented one way of selecting a predefined set of tool functionality as a framework for a systematic comparison of tools. It is clear that there cannot be one definite framework for OSD evaluation because each project has different needs depending on the particular project teams and settings. Also, a framework for evaluating tools needs to take into consideration which activities are going to be distributed and how.

The results from the tool comparison confirm that there is no definite solution for picking up a tool for offshore development. It has been demonstrated that the platform selection processes always involves additional tradeoffs along with the technology and functional capabilities. Considerations such as platforms costs, estimated learning curve or project team expertise would definitely have to be taken into account in the equation. Tool selection depends on whether the emphasis is on one particular functional area or a balance across all areas desired. During the tool evaluation process it becomes clear that most tool strengths reside in one particular functional area and two at the most. As a result, it is evident that any OSD project will require integration capabilities of the chosen tool to account for any flaws with a particular tool over a functional area. This is another aspect that was considered during this research but will also be taken into more consideration in future work.

Acknowledgments. The authors would like to thank Polytechnic University of Puerto Rico and collaboration with the Lehrstuhl für ABWL und Wirtschafts Informatik at the University of Mannheim for making this work possible. This work is also a result of the project CollaBaWue supported by the German state of Baden-Wuerttemberg. CollaBaWue is part of the research association PRIMIUM.

References

1. ArcStyler, http://www.interactive-objects.com
2. Berkling, K., Zundel, A., Rodriguez, F., Rivera, E., Bentine, N.: Experience Report: Offshore Software Development in the Classroom. Knowledge Sharing and Collaborative Engineering. In: Proceedings of KSCE, Acta Press, Virgin Islands (2006)
3. CodeBeamer, http://www.intland.com
4. CollabNet, http://www.collab.net
5. Cusumano, M., Yoffie, D.: Software Development on Internet Time. IEEE Computer Magazine, 60–69 (1999)
6. Doors, http://www.telelogic.com
7. Eproject, http://www.eproject.com
8. Erickson, J., Ranganathan,: Project Management Capabilities: Key to Application Development Offshore Outsourcing. In: Proceeding of the 39th Hawaii International Conference on System Sciences, Hawaii (2006)

9. Fairley, R.E.: Software engineering concepts. McGraw Hill, New York (1985)
10. GForge, http://www.gforge.org
11. Gopal, A., Sivaramakrishnan, K., Krishnan, M.S., Mukhopadhyay, T.: Contracts in Offshore Software Development: An Empirical Analysis. Management Science 49(12), 1671–1683 (2003)
12. Gotel, O., Finkelstein, A.: An Analysis of the Requirements Traceability Problem. In: Proceedings of the First International Conference on Requirements Engineering (ICRE'94), pp. 94–101 (1994)
13. Grehag, A.: Requirements Management In A Life Cycle Perspective – A Position Paper. In: Proceedings of the 7th International Workshop on Requirements Engineering: Foundation for Software Quality, Interlaken, Switzerland. Essener Informatik Beiträge, pp. 183–188 (2001)
14. Hameed, T., Nisar, M.: Agile Methods handling Offshore Software Development Issues, IEEE Instrumentation and Measurement Technology Conference, Pakistan (2004)
15. Heeks, R., Krishna, S., Nicholson, B., Sahay, S.: Synching or Sinking: Global Software Outsourcing Relationships. IEEE Software 18(2), 54–61 (2001)
16. Balzert, H.: Lehrbuch der Software-Technik II: Software-Management, Software-Qualitätssicherung, Unternehmensmodellierung, 769 S, Spektrum Akademischer Verlag Heidelberg (1998)
17. Hoffmann, M., Kuehn, N., Bittner, M.: Requirements for Requirements Management Tools. In: Proceedings of the 12th IEEE International Requirements Engineering Conference, pp. 301–308. IEEE Computer Society Press, Los Alamitos (2004)
18. Polarion, http://www.polarion.com
19. Rational Suite, http://www.ibm.com
20. Rhapsody, http://www.ilogix.com
21. Robbins, J., Feller, J., Fitzgerald, B., Hissam, S.A., Lakhani, K.R. (eds.): Adopting Open Source Software Engineering (OSSE) Practices by Adopting OSSE Tools, pp. 245–264. Free/Open Source Processes and Tools MIT Press (2005)
22. Seinwald, S., Wingerd, L.: High-Level Best Practices in Software Configuration Management. In: Jul, E. (ed.) ECOOP 1998. LNCS, vol. 1445, pp. 57–66. Springer, Heidelberg (1998)
23. Tosic, V., Mennie, D., Pagurek, B.: Software Configuration Management Related to the Management of Distributed Systems and Service Oriented Architectures (SOA). In: Westfechtel, B., van der Hoek, A. (eds.) SCM 2001 and SCM 2003. LNCS, vol. 2649, pp. 54–69. Springer, Heidelberg (2003)
24. Twiki, http://www.twiki.org
25. Visual Paradigm Team Work Center, http://www.visual-paradigm.com

Outsourcing and Offshoring: The Consultancies' Estimates

Christian Sommer and Georg Troxler

ETH Zurich, Switzerland

Abstract. Offshoring project work ideally would decrease the overall cost of a software project. We give a short survey of current trends based on different studies and our own poll, covering advantages, risk, and the impact for the job situation in saturated markets. Several questions show unity among the different consultancies where the opinions about trends are quite diverse.

1 Introduction

Offshoring is mainly supported by communication infrastructure, cost pressure after the internet hype, and new near-shoring alternatives in the east of Europe. However, during the first wave of outsourcing and offshoring, high expexctations for cost reductions often were not met. A study of The Boston Consulting Group [11] results in the following sentence:

> Most banks that have engaged in offshoring have not fully achieved their most important goals, such as significant reductions in labor costs.

Some companies even started to source their IT-infrastructure back in [8], however, they still intend to expand application outsourcing [15]. Sourcing models for the banking sector are analysed in more detail by Alt and Zerndt in [3].

The technical communication support is satisfactory, though, successful communication necessitates more than a reliable channel. Besides cultural discrepancies, difficulties in language and, thus, understanding need to be managed, as a study of The Boston Consulting Group [11] describes.

> ...first ensure that their institutions are ready, both organizationally and culturally.

Legal comprehension varies between different countries and often leads to misunderstandings. Asian countries, for example, consider contracts as a commitment to work together, whereas Europeans specify every single detail to ensure a positive outcome. Furthermore, the ongoing trade-off between cost and control has not been solved sufficiently yet. Both quality and security are difficult to control if a project or a process are not performed in-house. Within planning, it remains hard to keep the golden mean between cost and control.

B. Meyer and M. Joseph (Eds.): SEAFOOD 2007, LNCS 4716, pp. 109–113, 2007.

1.1 Our Contribution

We asked employees from different consultancies (Accenture, ALTRAN, A.T. Kearney, Bain, Bearing Point, ELCA, McKinsey, Roland Berger, The Boston Consulting Group) for their estimates about outsourcing and offshoring. Furthermore, studies of the aforementioned companies were used to get an overview. The results are presented briefly in this paper.

2 Reasons and Advantages

The main advantage always mentioned is significant cost advantage. To gain an insight about the reasons other than costs, we distinguish between outsourcing and offshoring. The consultants interviewed identified innovation, consolidation, and optimisation aspects especially for outsourcing. A capable outsourcing partner can influence future business activities.

An important strategic motive is to keep a company's core competencies and to rely on a partner for other tasks. An outsourcing of support processes results in flexible structures (on-demand), transparent and reduced costs, and risk reduction [14].

3 Risks

Groetschel from the Computerwoche magazine [7] identifies the most important problems with outsourcing projects as dissacordance within management, unsufficient strategic preparations before outsourcing, and contract negotiations under time pressure. IT-managers tend to premature implementations in order to present cost savings. However, without diligent preparations, specifications, and planning, outsourcing projects will fail. Iyengar et al. from Gartner offer an overview about different vendors for offshoring services [12] to support companies in the risky selection process.

An elaborate list of offshoring risks is presented in [14]. Besides the aforementioned aspects, vendor dependencies, loss of knowledge and control [5], doubtful cost advantage, difficult performance measurements, interface management, and resistance of employees are itemised.

According to the consultant's opinions, even successful implementations still hold risks such as loss of knowledge and control [5], increased complexity, and high communication overhead. However, the most important aspects to cover remain specified requirements, a clean contract, and coordination.

4 Countries

It is not surprising that India was mentioned by all consultants asked for our poll, followed by Vietnam and China. Asian companies offer the best price for offshoring services. Furthermore, India assures high quality standards with legions of well-trained IT specialists. An A.T. Kearney study [13] ranks India before China and Malaysia. Considering people skills and availability, India is followed by Canada and Australia. Drucker and Solomon's Wall Street Journal's article [9] mentions increasing salaries as follows:

> Indian software workers' salaries have increased over the past few years because of rising attrition rates, sparking some worries about cost pressures. But the strong demand for software services and increasing efficiencies by the Indian companies could offset some of the impact, say analysts.

However, a McKinsey study by Farrell et al. [10] recognises a few dangers for India's offshoring future:

> ... India's vast supply of graduates is smaller than it seems once their suitability for employment by multinational companies is considered. And in the country's most popular offshoring locations, such as Bangalore, rising wages and high turnover are evidence that local constraints on talent supply have already appeared. Worse for India, other low-wage countries such as China, the Philippines, and Hungary are gearing up to challenge its lead.

Since cultural differences are smaller wihin Europe, near-shoring, especially in eastern Europe, is an interesting alternative. A.T. Kearney identified the Czech Republic, Poland, and Hungary as most attractive countries [13].

> Eastern Europe as a whole offers cultural similarities, attractive costs, good language skills, solid technical capabilities, and minimal regulatory problems for European firms.

5 Impacts on Jobs

Our poll showed that when announcing an outsourcing/offshoring project, first of all, employees fear to loose their jobs. However, these feelings depend on the corporate culture and temper. In some companies, employees are sceptical and not too optimistic for the project's success, while in others, employees feel challenged and understand cost pressure and the outsourcing of non-core-competencies.

Agrawal et al. from McKinsey predict a change of the job market [2], however, mainly the kind of the jobs will adapt.

> Redeployed labor - U.S. workers who lose their jobs to offshoring will take up other jobs, which will in turn generate additional value for the economy.

However, a study by Frank from Deutsche Bank Research [14] sees 3.5% of IT-jobs in Germany endangered by offshoring trends.

Clearly, repetitive activities will wither from western countries. Main actions within IT will contain analysis, specification, and client contact. Consequences are that IT-workers are required to be well educated and to have excellent communication skills.

6 Trends

The interviewed consultants predict a variety of scenarios. Where today mostly simple tasks are offshored, in the near future this might change to more skilled labour. Others prophecy decreases in offshoring because many projects were unsuccessful. The majority forebodes a constant development.

Accenture [1] anticipates:

> Outsourcing and offshoring will become increasingly attractive ways to take advantage of the full global talent pool and to carry out work round the clock.

Bain proposes a more pragmatic IT-management, consequently oriented on business goals [6]. Finally, Arthur D. Little's study by Brabandt and Eichin [4] predicts a slow establishment of offshoring and sees the highest potential for cost savings within IT maintenance.

References

1. Accenture. The Major Trends that will shape IT (2006), URL http://www.accenture.com/Global/Services/Accenture_Technology_Labs/Services/FromIT.htm
2. V. Agrawal, V. Bansal, T. Beacom, D. Farrell (McKinsey & Company Global Institute). Offshoring: Is it a Win-Win Game? (2003), URL http://www.mckinsey.com/mgi/reports/pdfs/offshore/Offshoring_MGI_Perspective.pdf
3. Alt, R., Zerndt, T.: Beurteilung von Sourcing-Modellen in der Bankenbranche. Zeitschrift für Controlling & Management, Sonderheft Industrialisierung des Controlling (2006)
4. Brabandt, M., Eichin, R., Little, A.D.: Ready for Offshoring? (2005), http://www.adlittle.de/asp/studie_offshoring.asp
5. Bugajska, M., Schwabe, G., Voigt, B.J.J.: Demand analysis [DEAN] method for knowledge transfer in IT outsourcing relationships. IT-outsourcing case: Postfinance (to appear). Journal of Information & Knowledge Management (to appear, 2007)
6. Bain & Company.: Outsourcing allein reicht nicht! (2004), URL http://www.bain.de/documents/176_1075478223.pdf
7. Groetschel, E.: (Computerwoche). Warum Outsourcing-Projekte schei-tern (2006), URL http://www.computerwoche.de/it_strategien/outsourcing_offshoring/571060/
8. Richert, V.: (Computerworld). D-LUX: Insourcing bei der Credit Suisse (2006), URL http://www.computerworld.ch/aktuell/itservices/35848/index.html
9. Drucker, J., Solomon, J.: (The Wall Street Journal). Outsourcing Booms, Although Quietly Amid Political Heat (2004)
10. Farrell, D., Kaka, N., Stürze, S.: (McKinsey). Ensuring India's offshoring future (2005), URL http://www.mckinseyquarterly.com/links/18842
11. The Boston Consulting Group. IT Outsourcing and Offshoring: Hype or Opportunity? IT Cost Benchmarking in the European Banking Industry (2005), http://209.83.147.85/publications/files/IT_Outsouring_Excerpt.pdf

12. Iyengar, P., Karamouzis, F., Marriott, I., Young, A.: (Gartner). Magic Quadrant for Offshore Application Services 2006 (2006), URL
    http://www.gartner.com/ DisplayDocument?doc_cd=137244
13. Kearney, A.T.: Making Offshore Decisions, A.T. Kearney's 2004 Offshore Location Attractiveness Index (2004), URL
    http://www.atkearney.com/shared_res/pdf/Making_Offshore_S.pdf
14. Frank, H.-J.: (Deutsche Bank Research). IT-Outsourcing: Zwi-schen Hungerkur und Nouvelle Cuisine (2004) URL http://www.dbresearch.de/PROD/
    DBR_INTERNET_DE-PROD/PROD0000000000073793.pdf
15. Zeitung, N.Z.: Interview with Karl Landert (Credit Suisse). Schafft Offshoring bei uns Arbeitsplätze?,NZZ (November 10, 2006)

Questionnaire-Based Risk Assessment Scheme for Japanese Offshore Software Outsourcing

Hiroshi Tsuji[1], Akito Sakurai[2], Ken'ichi Yoshida[3], Amrit Tiwana[4], and Ashley Bush[5]

[1] Osaka Prefecture University, Graduate School of Engineering,
1-1 Gakuencho, Nakaku, Sakai, 559-8531 Japan
tsuji@cs.osakafu-u.ac.jp
[2] Keio University, Graduate School of Science and Engineering
4-1-1 Hiyoshi, Kohoku-ku, Yokohama, Kanagawa 223-8521, Japan
sakurai@ae.keio.ac.jp
[3] Tsukuba University,
3- 29-1, Otsuka, Bunkyo, Tokyo 112-0012, Japan
yoshida@gssm.otsuka.tsukuba.ac.jp
[4] Iowa State University, Postfach 10 52 80,
2340 Gerdin Business Building Ames, Iowa 50011-1350, USA
tiwana@iastate.edu
[5] Florida State University,
Tallahassee, FL 32306-1110, USA
abush@garnet.acns.fsu.edu

Abstract. As the volumes of software development increase and the cost reduction is required, most Japanese IT companies are interested in offshore software outsourcing. Although a lot of engineers have experienced the success and failure on their projects, their know-how still remains as tacit knowledge. This paper proposes a risk assessment scheme for new projects by externalizing such tacit knowledge. Such a scheme requires collaboration between industry and academia because the tacit knowledge is scattered over many companies and cannot be formalized by a single company or academic institute. Defining fourteen attributes related to software development and designing questionnaire about project evaluation, this paper clarifies how to quantify the risk of offshore software outsourcing. Risk assessment tool based on the proposed scheme will promote a knowledge spiral for project management.

1 Introduction

As the volumes of software development increases, most Japanese companies are interested in offshore outsourcing [9]. Their expected benefits in offshore outsourcing include flexible human resource procurement, cost reduction and an improved ability to meet short deadline [2, 5, 6, 7, 10, 11, 13, 14]. There are many excellent Java programmers in India and their salaries are generally lower than those of ordinary Japanese ordinal programmers. Furthermore, the shorter development time afforded by the extra man power can save a company from losing a market opportunity.

B. Meyer and M. Joseph (Eds.): SEAFOOD 2007, LNCS 4716, pp. 114–127, 2007.

However, there are still risks in offshore outsourcing: miscommunication, cultural difference in business customs, quality issues, and so on [2, 6, 7]. Although the offshore outsourcing is not a new concept and there are many experienced managers, such risks management know-how still remains as tacit knowledge [10, 11]. Then it is not easy to transfer such tacit knowledge from a project manager to others [8]. While nominal risk items are known, their magnitudes have not been measured. Note that some risks have a trade-off relationship. If one tries to avoid one kind of risk, one may increase other kinds.

Therefore, it is important to measure risks and analyze their relationship to the success or failure of offshore software outsourcing. Such a task cannot be completed by only academic people because they do not have real project experiences. And it cannot be done by only a corporate people either because they are reluctant to disclose their confidential experiences. The only possible way to do it is through an academia-industry collaboration.

This paper presents an overview of how we are promoting a project of the Joint Forum of Strategic Software Research in Japan. First, showing the black box in software development, section 2 presents our motivation, research framework and research steps. This project involves five academic people and thirteen industrial people (from Toshiba, Hitachi, Fujitsu, IBM-J and Mitsubishi). Next, section 3 introduces company visits for pre-analysis. The pre-analysis included structured interviews with a protocol and voting for the likelihood of successful outsourcing on virtual projects with nine attributes. Reviewing the pre-analysis, section 4 describes our design for a new questionnaire for externalizing tacit knowledge from skilled managers. The responses to the questionnaire were analyzed by three methods in section 5. Detailed discussions on the analysis are given elsewhere individually [14, 15]. Section 6 discusses what we did in the context of knowledge spiral.

2　Framework for Risk Assessment

Taking an engineering approach to risk assessment, we regard software development as a function with input, output and control parameters [11] as illustrated in Fig. 1. Our motivation is to clarify the causal relationship among input, output and control parameters. Once the structure of the function is identified, the output of new software development can be estimated by assigning values for the input and control parameters.

Fig. 1. Causal Relationship between Risk and Project

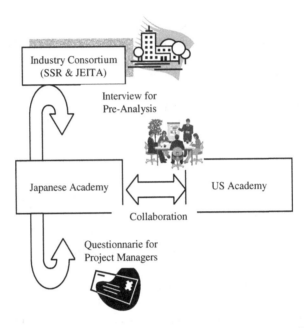

Fig. 2. Framework for Offshore Software Outsourcing Research

Table 1. Interview Protocol in Company Visit

Parts	Contents	notes
Project Background	- Vendor Type - Expected and actual man-month, budget and duration - Stage vendor become involved - Benefit - Satisfaction on outcome	Capital Relationship Both for client and vendor Design, Coding, Test, etc. Cost, vendor expertise, etc. Effectiveness and quality
Project Control	- Project decision - Outcome setting - Change Management -Contract Detail	Platform, Development methodology, etc Mile stones, budget, etc. Co-location, Weekly meeting US style vs. JP style
Collaboration	- Business custom - Domain Knowledge projection - Communication quality maintenance	Trigger, flexibility Intellectual propriety Bridge SE
Conclusion	Three top considerations	Success and failure

To identify the structure of the function, we established the framework for a re-search project as shown in Fig. 2. This framework is an instance of a joint forum called SSR (Strategic Software Research) in IISF (International Information Science

Foundation). SSR sends requests for proposal (RFPs) to Japanese academic institutes every year. The requirements in an RFP include: 1) the participants should involve industry people, and 2) the theme should be related to an international matter.

To promote the research, Japanese researchers collaborate with US researchers. The basic idea in this questionnaire scheme is borrowed from the original work of a US researcher [11]. To design the questionnaire and ensure a high response rate to it, we asked the industry members of JEITA as well as SSR to collaborate with us. JEITA (Japan Electronics and Information Technology Industries Association) has a committee on future human resource for software development and has interest in our work.

The research steps can be summarized as follows: 1) company visit for pre-analysis during one week, 2) repetitive face-to-face meetings and electronic meetings for questionnaire design during three months, 3) questionnaire delivery and collection during two months and 4) statistical analysis during two months. These steps are overviewed in the following sections.

3 Pre-analysis by Visiting Skilled Project Managers

Under the premise that the questionnaire is clue for risk assessment, one of our missions is to design a questionnaire. Since there already was a questionnaire for US project managers, we wanted to check whether it is applicable for Japanese project managers.

3.1 Interview Analysis

To overview the risk factors and find out the difference between Japanese offshore and America offshore outsourcing if any, we visited five Japanese client companies and two vendor companies (One Chinese and the other Indian) in October, 2005. The analysis was done as follows:

1) Each client company was visited by three or more of the authors who met at least two engineers there.
2) Each interview ran for thirty minutes. All questions and answers including translation were recorded using a voice recorder.
3) Each interview followed the structured protocol shown in Table 1.
4) To avoid hearsay and to obtain specific comments, the interviewee was asked to remind the last project and to describe it.

Then the followings are found while the interpretation of the reasons for the difference between Japan and American cases will be discussed elsewhere [13]:

1) There are three categories of attributes for offshore software development: software, vendor and project properties,
2) Each attribute seems to have a preference value for outsourcing and is not negligible in the decision to choose outsourcing,
3) Each company has a different strategy, especially for project control, for dealing with vendors.

3.2 Feasibility on Votes for Projects Evaluation

The questionnaire designed in the previous research makes use of three theories as shown in Table 2: transaction cost theory, agency theory and knowledge-based theory. We performed conjoint analysis on nine attributes based on these theories where each attribute has the value HIGH or LOW [11].

For the feasibility test, we asked skilled engineers to vote on the likelihood of success in the project using nine attributes where the range of vote was from 1 to 9. The results show the differences between Japanese and American outsourcing. This will be discussed elsewhere. It worked well for sophisticated professionals but still had some problems for various types of engineers.

1) It is difficult to imagine a project with nine attributes. Some participants in the experiments claimed that they could consider at most five attributes at once,
2) While HIGH means a positive value for outsourcing and LOW means the opposite from the view of a designer, these expressions confused interviewees somewhat,
3) A nine-point range was too wide for vote when there were twelve projects to evaluate.

Table 2. Project Attributes for Pre-Analysis

Category	Attributes
Transaction Cost Theory	Relative cost advantage
	Threat of opportunism
	Project complexity
	Project strategic importance
Agency Theory	Project outcomes measurability
	Vendor behavior observability
Knowledge Based Theory	Client technical knowledge
	Requirements knowledge specifiability
	Requirements volatility

4 Questionnaire Design

Based on the pre-analysis, we choose three property types for describing software development as shown in Table 3 instead of the previous nine attributes: software property with four attributes, vendor property with five attributes and project property with five attributes. The questionnaire has four parts and was designed so that a responder could answer all items in thirty minutes.

4.1 Part 1: Control Parameters

This part requires the personal information from the responder. These parameters are designed so as to adjust the bias of answers:

1) Numbers of years of IT experience, number of years of experience in the current company, and number of offshore projects experienced,
2) Position/ role: planner, project manager, project member,
3) Standard for evaluating vendors: ISO or CMM [4] ratings,
4) Type of projects: customer application, middleware or embedded software,
5) Vendor countries: China, India, Vietnam or others.

Table 3. Attributes of Offshore Software Development in Questionnaire

	Category	Attributes	Two levels for Attribute	
S1	Software Property	Software complexity and scale	Simple and small	Complex/ large
S2		Software quality measurablity	Easy to measure	Difficult to measure
S3		Requirement specifiablity	Easy to specify	Difficult to specify
S4		Requirement volatility	No change	Shall change
V1	Vendor Property	Communication skill	Good	Bad
V2		Project management capability	Much reliable	Unreliable
V3		Vendor flexibility on specification changes	flexible	Not flexible
V4		Attrition rate	Smal rate	Large rate
V5		Long term strategy	Yes	No
P1	Project Property	Deadline urgency	Urgent	Not urgent
P2		Relative cost advantage	High advantage	Low advantage
P3		Client side technical expertise	Lack	Suffcient expertise
P4		Strategic importance for future project	High	Low
P5		Ability to monitor vendor behaviour	Easy to monitor	Difficult to monitor

4.2 Part 2: Separate Evaluation on Attribute Importance

This part is designed to verify whether a responder knows the weight of each attribute in the outsourcing decision. The question is "According to your experience and knowledge, how important is each attribute in Table 3? Assume that you are the person in charge even if you should actually follow the decision made by a top manager". There are five options for the answer, ranging from 1 (negligible) to 5 (Very important).

4.3 Part 3: Evaluation of an Experienced Project

This part is designed to reveal the relative weight among software, vendor and project properties by evaluating fourteen attributes at once. While it was difficult for a responder to imagine a virtual project described by nine attributes in the pre-analysis, we suppose that it would not be difficult to imagine all attributes of a experienced project that they had actually experienced.

The question is "Think of one recently outsourced software development project. Keeping this project in mind, please evaluate its result in terms of fourteen attributes." Each attribute has two possible values as shown in Table 3. The development result is assigned by a value ranging from 1(fatal failure) to 5 (success beyond expectation)].

4.4 Part 4: Evaluation on Virtual Projects

This part is designed to identify the importance of attributes in the separate properties by conjoint analysis [1] [14]. Because the pre-analysis showed that it was difficult to image nine attributes at once, we classify fourteen attributes into four software attributes, five vendor attributes and five project attributes. Based on orthogonal planning of conjoint analysis, we prepare three sets of virtual projects.

An example question for the vendor property is "You will be presented with a series of 9 virtual vendor profiles in Table. Based on this information and your own experience and knowledge, please circle the appropriate numbers in the following table. How attractive would it be for your company to OUTSOURCE to this vendor?" The similar questions are provided on software property and project property, too. The evaluation for profile is assigned by value ranging from 1 (low possibility for success) to 5 (high possibility for success) .

5 Overview of Risk Extraction by Statistical Method

There are two approaches to sampling: random sampling and intentional sampling. In general random sampling does not include bias, but the return rate may be terrible because the contents requested by the questionnaire are too confidential for responders to disclose. Therefore, we use two channels for questionnaire delivery as mentioned before: SSR and JEITA. Each company in SSR collected twenty responses and JEITA collected thirty responses. There were other volunteers who answered the questionnaire. In total, we collected one hundred and seventy five responses. They are all Japanese client-side people.

5.1 Frequency Analysis

The first Analysis is a simple frequency analysis, Figure 3 shows the distribution of software category and Figure 4 shows that of vendor countries. Note that about sixty percent of outsourced software to foreign countries is customer applications and fifty percent are outsourced to china.

Table 4 shows attribute importance by separate evaluation for Part 2 questions described in 4.2. It shows that there is little difference in importance among attributes for any property. In a sense, this confirms that separate evaluation has no meaning in determining risk magnitude.

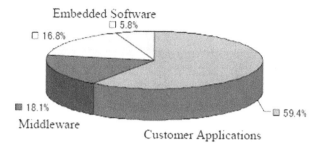

Fig. 3. Rate of Software Categories

Table 4. Attributes Importance by Separate Evaluation

Score in Software	Software complexity and scale	Quality measurability	Requirement Specifiability	Requirement volatility
5	59	38	53	54
4	49	67	67	50
3	34	32	24	34
2	10	14	8	13
1	4	5	4	5
Average	3.96	3.76	4.01	3.87
Rage	0.25	0.24	0.26	0.25

Score in Vendor	Communication skill	Project management capability	Vendor flexibility	Attribution rate	Long term strategy
5	90	82	47	23	48
4	56	53	60	68	51
3	9	20	40	49	47
2	1	1	8	13	6
1	0	0	1	3	3
Average	4.51	4.38	3.92	3.61	3.87
Rage	0.22	0.22	0.19	0.18	0.19

Score in Project	Deadline urgency	Relative cost advantage	Client side technical expeitise	Strategic impoitance for future project	Ability to monitor vender behavior
5	66	64	51	18	35
4	36	56	68	54	64
3	47	29	29	60	50
2	4	6	6	17	7
1	3	1	2	7	0
Average	4.01	4.13	4.03	3.38	3.81
Rage	0.21	0.21	0.21	0.17	0.2

5.2 SEM Analysis

This analysis is done for the experienced projects collected by Part 3 of questionnaire. The main concern is to determine the degree of importance among three property types: software, vendor and project properties. Introducing four latent variables

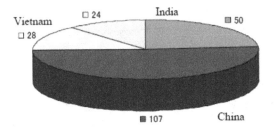

Fig. 4. Rate of Vendor Countries

(software, vendor, project and satisfaction) that are not observed in answers from responders, we refine path diagrams step by step. The modifications and findings are discussed in detail elsewhere [15].

The final model is shown in Fig. 5. The findings are summarized as follows:

1) Vendor property such as communication ability and project management ability mainly affected the result of development,
2) Software property such as requirements specificity and requirements volatility did not affect the result directly but did affect it indirectly through project property such as relative cost advantage and project strategic importance,
3) Control parameters such as vendor companies and software type did not improve the precision of the models.

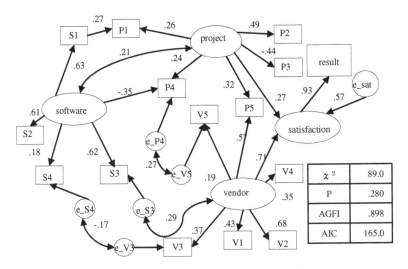

Fig. 5. Result of Structural Equation Modeling

5.3 Conjoint Analysis

As introduced in the description of Part 4 of the questionnaire, this analysis is done for the assessment of virtual projects generated by orthogonal planning [1]. There are three sets for virtual projects. One set is described in software attributes defined in

Table 3, second set is described in the vendor attributes and the final set is described in the project attributes.

The main concern is to detect the relative importance of attributes in their properties. Conjoint analysis [1] calculates the relative importance rate and partial utility of attributes. The sum of partial utility decides the range of total utility. The total utility is an estimated value for project evaluation.

$$TotalUtility = \sum PartialUtility + Const$$

Table 5 shows an example result of a conjoint analysis result where the samples are classified by software category: customer application, middleware and embedded software. From this table, we obtained followings:

1) There are different risk magnitudes for attributes in each category. For example, in outsourcing embedded software, the attrition rate cannot be used to evaluate a vendor. Instead, communication skill and project management capability are the key attributes for selecting vendors for this category,
2) Because the sum of partial utilities and a constant for middleware is smaller than those for the other two categories, the success beyond expectation is unlikely to occur in the middleware category.
3) According to Pearson's R and Kendall's taw, the fitness of the model is excellent for any category.

Let us show another example result of conjoint analysis results. Fig. 6 shows the individual partial utilities in software property: software complexity and scale, and requirement volatility.

Table 5. An Example Result of Conjoint Analysis

():Sample size

Vendor Property	Customer Applications (92)		Middleware (28)		Embedded Software (26)	
	Importance Rate	Partial Utility	Importance Rate	Partial Utility	Importance Rate	Partial Utility
Communication skill	25.02	.3638	24.05	.2404	28.26	.4459
Project management capability	19.95	.2992	21.44	.3173	24.21	.3986
Vendor flexibility on specification changes	18.61	.2795	18.2	.2788	18.72	.2703
Attrition rate	16.74	.2093	19.83	.2500	9.89	.0946
Long term strategy	19.68	.1896	16.48	.1731	18.92	.1959
Sum of Partial Utilities	1.3414		1.2596		1.4053	
Constant	2.4480		2.3654		2.500	
Pearson's R	.983		.994		.997	
Kendall's tau	1.000		.982		1.000	

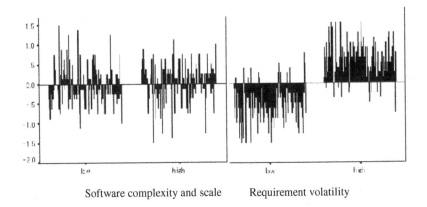

Fig. 6. Examples of Partial Utility in Software Property

Each bar expresses a responder's utility value. An upward bar expresses negative feeling for offshore outsourcing because there must be risk while a downward bar expresses positive feeling. Most people agree that the potential requirement volatility is risk. On the other hand, there are two different views of whether or not software complexity and scale is a risk.

To confirm the fitness of the model for vendor property, let us depict the frequency diagram as shown in Fig 7. The x-axis is the estimated total utility based on the previous formula and the y axis is the occurrence count. There are five lines and each expresses the same result of a project where the range is from1 to 5.

6   Discussion

Let us discuss what we did. Again, our basic assumption is that the experienced managers know risk factors and their magnitudes as their tacit knowledge. Asking them to answer the designed questionnaire forced them to externalize their knowledge. Then the written knowledge can be shared with other people. However, it is difficult to use such written knowledge separately because it is too subjective.

There is a hint in the SECI model proposed by Nonaka [8] where SECI means socialization, externalization, connection and internalization. To connect individual items of externalized knowledge, we have used statistical analysis methods like SEM and conjoint analysis. The connected knowledge based on statistical analysis can be shared as discussed in the previous section.

Furthermore, there should be internalization for knowledge transfer. Internalization allows persons to learn connected knowledge and increase their tacit knowledge. In our case, risk assessment for new project corresponds to the internalization. The model of knowledge spiral is shown in Fig. 8. Thus, we have chance to design and to install risk assessment tool.

Assigning values to the attributes of a new project, IT manager has chance to get diagnosis result. The risk assessment tool refers to the relative importance among

Frequency of Responders

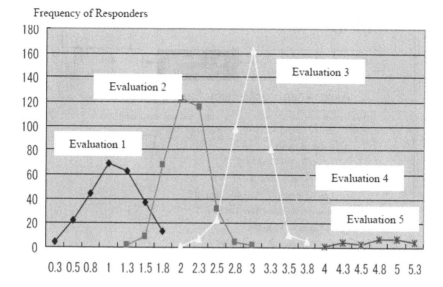

Fig. 7. Freuuency of Estimated Preference by Vendor Property

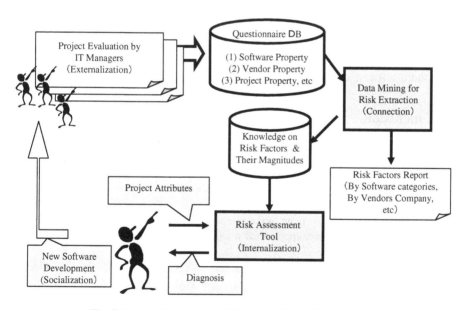

Fig. 8. Knowledge Spiral in Offshore Software Development

three properties discussed in 5.2 and the partial utilities values for attributes discussed in 5.3. The basic idea for tool itself is borrowed from [12] and the example screen is shown in Fig. 9.

Persons who internalize the experience in the past projects will collaborate with other people and outsource new project to a vendor. In SECI model, this collaboration

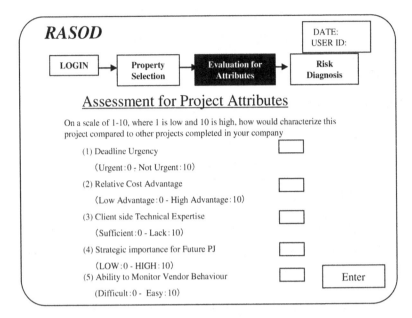

Fig. 9. An Example Screen for Offshore Software Outsourcing Assessment Tool

is socialization. Thus, their tacit knowledge will propagate among their brain. Then their externalization in the future should be new. This will lead to a knowledge spiral in offshore software outsourcing.

7 Conclusion

This paper has presented a questionnaire-based risk assessment scheme. Our contributions are as follows:

- We established an academia-industry collaborative framework for research on offshore software outsourcing.
- To approach the issues from an engineering viewpoint, we presented how to collect sample data from experienced managers and how to identify risks and their magnitudes.
- By visiting companies for pre-analysis and by testing its feasibility on collecting reasonable responses, we have designed a four-part questionnaire.
- Delivering the designed questionnaire through two intentional channels, we collected one hundred and seventy five responses.
- The collected samples were analyzed by three statistical methods: frequency analysis, structural equation modeling and conjoint analysis. This paper has shown an example of the statistical analysis results and what they reveal.
- This paper also showed that our research plays the role of a knowledge spiral in the context of the SECI model. The development of the risk assessment tool is on going.

Acknowledgements

The authors would like to sincere thanks to members of Strategic Software Research forum (SSR) and Japan Electronics and Information Technology Industries Association (JEITA) who contributed to collect responses of questionnaire. Special thanks are also due to Mr. Yoshihisa WADA and Mr. Daiki Nakahigashi who helped our statistical analysis and developing risk assessment tool.

References

1. Andrews, R.L., Ansari, A., Currim, I.S.: Hierarchical Bayes Versus Finite Mixture Conjoint Analysis Models: A Comparison of Fit, Prediction, and Partworth Recovery. Journal of Marketing Research XXXIX, 87–98 (2002)
2. Aspray, W., Mayadas, F., Vardi, M.Y. (eds.): Globalization and Offshoring of Software, Report of the ACM Job Migration Task Force, Association for Computing Machinery (2006)
3. Bharadwaj, A., Tiwana, A.: Managerial Assessments of E-Business Investment Opportunities: A Field Study. IEEE Trans. on Engineering Management 52(4), 449–460 (2005)
4. Carnegie Mellon University: The Capability Maturity Model: Guidelines for Improving the Software Process, Addison Wesley Longman, Inc. (1994)
5. Gold, T.: Outsourcing Software Development Offshore - Making It Work. Auerbach Publications (2005)
6. Krishna, S., Sahay, S., Walsham, G.: Managing Cross-Cultural Issues in Global Software Outsourcing. CACM 47(4), 62–66 (2004)
7. Mayer, B.: The Unspoken Revolution in Software Engineering, Computer, pp. 121–124 (January 2005)
8. Nonaka, I., Takeuchi, H.: The Knowledge-Creating Company: How Japanese Companies Create the Dynamics of Innovation. Oxford Univ. Pr., Oxford (1995)
9. Software Business Comittee: Report on Software Development Resource, Japan Electronics and Information Technology Industries Association, No. 06-P-9 (2006)
10. Thondavadi, N., Albert, G.: Offshore Outsourcing - Path to New Efficiencies in IT and Business Processes, 1st Books Library (2004)
11. Tiwana, A.: Beyond the Black Box: Knowledge Overlaps in Software Outsourcing. IEEE SOFTWARE 21(5), 51–58 (2004)
12. Tiwana, A., Keil, M.: The One-Minute Risk Assessment Tool. CACM 47(11), 73–77 (2004)
13. Tiwana, A.B., Tsuji, H., Sakurai, A., Yoshida, K.: Myths and Paradoxes in Japanese IT Outsourcing.Communications of the ACM (forthcoming)
14. Tsuji, H., Sakurai, A., Yoshida, K., Tiwana, A., Bush, A.: Risk Factors on Offshore Software Development by Conjoint Analysis (In Japanese). Transaction on Information Processing Society for Japanese 48(2), 823–831 (2007)
15. Wada, Y.D.N., Tsuji, H.: An Evaluation Method for Offshore Software Development by Structural Equation Modeling. In: Proc. of the First Software Engineering Approaches For Offshore and Outsourced Development, vol. 4716, pp. 114–127 (2007)

An Evaluation Method for Offshore Software Development by Structural Equation Modeling

Yoshihisa Wada, Daiki Nakahigashi, and Hiroshi Tsuji

Graduate School of Engineering, Osaka Prefecture University,
1-1, Gakuencho, Naka-ku, Sakai,
599-8531 Osaka, Japan
{Wada,Nakahigashi,Tsuji}@mis.cs.osakafu-u.ac.jp
http://www.cs.osakafu-u.ac.jp/mis/

Abstract. To determine the magnitude of risk factors in offshore software development, we explain how structural equation modeling works for questionnaire samples. Each response to our questionnaire consists of one offshore software development instance including its result in terms of success/failure and fourteen attributes. The attributes are classified into software, vendor or project properties. Collecting 172 responses from Japanese project managers and following a series of modifications from a basic model to the final model, we have found the followings: 1) the vendor properties mainly affect the result of development, 2) the software properties do not affect the result directly but did affect it indirectly through the project properties, and 3) control parameters such as vendor companies and software type do not improve the fit indices of the models.

1 Introduction

These days, there is a strong trend in the Japanese software industry for offshore software development, in which client companies outsource their software development to vendor companies in developing countries like India, China and Vietnam. The main reasons for this trend are a shortage of human resources at home and the need to reduce costs and meet shorter deadlines.

While there have been some great successes in offshore software development projects, there have also been some fatal failures because of mis-communication, cultural differences, quality issues, and so on. To avoid failure and achieve success, one must consider research from various fields including science and engineering [1] [2] [5] [6] [9] [10] [11]. In fact, social science and economics as well as software engineering will contribute to improve the success rate of offshore software development. Decision science and knowledge engineering will also be useful to clarify the risks in offshore software development.

As the first step of a field approach, SSR (Strategic Software Research forum) established a project in 2005 [14]. It consists of three Japanese professors, two US professors, and twelve engineers from IT companies (Toshiba, Mitsubishi, Fujitsu, Hitachi and IBM-Japan). In order to acquire knowledge about risks from project

B. Meyer and M. Joseph (Eds.): SEAFOOD 2007, LNCS 4716, pp. 128–140, 2007.

managers, they designed a questionnaire, delivered it to many experienced project managers, and collected the results [15].

Thus we have the opportunity to mine the risk factors in the responses. The questionnaire asked for votes on two kinds of offshore software development: existing development and virtual development.

This paper concerns structural equation modeling (SEM) [3] [8] [13] [16] for the former while another paper [14] discusses conjoint analysis [4] for the latter. First, this paper defines our goal and means. Then, we introduce the means, namely the questionnaire and statistical method, SEM. In section 3, we explain how to build an initial basic model and how to refine it to the final model. Finally, section 4 discusses the fit indices and effects of latent variables for the final model and three findings.

2   Approach for Evaluation

Our goal is to reduce the risks of offshore software development. To achieve this goal, it is helpful to use an offshore software development evaluation tool such as the one discussed in [12]. The evaluation tool should be based on statistical analysis methods and sample data. In our case, the method is SEM and the sample data come from replies to a questionnaire. An overview of our approach is shown in Fig. 1.

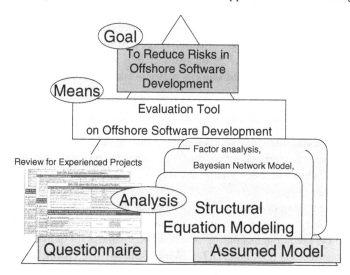

Fig. 1. Approach for Evaluation

2.1   Questionnaire Design

Our basic premise is that the experienced people know the risks of offshore software development as their tacit knowledge. Therefore, the first issue is how to acquire this knowledge from them. A questionnaire is a simple but powerful means of obtaining it.

We made the following assumptions about the questionnaire:

1) The responses may differ according to the responders' backgrounds. For example, there may be differences in software types and vendor countries. Their experience and careers may also cause differences.

2) It is not easy for people to answer general questions but it is possible to give facts about projects of which they have experience.

For the first assumption, we included the following items in our questionnaire to handle the responders' demography: number of years of IT experience, number of years of experience in the current company, number of offshore projects you have previously been involved with in the outsourcing decision process, current position/role, vendor ISO/ CMM ratings, type of software and vendor countries.

For the second assumption, we ask each responder to remember his/her last project and describe it including its result and attributes. In our questionnaire, these attributes are classified into software, vendor, and project properties as shown in Table 1. How to design these attributes is discussed elsewhere [15]. While the software and project properties can also be applied to onshore software development, there are differences in the vendor properties between them. Communication skills cover cross-cultural problems and Japanese language ability for offshore software development. Furthermore, although the worker attrition rate is low and thus not an important attribute in onshore cases, that for offshore is considered as ineligible. The selectable values for describing the result ranged from 1(fatal failure) to 5(success beyond expectation). Two-level evaluations (High- or low) were used for the observed variables to show clear differences between successes and failures.

2.2 Sample Sources

There are two ideas for collecting samples: random sampling and intentional sampling. In general, random sampling provides impartial precision but leads to a low response rate, while the intentional sampling may be biased, but should produce a higher return rate.

Since most companies want to keep project results confidential, random sampling would seem likely to get a very low response rate in our situation. Therefore, we chose to use the intentional sampling. We had two channels for delivering and collecting questionnaires: via SSR and JEITA. While SSR has five channels, which are major Japanese IT companies (Hitachi, Fujitsu, Mitsubishi, IBM-Japan, and Toshiba), JEITA has about five hundred affiliated companies. We asked representative persons of these consortiums to collect responses, and we got one hundred and seventy five responses. Of these, thirteen were considered unusable because of various deficiencies, leaving one hundred sixty two responses for analysis. The correlation among the results and attributes is shown in the Appendix. The distribution of the project results is shown in Table 2.

Table 1. Attributes in Questionnaire

Software	
S1	Software complexity and scale
S2	Software quality measurability
S3	Requirement specificity
S4	Requirement volatility
Vendor	
V1	Communication skill (Including language ability)
V2	Project management capability by vendors accomplishment
V3	Vendor flexibility on specification changes
V4	Work attrition rate
V5	Strategic long-term relationship
Project	
P1	Deadline urgency
P2	Relative cost advantage
P3	Client side technical expertise
P4	Strategic importance for related future project
P5	Ability to monitor vendor behavior

Table 2. Distribution of Result Index in Questionnaire

Result	Meaning	Frequency	Proportion (%)
1	Fatal Failure	6	3.70
2	Failure	16	9.88
3	Not Bad	71	43.83
4	Success	64	39.51
5	Great Success	5	3.09
Total		162	100.00

3 Structural Equation Modeling

There are many methods like multi-regression analysis and conjoint analysis for statistical methods [4] [7] [13]. Although the former is simple and popular, it cannot to express a chain structure or the ring structure among variables. On the other hand, the latter is powerful for market research like product design, but it absolutely requires complete combinations of attributes for samples. Therefore, we chose to use another method. For research of this type, we prefer a visualization method for capturing hidden knowledge structures about risks from project managers. In our risk analysis of offshore software development, visual models with precise indices are helpful to establish an initial model and modify it. So it is very meaningful to introduce a quantitative and visual approach for our task. The correlation coefficient is also useful to figure out the characteristics of samples (Refer to the Appendix). While we considered the correlation coefficient in the first phase of analyzing data, it is not very versatile. Therefore, we decided to use SEM to reveal causality among variables in a visual manner. Moreover, it enabled us to find many compiled observed variables at the same time based on the notion of structure. The main features of SEM are as follows [3] [8] [13] [16]:

(1) It is a modeling method based on regression analysis and factor analysis. These are traditional multivariate analyses.

(2) It uses not only directly observed variables but also latent variables that are unobserved.

(3) Both variables are connected by arrows, called paths, which express linear relations and the bases of fitness.

(4) The path coefficient, which is the degree of causality for making a better model, should be calculated. A better model fits the sample data better and shows the causality.

(5) Squares and ellipses should be drawn for observed and latent variables, respectively, in the path diagram. The path coefficient is on its path and is regarded as effective when it is close to one.

In particular, we considered item (2) to be a key feature of SEM. Latent variables are typical characteristics of SEM for visualizing hidden factors. By showing the path-coefficient among variables, SEM suggests that we should explore data analysis and modify the models.

3.1 Skeleton of Model

The basic procedure for SEM is as follows:

1) Assume a causal model,
2) Verify it,
3) If the conditions are satisfied, stop modification, else modify the model and return to 1).

Thus we should establish the skeleton of the model first. As we have already obtained the observed variables, we need to know how to introduce latent variables and how to incorporate them in the model. Because the attributes in the questionnaire were classified into three property types, we introduced three latent variables: software, vendor, and project.

We also introduced a latent variable called satisfaction because there should be a unique variable that affects the observed variable "result". We were, however, concerned the model would have been almost equal to one of the multi-regression models if we had ignored the latent variables. Therefore, we established the model skeleton shown in Fig. 2.

Here, we discuss the value of the observed variable "result" in Fig. 2. As shown in Table 2, the possible values of result is from 1 to 5. Therefore, there are some alternatives for handling the value because it is not a cardinal number but an ordinal number. One idea is to use the original five numbers. Another is to separate them into success and failure by ignoring the middle result value "3". A third idea is to unify the frequency of result.

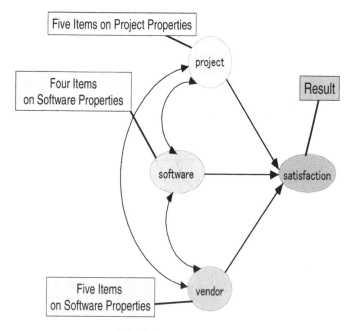

Fig. 2. Assumed Model

Based on preliminary-experimentation for evaluating these alternatives, we decided to use the original five numbers. This idea is valid because SEM works well under the premise that the distribution is normal.

3.2 Scratch Building

To confirming the fit indices, we scratch built the model for the samples. In this section, we focus mainly on path coefficients and sometimes on chi-square goodness of fit and significance level (P). Note that chi-square goodness of fit shows the degree of agreement to the original population and is close to 0 if the model is appropriate. The significance level (P) should be greater than 0.05 for the 5% confidence level.

(1) Basic Model. As shown in Fig. 3, it is a simple model in the view of the skeleton. Three latent variables are connected to the latent variable "satisfaction" and there are no paths among them. We used AMOS 6.0 [8], which is a commercial software package for SEM. This gave us the coefficients shown in Fig. 3.

As a result, chi-square goodness of fit was 183.063 and its significance level (P) was 0.000. Therefore, we should regard this model as improper. In particular, we found that the coefficient between "satisfaction" and "software" was too small.

(2) Modified Model. Because the coefficient between "satisfaction" and "software" was small, we cut the path. Because the relation between "project" and "software" seemed to be stronger than the relation between "software" and "vendor", we connected a path for the former relation. Comparing a bi-directional path with a unidirectional one, we found better fit indices for the former. Note that one feature of SEM is

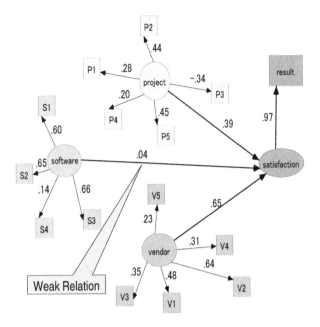

Fig. 3. Basic Model

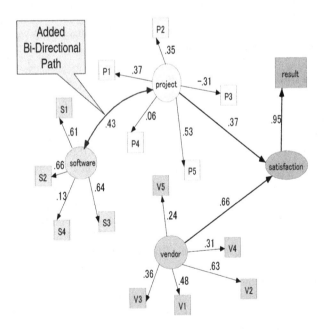

Fig. 4. Modified Model

that it can handle bi-directional relations while the multi-regression model can handle only unidirectional ones. The model is shown in Fig 4 with its coefficients.

(3) Final Model. Based on the modified model, we took two different approaches to improving fitness. One was based on a modification index and the other on the domain principle.

The modification index in SEM shows the sensitivity of fitness for adding new paths. Adding a variety of new paths to the modified model revealed four causal relations for improving fitness.

1. Relation from observed variable "S1" (software complexity and scale) to observed variable "P1"(deadline urgency),
2. Relation from latent variable "software" to observed variable "P4" (strategic importance for related future projects),
3. Relation from latent variable "vendor" to observed variable "P5" (ability to monitor vendor behavior),
4. Relation between latent variable "vendor" and error variable "e_S3" for "S3" (requirements for specificity),

From the viewpoint of principles, we added new paths. The principles were based on background knowledge about software development. Referring to the attributes in the questionnaire, we reminded some principles. Among them, there were two modification indices.

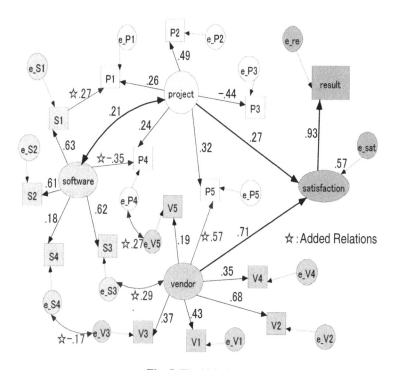

Fig. 5. Final Model

First, we set the causality between error variable "e_S4" for "S4" (requirement volatility) and error variable "e_V3" for "V3" (vendor flexibility on specification changes). This is because we considered that these variables concern the complexity of the software requirement.

Second, we set the causality between the error variable "e_P4" for "P4" (strategic importance for related future projects) and the error variable "e_V5" for "V5" (strategic long-term relationship). This is because we considered that these variables concern future projects (Fig. 5).

Note we should consider these two approaches in a complementary manner. If the modification index is high but there is no domain principle, then no modification should be made. Furthermore, if there is a domain principle but the modification index is low, the modification should not be made.

(4) Expansion based on control parameters As introduced in **2.1**, there are parameters related to responders. In particular, we paid attention to the software category and vendor countries because they affect the model. For such parameters, SEM accepts a special variable called dummy. We refer to the expanded model with the dummy variables.

We built another two models by adding observed variables related to the responders' demography. Suppose that there are m-1 variables $D_1, D_2,..., D_{m-1}$ when one parameter X has m categories. $D_i = 1$ or $D_j = 0$ $(j \neq i)$ was represented when the case is category i. For example, dummy variables $D_{India}=1$ and $D_{China}=0$ for Indian vendors if there are three alternatives for vendor countries. Locations (India, China, others) are introduced. Dummy variables and their relations were added as follows:

Table 3. Fit Indices

Model	Chi-square	P	AGFI	AIC
Basic	183.1	.000	.820	247.5
Modified	175.5	.000	.826	239.5
Final	89.0	.280	.898	165.0
Expanded-1	155.9	.003	.857	239.8
Expanded-2	99.7	.376	.894	179.7

Expanded 1.   From software types to satisfaction (customer applications, middleware, embedded software)

Expanded 2.   From vendor countries to satisfaction (India, China)

These two expanded models were not effective because the coefficients for the paths added by dummy variables were close to 0.1 and these coefficients were regarded as insignificant. Note that models with the following paths are less appropriate than the models we presented: from software type to software, and from vendor countries to vendor.

4 Discussion

Let us discuss which model is appropriate for the samples based on fit indices and which latent variables affect the result based on path coefficients.

4.1 Fit Indices and Path Coefficient

For the fit indices, SEM has the chi-square goodness of fit, significance level (P), AGFI (Adjusted Goodness of Fit Index) and AIC (Akaike Information Criterion). The AGFI score should be greater than 0.9 if the model is appropriate while a lower AIC implies a better model.

The indices for the five discussed models are shown in Table 3. The final model is much better than the basic model. This means that the software properties do not affect the result directly but affect it indirectly through the project properties. Furthermore, the final model is slightly better that the expanded models. This means that the control parameters do not work in our case.

4.2 Effects of Variables

For checking the path coefficients, let us review Fig. 5. The path coefficient between the satisfaction and the project is 0.27, while the path coefficient between the satisfaction and the vendor is 0.71. The causality between the project and the software is 0.21. In addition, the square of multiple-correlation-coefficients of the satisfaction is 0.57 (shown at the upper right of satisfaction). It is calculated as $0.71^2 + 0.27^2$. This means that these variables account for 57% of the satisfaction.

For the magnitude of risk, the path coefficient could be clue for the estimation. For SEM, there are two kinds of effects: direct effect and indirect effect. While the direct effect is the path coefficient itself, the indirect effect is calculated by summing the products of the path coefficients through passing variables. For example, the latent variable 'software' affected 'project' by 0.21 while it affected 'satisfaction' by 0.21*0.27. Note that there is only one path from 'software' to 'satisfaction'. If there are multiple paths, such product should be added.

We got the effects of latent variables for the observed variable 'result' as shown in Table 4. We found that vendor properties were the main property type affecting the result of development.

To validate our analysis, we checked correlation coefficients. As path-coefficients, some of them explain how to scratch build models in section 3. Actually, the correlation coefficients between Result and V1-V5 are high while those of between Result and S1-S4 are low. On the other hand, correlation coefficients between S1-S4 and P1-P5 are not low, and they provided clues for changing models in the Basic Model. Of course, those between Result and P1-P5 are significant and are not low. The exploratory data analysis in this research is very useful and relates to correlation coefficients.

4.3 Experimentation in Progress

Although our analysis is still in progress, we briefly disclose here what we are doing. We have explored models to get higher indices by SEM with intuitive latent variables. On the other hand, it is important to define latent variables rationally as assumptions under SEM. In addition, finding and introducing unique variables that affect only satisfaction and do not relate the other variables may give better models. For this purpose, factor analysis will be used in the future. It should help to reveal common combinatorial notions for observed variables like latent variables in SEM. Before using SEM, we can get common factors and unique variables through factor analysis. Then, to verify the effectiveness of the Final Model, we must plan to compare it with models suggested by factor analysis. If this factor analysis approach is different from our exploratory data analysis, there may be a chance to get a better model. Otherwise, it will provide a double checked that our results are significance.

Table 4. Effects of Latent Variables for Result

Latent Variable	Direct effects	Indirect effects	Total effects
Project	.27		.27
Software		.06	.06
Vendor	.71***		.71

***P<0.001

Second, questionnaire data are essential to justify this research. In this questionnaire, two-level evaluations (high or low) were used for the observed variables to show clear differences between successes and failures. On the other hand, if we choose n-level evaluations ($n>2$), we may get more precise indices for showing the model. This would also enable use to figure out the validity of the Final Model.

Finally, we should consider the demographic data mentioned in section2.1. Although we tried introducing dummy variables to treat parameters related to responders, we have not gotten good results. That is to say, few indices were changed by introducing dummy variables. There might be a better way to introduce dummy variables for SEM. There is an inherent problem of SEM. We should consider the actual meanings of indices and models because SEM is a very flexible method. Analyzing partial correlation coefficients as well as introducing dummy variables may lead to a better model.

5   Conclusion

This paper has described SEM analysis for offshore software development. The purpose of the analysis is to determine the magnitude of risk factors where the risks might have been hidden in past projects or remained as tacit knowledge of project managers. The other purpose, or rather the goal of this research, is to apply the findings to new offshore software development in order to assess the risks and reduce them.

To apply SEM to offshore software development, we designed a questionnaire for collecting the experiences of project managers. The questionnaire contained four software attributes, five vendor attributes and five project attributes of outsourced development and its results. Each attribute had a binary value and the results ranged from 1 to 5. Starting with a simple model in which three properties were directly connected to the result, we modified the domain model step by step based on path coefficients and the principle of attributes. Finally, we identified the model that satisfied the statistical fit indices such as chi-square goodness of fit and AGFI. According to the results of analysis:

1)   vendor properties such as communication ability and project management ability mainly affect the results of development,
2)   software properties such as requirements for specificity and requirements volatility do not affect the result directly but did affect it indirectly through the project properties such as relative cost advantage and project strategic importance,
3)   control parameters such as vendor companies and software type do not improve the precision of the models.

For the goal of this research, we are going to develop risk assessment tool.

Acknowledgement

The authors would like to sincere thanks to Prof. Akito Sakurai, Prof. Kenichi Yoshida, Prof. Amrit Tiwana and Prof. Ashley Bush who gave valuable comments on designing questionnaire. Special thanks are also due to members of Strategic Software Research forum (SSR) and Japan Electronics and Information Technology Industries Association (JEITA) who contributed to collect responses of questionnaire. This work is partly supported by the ICOM Electronic Communication Engineering Promotion Foundation, Japan.

References

1.   Aspray, W., Mayadas, F., Vardi, M.Y. (eds.): Globalization and Offshoring of Software, Report of the ACM Job Migration Task Force, Association for Computing Machinery (2006)
2.   Gold, T.: Outsourcing Software Development Offshore - Making It Work. Auerbach Publications (2005)
3.   Hiramatsu, A., Oiso, H.: Analysis of Customer Unsubscription Intention for a Mobile content service, The Papers of Technical Meeting on Information Systems, IEE Japan, IS-05-23 (2005)
4.   Kinosita, A., Ono, E.: AHP and Conjoint Analysis (In Japanese). Gendaisuugakusya Co., Ltd. (2004)
5.   Krishna, S., Sahay, S., Walsham, G.: Managing Cross-Cultural Issues in Global Software Outsourcing. CACM 47(4), 62–66 (2004)
6.   Mayer, B.: The Unspoken Revolution in Software Engineering, Computer, 121–124 (January 2005)
7.   Nagano, H.: Introduction of Statistics (In Japanese). KyourituShuppan Co., Ltd. (2003)
8.   Oshio, A.: Psychological and Survey Data Analysis using SPSS and Amos (In Japanese). TokyoTosho Co., Ltd. (2005)
9.   Shindo, T., Takei, T.: the Division of Labor of Software Development in the World, NIKKEI ELECTRONICS, pp. 107–121 (2004)
10.   Thondavadi, N., Albert, G.: Offshore Outsourcing - Path to New Efficiencies in IT and Business Processes, 1st Books Library (2004)
11.   Tiwana, A.: Beyond the Black Box: Knowledge Overlaps in Software Outsourcing. IEEE SOFTWARE 21(5), 51–58 (2004)

12. Tiwana, A., Keil, M.: The One-Minute Risk Assessment Tool. CACM 47(11), 73–77 (2004)
13. Toyota, H.: Covariance Structure Analysis [introduction] (In Japanese). Asakura Shoten Co., Ltd. (2004)
14. Tsuji, H., Sakurai, A., Yoshida, K., Tiwana, A., Bush, A.: Risk Factors on Offshore Software Development by Conjoint Analysis (In Japanese). Transaction on Information Processing Society for Japanese 48(2), 823–831 (2007)
15. Tsuji, H., Sakurai, A., Yoshida, K., Tiwana, A., Bush, A.: Questionnaire-based Risk Assessment Scheme for Japanese Offshore Software Outsourcing. In: Meyer, B., Joseph, M. (eds.) SEAFOOD 2007. LNCS, vol. 4716, pp. 128–140. Springer, Heidelberg (2007)
16. Yamamoto, K., Onodera, T.: Covariance Structure Analysis and the Case of Analysis by Amos (In Japanese). Nakanishiya Syuppan Co., Ltd. (2002)

Appendix

Table A2. Correlation among Result and Attributes

	RESULT	S1	S2	S3	S4	V1	V2	V3	V4	V5	P1	P2	P3	P4	P5
RESULT	1.000	0.094	0.061	*0.182	-0.060	*0.335	*0.424	*0.331	*0.197	0.210	*0.152	*0.149	-0.037	*0.184	*0.439
S1	0.094	1.000	*0.411	*0.393	*0.170	0.064	0.115	-0.128	*0.169	-0.025	*0.304	-0.016	*-0.168	*-0.237	0.101
S2	0.061	*0.411	1.000	*0.418	-0.015	0.047	0.013	0.069	0.122	0.008	*0.173	0.060	-0.013	-0.099	*0.264
S3	*0.182	*0.393	*0.418	1.000	0.093	0.073	0.199	0.109	0.056	0.026	*0.181	-0.012	0.008	*-0.179	*0.212
S4	-0.060	*0.170	-0.015	0.093	1.000	-0.039	-0.079	*-0.182	-0.067	-0.006	0.081	0.015	*-0.119	*-0.151	-0.076
V1	*0.335	0.064	0.047	0.073	-0.039	1.000	*0.350	0.073	*0.155	0.128	0.040	0.027	-0.021	0.034	*0.200
V2	*0.424	0.115	0.013	*0.198	-0.079	*0.350	1.000	*0.219	*0.275	0.094	0.100	-0.051	0.080	0.035	*0.398
V3	*0.331	-0.128	0.069	0.109	*-0.182	0.073	*0.219	1.000	0.074	*0.167	0.121	0.107	0.039	0.082	*0.266
V4	*0.197	*0.169	0.122	0.056	-0.067	*0.155	*0.275	0.074	1.000	0.002	0.035	0.022	*-0.144	0.000	*0.292
V5	*0.209	-0.025	0.008	0.026	-0.006	0.128	0.094	*0.167	0.002	1.000	-0.044	0.047	-0.040	*0.276	*0.154
P1	*0.152	*0.304	*0.173	*0.181	0.081	0.040	0.100	0.121	0.035	-0.044	1.000	0.109	*-0.176	-0.058	*0.146
P2	*0.149	-0.016	0.060	-0.012	0.015	0.027	-0.051	0.107	0.022	0.047	0.109	1.000	*-0.231	0.086	*0.171
P3	-0.037	*-0.168	-0.013	0.008	-0.120	-0.021	0.080	0.039	*-0.144	-0.040	*-0.176	*-0.231	1.000	-0.063	-0.118
P4	*0.184	*-0.237	-0.099	*-0.179	*-0.151	0.034	0.035	0.082	0.000	*0.276	-0.058	0.086	-0.063	1.000	0.063
P5	*0.439	0.101	*0.264	*0.212	-0.076	*0.200	*0.398	*0.266	*0.292	*0.154	*0.146	*0.171	*-0.117	0.063	1.000

Note: Symbols such as S1 and S2 come from Table 1.
*: $P<0.05$

The Value of Outsourced Software

Gio Wiederhold, Amar Gupta, Rajat Mittal, and Erich Neuhold

[1] Computer Science Department, Stanford University
[2] Entrepreneurship, MIS, and MAP Departments, University of Arizona
[3] Eller College of Management, University of Arizona
[4] University of Vienna, Vienna, Austria
gio@cs.stanford.edu, gupta@eller.arizona.edu,
rajatprm@email.arizona.edu, erich.neuhold@univie.ac.at

Abstract. Outsourcing of work to support software development and services is seen primarily as a transfer of labor to another shore. But intellectual property, as software, is transferred as well. There are risks when IP is transferred. In order to assess the extent of those risks, one needs to know the value of that concerned software. Software is an intangible good, and the value of intangibles is based on the income they are expected to generate in the future. This paper exploits a model for software valuation based on principles of IP valuation, sales expectations, net present value, and related parameters. Having a quantitative model on a spreadsheet allows for the exploration of business alternatives in outsourcing. The motivation for this paper is to increase the awareness of members in the computing community. Software valuation plays a role in a global economy where the developers of the software and the users of the company reside in different countries.

1 Introduction

Outsourcing of work to support software development and services to other countries has been presented primarily as a transfer of labor to another shore. However, such offshoring also requires transfer of supporting materials. Much of that material has value, and represents intellectual capital. While Marx was concerned about labor and financial capital as the drivers of the economy, in today's knowledge-driven environment it is the intellectual capital that counts. A significant part of that intellectual capital is software, and is property (IP) of the outsourcer. This paper discusses the relevance of valuing software when offshoring. The actual valuation method has been presented in a recent paper by one of the authors [13]. The analyses that led to the development of the software valuation method was indeed motivated and supported by the need to assess software IP exports.

Little specific guidance existed for software valuation. It was left to lawyers, economists, software vendors, or promoters to quantify the benefits of software in commerce. The results were mostly inconsistent [8]. To value software information from domains that rarely interact directly: software engineering, economics, business practice, and legal sources, had to be brought together. Now, the more formal

B. Meyer and M. Joseph (Eds.): SEAFOOD 2007, LNCS 4716, pp. 141–151, 2007.
© Springer-Verlag Berlin Heidelberg 2007

methods presented can be exploited, and further developed to put the aspect complementary top labor transfer into a manageable setting. More than software alone is involved in IP transfer, but this paper will focus on that aspect. When software is exported or imported during outsourcing, assigning an appropriate value is crucial. Software that is broadly used can have values ranging to millions of dollars, and companies can thrive or collapse based on those results.

1.1 Outline

The next section will discuss the motivation and types of off shoring as relevant for software and IP transfer. Section 2 provides a brief introduction to the principles of IP valuation, both for the creator and the user. The issue of offshored maintenance is also addressed. Section 3 summaries valuation principles.

Section 4 presents the changes to the value of software over time, as they pertain to an offshored operation. The conclusion in Section 5 summarizes the use of software valuation when offshoring is planned or re-evaluated.

2 Outsourcing and Software

In this section we cover the generalities that are relevant when the value of outsourced software is an issue.

2.1 Why Should Software Exporters Care?

In general, exporters have a good idea of the value of their products. That knowledge is lacking is software, so that software and related IP necessary for a successful offshoring project is often transferred without valuing that property, although the risks of losing that property is often discussed.

For a software company, its entire value depends on its products. A first-order estimate of the value is then the company's market capitalization – the number of shares times the value of each share, as determined by its investors. Losing a significant fraction could be devastating. But other companies, as manufacturers and financial institutions, also depend on software for their revenues. If they distinguish themselves from others by IP embedded in software they are equally at risk. If outsourcers know the value of their implicit IP exports, they will be better prepared to make decisions about those exports, expected income, and resulting taxation. They will also be able to better report to their stockholders the costs, risks, and benefits of their actions.

2.2 Outsourcing Operations That Involve Software

Common applications for the information technology involving software exports include:

A. Call Centers, where the servitor provides assistance to customer having problems with a product.

B. Production settings, where software supports a manufacturing or service process, including software production, but also financial or supply-chain services.

C. Software Maintenance, where existing software products are repaired, adapted, or extended [1].

D. Software creation, where new products are developed.

E. Software localization, with regional marketing and sales.

F. Web services, where products are made available to process customer data.

In this paper, a general model is described that can be applied to any such application even though the parameters, the dependencies, and the risks among the partners differ.

2.3 Risks

Since the cost of copying software is very low, it is easy to copy. But software also looses its value rapidly. Software must be maintained to keep up with changes expected by users and the setting where the software is being used. While a book written and printed two years ago can be profitably sold for, say 80% of its new price, a prior version of software has little value for a user. Version life is hence an important aspect of software valuation in outsourcing. Software life is also important for valuation within a company, but has to include successive versions, since a new version of the software product includes much of the code and all of the functionality of its prior versions. The base paper covers software life for valuation only for the owners of the software. When risk assessment has to be done the metrics change, based on the type of risk being considered. This paper does not deal with risk models.

2.4 Locations

The basic model is that outsourced work is performed under contract by a wholly Independent Foreign Company (IFC). While that approach was common initially, it also carries the greatest risk. An IFC will seek to serve multiple customers, and maintaining fences to protect each customer's IP will be hard. For call centers such an approach is still common, and it is also used when the software does not represent important IP of the owner. Unless the IFC accepts liability for losses in its contracts little valuation effort is required.

When significant IP is involved most outsourcing companies have set up a fully owned, but independent entity, a Controlled Foreign Corporation (CFC), as shown as Alternative 1 in Figure 1. Such a company operates now a complete business, with records of costs and revenues. Payment for the use of intangibles that remain at the source can be in the form of royalties. The royalties should fairly reflect the contribution to income at the CFC. That income determines the value of the software and other IP being used. Such an arrangement typically requires valuation of all the IP used, including the software. Such software will be maintained at the source, and the valuation model should include that ongoing effort. If the royalties are set too low, the CFC will show a higher profit than it should, and the owner of the IP will show less profit. If the royalties are set too high, the CFC will show a lower profit than it should, and the income shown at the source will be excessive.

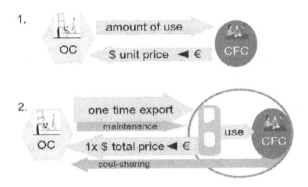

Fig. 1. Alternative IP locations and payment flow

The second alternative for the CFC is to invest in importing the software. Since in general investments are needed to create a profitable entity, purchasing IP is a common strategy. A one-time investment charge will appear in the books of the CFC, and the source will show a sale to the CFC. Ongoing costsharing payments are needed to compensate for software maintenance. Differences in the income streams and hence taxation can affect the total profit of the company, but are not addressed in this paper.

3 Principles of IP Valuation

Assigning value to intangible property is assuming greater importance as our society moves from dependence on hard, tangible goods to a world where knowledge and talent create intangible goods that everyone needs and desire. Many approaches for IP valuation compete [3].

To be considered property the intellectual good has to be owned, and its ownership has to be protected. Evidence of protected ownership is having patents, copyrights, and coverage by trade secret. Since patents and copyrights are unsuitable in many instances, trade secret, enforced by having personnel sign non-disclosure agreements is the primary means of protection.

The intangible property owned by a company in the knowledge-based domain includes the technical knowledge of its staff, the competence and insights of its sales force, the business knowledge of its management, the worth of its trademark, its reputation, and the value of its software inventory.

3.1 The Value of Software IP for Software Producers

Since the value of IP cannot be assessed by its development cost, it has to be valued by its contribution to the income of a business. The general rule is: The value of Intellectual Property is the income it generates over its lifetime [10]. From the viewpoint of software seller, the income generated from the software depends on the sales revenue, i.e., the product of software sales and its unit price. In the base paper the value of the IP inherent in software is estimate by considering its price, its useful life, and the expected sales [13]. While many assumptions are required, there are useful guidelines and rules that can support valuations. When the outsourced software has been in use prior to its transfer to a foreign shore, information for estimating the required parameters can be made available.

In an outsourced setting, some of the ongoing costs will be incurred at the home site and some at the remote site, the CFC. A standard approach is *costsharing*. For costsharing all the research and development costs are first aggregated and then allocated according to revenues in the home and CFC geographical areas. Any costs that exceed the revenue apportionment are then reimbursed from the other side. While in principle this arrangement is simple, it becomes complex when multiple sources of IP exist, since IP is also generated by brand and product marketing, which will have different lives than the technological components. Since no amount of marketing can overcome poor product quality, we concentrate on software.

3.2 The Value of Software IP for Software Users

Since the value of IP cannot be assessed by its development cost one has to focus on income. But for companies that use software, as listed as categories A and B in Section 2.2, only a fraction of the company's income can be attributed to the software. In that case an allocation has to be made. Then income can be assigned based on the assumption that the management of a company is rational in the allocation of its resources, a standard textbook assumption. If a company spends more than is optimal on software and less on people or marketing, its potential income is reduced. Given that rule, corporate net income created by diverse expenses can be allocated according to the proportion of costs incurred. The fraction spent on software from year to year will vary, but over its life such variations even out. If a company behaves irrationally in its spending, it is bound to have lower net profits, and both its IP and its prospects will suffer as a result.

3.3 Revenue and Gross Profit

Once the value of the concerned software is estimated, one can compare that value with the cost of its creation and evaluate if the overall project is at all profitable.

In most businesses manufacturing expenses have to be deducted as Cost of Goods Sold (CoGS) before the net revenue can be determined. Determining software income can typically be simplified, once a single copy exists. Every subsequent instance of software is assumed to be produced at a negligible incremental cost. If software is distributed over the Internet, there are no incremental costs involved for each sale. Consequently, revenue and gross profit become similar. Now common financial indicators such as gross margin becomes close to one, and thus meaningless.

However, there will be substantial ongoing costs to keep the software viable. Such maintenance costs typically amount to about 15% annually of the original development cost. The financial picture would be clearer if such cost would be considered as part of the CoGS, but current accounting practice lump development and maintenance costs [8]. When IP is paid for in a royalty scheme, maintenance costs are included, and product improvements are made available at no extra charge. If a CFC or CFH has imported a version of the software, it must pay for any needed maintenance as a distinct activity.

3.4 Offshoring Maintenance

From financial analyses we find that maintenance of long-lived software has substantial costs, but the resulting longevity of software provides major benefits to the owner. Quality maintenance is a major contributor to software costs and its benefits. With five years cost of maintenance exceeds the original investment [13]. But by year 10 the income from maintenance licenses can exceed the income from sales, as sketched in Figure 2 [12].

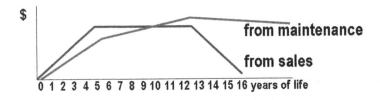

Fig. 2. Income for a software company that charges maintenance fees

It is commonly accepted that over the lifetime of software maintenance costs are 60-80% of total cost [9]. Managers bemoan the high cost of maintenance, since they are not clear about the benefits [11]. Education also ignores this cost component of software. It is an illusion that cheap labor reduces the overall costs; it essentially reduces the benefits of maintenance [7].

Input to the IP created during maintenance flows from many sources, customers, participation in standards committees, and business intelligence. When offshoring of maintenance is being considered care must be given that these flows will not be hindered, so that the software retains its quality in the competitive market place.

4   Diminution of Software Value

If the software has been imported by the CFC or CFH, the value of the initial investment will diminish. Ongoing maintenance will keep the software effective, but also requires an ongoing reimbursement by the importer.

4.1   Estimating the Diminution

Since the software IP was embedded in the original code, and that body of code changes over time, the base paper predicts typical code contributions due to maintenance [13]. For current assessments the actual code can be analyzed. The fraction of original code remaining is taken a surrogate for its relative value, as shown in Figure 3.

The unit price for much software tends to be stable. Customer expectations and competitive threats make it hard to raise software prices for the same functionality, even if the software now has fewer problems, increased capacities, and a smoother interface.

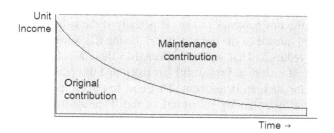

Fig. 3. Diminution of the value of the original IP contribution in software

Combining the relative growth and constant price allows an assessment of the value remaining of the original investment and setting of appropriate royalty rates.

The maintenance effort is likely carried out by the CFC as well as by the original creators. An easy way to account for the relative contribution is to pool all maintenance costs, and use those as the basis for cost-sharing. Maintenance income and revenues beyond the diminished software value are then contributed to that pool. Out of that pool the contributors can be reimbursed.

A typical life span for a successful software product is about 15 years. Over that life, there may be 10 significant version releases. Early in its life, there maybe several versions in a year and later in life, several years may elapse before a new version is warranted. Software that has significant dependencies to external conditions will require more frequent update, and hence a higher level of royalties or cost-sharing. For instance, software that supports logistics will require updates whenever capabilities of carriers change.

Note that there is no attempt to actually value the software by quantity. Only the relative size matters, so that contributions to be allocated to the original IP can be determined as part of the software at some future point.

Software does not wear out, but rather improves over time due to maintenance. But the original content diminishes in value. The end-of-life for software occurs when its sales no longer bring in sufficient income to warrant the ever-increasing maintenance costs. Hence, the estimation of the IP value of software requires estimates of the current sale price, future version frequencies, maintenance cost expectations, and sales volumes over time. A spreadsheet is available with one of the authors [13] to assess the values of possible business alternatives.

4.2 Importing Mature Software

The curve in Figure 3 shows the diminution of value from the point of initial creation. If the export pertains to software that has reached a more mature point, the curve from that point on will be less steep, and the relative diminution with each new version will be less. But the remaining life will also be less. Such a situation is actually typical, since during initial development creators will have given little thought to outsourcing possibilities. Only when the software is successful, and call center and maintenance demands grow, is outsourcing considered.

At that time the business risk is less. Especially if the software has already been successfully used outside of the country of origin, the risk normally associated with a new venture is reduced. That will be reflected in the cost of funds needed for the import. Funding of mature software still has risks, and discount rates as high as 15% are appropriate for such an investment. That cost has to be included in the business models. Again, without having valuations of the IP needed at the CFC a business model which only considers labor costs will be incomplete.

4.3 Outsourced Operations

Section 1.2 lists some of businesses operations that are often outsourced. Each of these is associated with specific types of intellectual property. After describing the principle of valuation of intellectual property, including software, a business case "for" or "against" outsourcing those components can be made, especially when offshoring.

There are two aspects here, first the risk that valuable IP will be lost, and then, the value of the IP exports that will be needed to achieve the business goals.

Information about the current operations can provide the quantitative information needed. If there is an existing call center, there has been training experience; as such, there is a record of the information needed and of supplementary material that was produced. Since a call center also provides valuable information for improving products, IP input from the call center should also be valued. Losing contact with customers is potentially a great loss, and needs to be quantified as well. Often, the expected output from a call center focuses merely on sales leads, and not on technology drivers.

If maintenance of an existing product is outsourced, then there tends to be an experience base that allows the valuation of the IP being transferred to the servitor. Here again, there is significant risk of creating disconnects. It is hard to transfer all the needed IP effectively, because it cannot be adequately documented. For instance, a reason for not employing a certain method is rarely documented. Such a determination may have been done, but it does not appear with the code, since another method was chosen and documented. It has been observed that successful software companies keep maintenance responsibilities with the creators, who are in a better position to respond and to enhance products than new hires or remote experts. However, in a setting where novelty is valued above all, it is hard to assign maintenance tasks to the best qualified staff.

When ongoing work is performed both by the owner and the servitor, then a split of IP inputs is needed to allocate income from the resulting IP. When the proportions of effort change, the allocation from each year should change as well. Since there are already many assumptions about the life of the software, it is probably best to use the simplest possible model. Clarity and stability have more utility than fictional accuracy.

4.4 Market Allocation

It is effective for the CFC to market and sell the products in its local region. Especially when software interfaces have to be translated and adapted to local requirements local knowledge and feedback loops are most effective. Now also the income has to be split. Estimation of income from software marketed to customers requires an estimation of future sales of copies of the software.

When setting up a CFC which depends on local sales additional planning is needed. How much effort at the CFC will be expended for local sales? That effort represents investments towards new IP, not useful to the source software. At the same time, feedback to the source can initiate changes that will greatly assist translation and adaptation. If, for instance Unicode is used throughout the software, it becomes much easier to adapt to foreign alphabets. If the direction of printing is a parameter, the efforts at CFCs will be greatly reduced,

Income estimation requires prediction of sales. This aspect is always risky, but even more so when operations are moved to foreign settings. Common ways include using information about a predecessor product, estimating the number of businesses that need the functionality of the new product, the number of customers who can afford the product, the number of certain type of computers or operating system in use, and similar bounds.

4.5 Complementary IP

IP is not only generated by software investments, but also by marketing investments. The distribution of investments for a CFC may well differ form the overall expense allocation of the company. At a first estimate we find that companies spend similar amounts on research and development as on marketing. If a company or product is already well known internationally, the CFC may have to spend less. In that case the CFC profits from trademarks and brand names have been previously established. These also represent IP and should be reimbursed.

Advertising expenses are typically taken as current expenses, even though they increase the IP value of the company. However, the effects of advertising tend to be short-lived, and have less importance than word-of-mouth recommendations for quality software.

The allocation and reimbursement policies for such market-related IP are beyond the scope of this presentation, but will convolute the valuation of software exports and imports.

5 Conclusions

We believe that transfer of capital, intellectual and real, should not be ignored when outsourcing is discussed. While transfer of jobs has a high emotional interest, the long-range aspect of capital transfer may well be of greater import.

Valuation is essential to assess the risk of offshoring: With the continuing trend towards globalization, a company in a developed country is increasingly likely to have a piece of software developed in a country that offers lower costs.

Valuation is essential to assess the investment needed for offshoring: Obtaining proprietary software or other IP for an outsourced operation requires ongoing payments or an investment. A valuation is needed both to determine the cost and the life of such an investment. The maturity of the software must be assessed to set an appropriate discount rate in making the investment decision.

Valuation of software is not easy, and requires many assumptions. But not knowing what IP exports are worth is dangerous. The cost-benefit and risk analyses required for outsourcing software and software production depend on such valuations.

Having a documented quantitative model allows rapid re-evaluation of offshoring benefits when labor rates, product prices, sales volume, levels of IP protection, and tax regulations change. Without a model, decisions will be based on obsolete assumptions, a situation not acceptable in a rapidly changing world.

Acknowledgements

Discussions with Treasury economists helped in establishing the principles discussed in the paper. We received constructive feedback from Bhavin Mankad, Ravi Sheshu Nadella and other readers. Any errors in this paper are our responsibility, but we will not assume any responsibility for business decisions based on applying the presented concepts. This work is based on the confluence of material from many sources. Only a few are cited below. Many more are listed with the full version of the base paper, available at http: infolab.stanford.edu/pub/gio/inprogress.html#worth.

References

1. Basili, V.: Viewing Maintenance as Reuse-Oriented Software Development. IEEE Software 7(1), 19–25 (1990)
2. Public Scorn for Private Equity. Business Week (December 4, 2006)
3. Damodaran, A.: The Dark Side of Valuation: Valuing Old Tech, New Tech, and New Economy Companies. Prentice-Hall, Englewood Cliffs (2002)
4. Gimme Shelter: The Economist (January 27, 2000)
5. Feinschreiber, R.: Transfer Pricing Handbook, 3rd edn. Transfer Pricing Consortium. John Wiley Publishers, Chichester (2001)
6. Kroppen, H.-K., Eigelshoven, A., Roeder, A.: Chapter 24 in [5] Transfer Pricing Handbook, 3rd edn., vol. 2, Germany (additions in 2002 supplement)
7. Landsbaum, J.B., Glass, R.L.: Measuring and Motivating Maintenance Programmers. Prentice-Hall, Englewood Cliffs (1985)

8. Lev, B.: Intangibles, Management, Measurement and Reporting. Brookings Institution Press, Washington, DC (2001)
9. Pigoski, T.M.: Practical Software Maintenance - Best Practices for Managing Your Software Investment. IEEE Computer Society Press (1997)
10. Smith, G., Parr, R.: Valuation of Intellectual Property and Intangible Assets, 3rd edn. Wiley, Chichester (2000)
11. Spolsky, J.: Joel on Software. Apress (2004)
12. Wiederhold, G.: The Product Flow Model. In: Proc. 15th Conf. on Software Engineering and Knowledge Engineering (SEKE), Keynote 2. Knowledge Systems Institute, Skokie, IL, pp. 183–186 (2003)
13. Wiederhold, G.: What is Your Software Worth. Comm. ACM 49(9), 65–75 (2006)

Reducing the Cost of Communication and Coordination in Distributed Software Development

Yunwen Ye[1,3], Kumiyo Nakakoji[1,2], and Yasuhiro Yamamoto[2]

[1] SRA Key Technology Laboratory, Inc.
3-12 Yotsuya, Shinjuku, Tokyo 160-0004, Japan
[2] Research Center for Advanced Science and Technology, University of Tokyo
4-6-1 Komaba, Meguro, Tokyo, 153-8904, Japan
[3] Center for LifeLong Learning and Design, University of Colorado at Boulder
Boulder, CO80309-0430, USA
`yunwen@colorado.edu; kumiyo@kid.rcast.u-tokyo.ac.jp;`
`yxy@kid.rcast.u-tokyo.ac.jp`

Abstract. Decades of software engineering research have tried to reduce the interdependency of source code to make parallel development possible. However, code remains helplessly interlinked and software development requires frequent formal and informal communication and coordination among software developers. Communication and coordination cost still dominates the cost of software development. When the development team is separated by oceans, the cost of communication and coordination increases dramatically. To better understand the cost of communication and coordination in software development, this paper proposes to conceptualize software as a knowledge ecosystem that consists of three interlinked elements: *code*, *documents*, and *developers*. This conceptualization enables us to understand and pinpoint the social dependency of developers created by the code dependency. We show that a better understanding of the social dependency would increase the economic use of the collective attention of software developers with a proposed new communication mechanism that frees developers from the overload of communication that does not interest them, and thus reduces the overall cost of communication and coordination in software development.

Keywords: distributed software development; knowledge collaboration; cost of communication and coordination; attention cost.

1 Introduction

When a large software project is created by developers separated by oceans and time zones, communication and collaboration becomes the more dominant forces in determining the productivity and quality of software development [13]. Most of the current research in supporting offshore outsourcing software development has mainly focused on the brawny power brought by *many hands* through collaboration. The major concerns have been on the cooperation, communication, and coordination problems brought by the consequences of division of labor [12, 34].

B. Meyer and M. Joseph (Eds.): SEAFOOD 2007, LNCS 4716, pp. 152–169, 2007.
© Springer-Verlag Berlin Heidelberg 2007

This paper focuses on another aspect of collaboration in offshore outsourcing software development that has not been paid enough attention—the brainy power brought by *multiple heads* of software developers; that is, the knowledge collaboration that takes place during the process of software development.

Software development is a knowledge-intensive and creative activity [22]. It requires knowledge from several different domains, including both the computing domain and the application domain. As computer applications get larger and more complex, the amount and kinds of knowledge required grow [38]. Few developers, if any, have all the knowledge needed in their own heads. The knowledge necessary for software development is distributed between the developer and the external world, and the development of a software system requires learning from and integrating the knowledge from various external sources in the world. Knowledge in the world comes from cognitive tools that support programming and from peer developers. The development of software is therefore no longer confined to an individual developer but has to rely on distributed cognition by reaching into a complex networked world of information and computer mediated collaboration.

With the current trend of offshore outsourcing, software projects are increasingly become distributed along different times zones, locations, and cultures. The distribution of software projects has become necessary due to not only the needs of shifting labors to places that have lower costs, but also the pursuit of local talents that are otherwise unavailable. In other words, in addition to delegating the task of development to the most economically viable places, which is the current driving force of outsourcing, software development companies need also to ship the task to the most talented and suitable people regardless of location, time zone, and national boundary. This, we strongly believe, will soon be the upcoming driving force of offshore outsourcing. Knowledge-based collaboration is becoming as important as, if not more than, the current labor-based collaboration in outsourcing.

2 Knowledge Distribution and Collaboration

Software development involves the application of knowledge from a variety of sources, which are constantly changing. For example, application domains are subject to rapid change; a vast amount of third-party libraries are continually updated; new features and functionalities continue to be introduced in programming tools and environments. Software development therefore is a continual learning process during which developers have to constantly acquire new knowledge [39].

The knowledge required in software development is not only about the process knowledge and domain knowledge that are applied in the software system; it also includes knowledge about the software system itself that developers are currently creating. One may argue that since the software developer participates in the creation of the system, he/she should know the system inside out. However, because large systems are created collaboratively by many developers, not all developers, if any, would have complete knowledge about the whole system. Meanwhile, with the increasingly accepted view of software systems as evolving entities, the percentage of incremental, continuous development in software has risen quickly. Such software systems need to be continuously developed with iterative processes. Coupled with the high turnover rate in software industry, many software developers find themselves working to make incremental changes to systems that have been partially developed. This is especially true in offshore outsourcing software development: local developers do not have the global knowledge of the whole system.

Software development, therefore, should be viewed as a distributed cognitive activity [10, 16]. The overall capability of a project team, termed as *group knowing*, is determined not only by the sum of the capability of individual developers, but also by the socio-technical environment consisting of the developers, tools, and accessible communication channels that affect how they contribute their knowledge to the project and how they collaborate with each other.

In offshore outsourcing development where software developers are dispersed geographically, they lost the opportunities of spontaneous and informal fact-to-face communication that has been shown critical in sharing context awareness and knowledge in software development [18]. The lost of communication opportunities, however, is not unique to offshore development; it is similarly detrimental to large software projects where all developers cannot be collocated in closeness. Allen [1] reported that when engineers' office were about 30 meters or more apart, the frequency of informal communication dropped to nearly the same level as people with offices separated by many miles.

The key challenge of supporting offshore development, therefore, lies not in developing tools that make offshore development same as same-site development, but in seamless integration of individual knowledge to enhance the group knowing regardless of location. Software developers, especially in offshore development, do not have a uniformed knowledge structure; each of them has a unique set of skills and expertise. The key is how to integrate this diversity of expertise and synthesize it into the group knowing of a software project team through knowledge collaboration in which ideas and inspiration cross fertilize and feed on each other.

3   Software = Code + Documents + Developers

3.1   Knowledge Resources for Software Development

As a knowledge artifact, software code is the ultimate knowledge resource about the system. Due to the essential invisibility of software code [3], however, it is not easy to recover knowledge about the system by simply reading the code. It has long been recognized that documents that provide high level descriptions of the code and the design rationale are needed to coordinate the development.

Code and documents, however, are often insufficient for supporting knowledge collaboration. Documents do not always exist, or quickly fall out of sync with the code. Much of the knowledge about the code and the design decisions remain in the head of developers. Many empirically studies have shown that software developers routinely access their peer developers for knowledge during the development process through informal communications [19, 21]. Peer developers remain the most commonly used and valued sources of expertise in software projects [32].

3.2 Software Project as an Evolving Knowledge Ecosystem

We conceptualize a software project as a self-organizing and evolving knowledge ecosystem [4] that consists of three interlinked elements: *code*, *documents* and *developers*. In such a knowledge ecosystem, knowledge is embedded in both its constituting elements and its structure that regulates their inter-relationship, and flows along the hyperlinked relationship. As developers create artifacts (code and documents), their knowledge gets distilled into the artifacts. Knowledge gets shared, exchanged and combined through the dynamic interactions between software developers, mediated by code, document, and communications.

This conceptualization enables us to model a software project as a socio-technical information space that has triangulated relationships among code parts, documents and developers. The nodes that constitute the socio-technical information space associated with a software system include not only parts of code at different levels of granularities, but also the documents that have been generated during the development process, as well as the developers that hold knowledge about them. Code, documents, and developers are therefore equally important knowledge resources that should be utilized during software development.

In this knowledge ecosystem, relationships among code, documents and developers dynamically change as the development process proceeds. The interacting developers form a knowledge community, defined as a group of people who collaborate with one another for the construction of knowledge artifacts. In a knowledge community, people are bonded through the construction of common artifacts. This is especially true in the case of offshore outsourcing development because, unlike a collocated software project in a single organization, those developers often do not have a shared identity defined by their shared belongingness to the organization. In most cases, they have different organizational and cultural identities [8]; and when they come together for a software project, they are bonded by the needs of constructing a common artifact.

3.3 Evolution in Software Projects

The knowledge community aspect has important implications when viewing software development as collective creative knowledge work that depends on the learning of developers through knowledge collaboration. The roles of individual developers, both formally assigned ones and informally perceived ones, change over time during a project. The social relationships among the developers grow through their engagement in the project, affecting how they collaborate, communicate, and coordinate with each other, which results in different ways of sharing and integrating knowledge.

All three elements constantly evolve during the process of software development (Fig. 1). Artifacts (code and elements) change over time throughout the

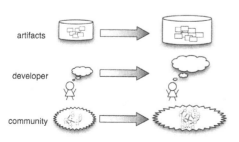

Fig. 1. Software Project as a Knowledge Ecosystem

development. Individual developers—or, more precisely, what individual developers know—grow by gaining experience through the engagement with artifacts and peer developers. The community of developers changes when new members join, old members leave, both the assigned or perceived roles of members change, and members' relationships change.

Existing studies on understanding and supporting software evolution have primarily focused on the evolution of artifacts. More recent work has started to look at how individuals change through learning about the system. People learn by reading source code and documents, and they learn by asking peers questions. They also learn by solving new problems and experiencing unfamiliar situations. Their old knowledge is replaced with new knowledge and is restructured during the development process. A community evolves through individual activities in software development that result in the change of software artifacts and/or in the individual growth of knowledge about the system. This paper views the evolutionary process of the developer community and software systems from the following three relationships (Fig. 2):

(1) *The relationship of an individual with artifacts.* How one relates with artifacts is concerned with what knowledge, expertise, and experience the individual has on what artifacts. This information is useful in identifying a set of people who are likely to have expertise with a certain artifact.

(2) *The relationship of an individual with other developers.* How one relates with other developers impacts knowledge collaboration among developers. This information helps a developer determine whom to ask for help about a certain artifact as well as decide whether and how to respond to a question posed by an asker.

(3) *The relationship of an individual with the community as a whole.* How one relates with the community is concerned with that individual's role within the community: whether he/she is a peripheral member, a core member, or a member in between. This relationship helps a developer decide how much he/she should contribute to the community by gaining trust and social reputation within the community.

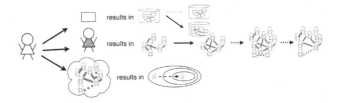

Fig. 2. Evolutionary Process in a Software Project

3.4 Socio-technical Costs in Knowledge Collaboration

When peer developers become critical resources for expertise, simply knowing who has the knowledge is not enough. The knowledge seeker needs to contact the knowledge providers and ask the question, and the knowledge providers then have to consent to engage in knowledge collaboration activities [17]. These steps become exceptionally costly in a globally distributed development project because developers in one site often do not "know" about those located in another site.

This knowledge collaboration act is affected by and affects the characteristics of the social relationship between developers and of their relationships with the community. The communication channels used, the contents of the question and answer, the ways the questions is asked and the answers provided, as well as the timing of asking and answering depends on a set of perceived social variables.

All the communication and coordination required for knowledge collaboration among developers come with a great cost that demands attention and time that can otherwise be used for development [19]. The technology used in supporting knowledge collaboration could affect positively or negatively of the perception of social variables, and the associated total cost of communication and coordination [33]. From the socio-technical perspective [24], we analyze those social factors that affect knowledge collaboration behaviors and cost (both social and attentional).

Awareness. For a developer to seek external expertise from peers, he/she has to know who might have the expertise. From a set of potential expertise providers, he/she needs to choose whom to ask, and then make the decision to ask. This conscientious decision making process is related to the following social and technical factors.

The asker needs to find where the needed expertise is located, and who potentially has the expertise. Previous research has shown that such transactive knowledge takes extensive time to develop [21, 30], and its utilization consumes intensive attentional cost [23]. The geographical distance in offshore development lowers significantly the knowledge of knowing who are the experts [18].

Asking a question shows that the developer is missing some knowledge, and he/she risks of appearing ignorant that impacts his/her overall relationship with the community. People demonstrate different asking behaviors when they are in public or in private; to a stranger or to a friend. Generally speaking, people are more willing to ask questions covertly to those that they are closely related because the close social relationship provides a psychological safety of admitting a lack of knowledge [6].

Asking question is also challenging because the expertise seeker needs to assess the reliability of and then understand the answer. Research has shown that a strong tie between the expertise seeker and the provider resulted from previous interactions leads to easier quality judgment and helps the interpretation of answers [29].

Asking. When a developer decides to ask a question, he/she needs to make contact with the experts. A study by Herbsleb and Grinter [14] observed that collocated developers feel socially comfortable to initiate contact easily because they know each other, know how to approach them, and have a good sense of how important their question is related to what the experts seem to be doing at the moment. When collocation is replaced with remote communication tools in offshore development, initiating a contact became more difficult due to the loss of such social cues.

The way that the question is presented has a direct impact on the response it will receive. Rhetorical strategies, linguistic complexity and word choice of the question all influence the likelihood of others responding to a question [2]. The needs for a developer to seek expertise mostly arise from a problematic situation that needs to be resolved in a specific timeframe. The expectation of how soon a help would come is shaped by a history of interactions with the other party [36].

Engagement. Upon receiving a question, the experts need to decide whether to engage in collaboration with the expertise seeker based on social factors: their perceived social relationship with the expertise seeker and the community at large.

The theory of social capital provides an analytic framework to understand this decision-making process. Social capital is the "sum of the actual and potential resources embedded within, available through, and derived from the network of relationships possessed by an individual or social unit [25]" and is regarded as important as financial capital and intellectual capital for an individual as well as a social organization because it promotes cooperation and reduce transaction cost. Social capital manifests itself in forms of obligations, expectations, trust, norms of generalized reciprocity, and reputations.

Social capitals are derived from social interactions. If *A* helps *B*, *A* then holds a credit slip for *B* to reciprocate the favor in the future. In other words, *A* can have a reasonable expectation that *B* will do something for him or her down the road, and *B* will feel an obligation to help *A* [5]. Regularly reciprocated fulfillment of obligations leads to the development of trust among the interacting parties. When this direct interpersonal reciprocity becomes a norm, it promotes generalized reciprocity. Persons with a large amount of credit slips are easier to draw collaboration in the social unit. The norm would also apply social pressure for those who have a large amount of obligations to engage actively in collaboration with others.

Engagement consumes time and attention. No action, however, has social cost too. Saying no untactfully to a peer who seeks for your help deteriorate your relation with him or her, and affects negatively your social reputation among other peers because it deviates from social norms.

Collective Attention Cost. Asking and answering a question takes cost. In addition to the time and attention for the asker to formulate and compose the question, and the expertise provider to read, think and post the reply, considerable collective cost is also incurred.

All the people who have received the question would at least spend some attention about the question before they decide to answer or not. When the number of people who receive the question becomes large, the collective attention consumed also becomes considerably large. Given the fact that we are now entering a world where our lives are guided more by the laws of the economics of attention because attention is quickly becoming the scarcest resource in our society [11], it is imperative for system designers to take this factor into consideration because the project has a limited supply of collective attention and should be used economically.

A question means an interruption. The cost of interruption includes both the loss of working context and the destruction of flow [35]. When multiple project members receive the request for help, for example, if the request is sent through the project mailing list, this interruption cost is multiplied with the number of receivers. Collectively, this cost might outweigh the benefits of knowledge collaboration and decreases the overall productivity of the whole project [33]. Communication mechanisms used for knowledge collaboration have to be carefully designed and chosen by paying attention that the communication would not impact negatively the overall performance of the project team.

4 A Socio-technical Framework to Supporting Knowledge Collaboration

We have developed the Dynamic Community framework to help software developers engage in knowledge collaboration during the process of software development through sharing and exchanging expertise required for the project. The goals of the framework are twofold: to increase the ease of accessing external expertise either through a knowledge repository or from peer experts, and at the same time to reduce the total cost of experts being interrupted and that of providing help. The essential guidelines of the Dynamic Community framework are:

(1)   Expertise is not an absolute attribute but a relative attribute of a developer. A group of experts can be identified only after the task is known.
(2)   Knowledge collaboration is not the goal; it is only the means to support developers to solve their current task. The social and technical cost of knowledge collaboration has to be balanced with the primary goal: to improve the productivity of the team.
(3)   Existing social relationships among developers play an important role and should be taken into consideration to facilitate knowledge collaboration.
(4)   The success of one knowledge collaboration transaction should not come at the price of developers' reluctance of further participation in future knowledge collaboration. The goodwill and limited attention of experts should be economically utilized to achieve sustainable and long term success. Rather than focusing only on the success of one act of knowledge collaboration; we focus on the sustainability of knowledge collaboration because it has to recur repeatedly during the whole lifecycle of the project.
(5)   Social support is costly and should only be used as a back up mechanism for technical approaches.

4.1 Modeling the Knowledge Ecosystem of a Software Project

The knowledge elements in a software project create a knowledge ecosystem with complicated interdependency. It consists of a group of developers, their code, related documents, and the relationships among them (Fig. 3). Three kinds of relationships exist: those between programmers, those between a programmer and information, and those between information. We use the term information to refer to both code and documents (such as design documents, configuration management logs, bug reports, and email archives that are associated with the development of the code). The relationship between programmers captures the social relationship between them, including who helped whom, and who sent emails to whom, as well as their social dependency derived from the

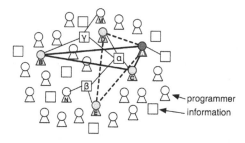

Fig. 3. An Actor-Network of a Software Project

technical dependency of the code and documents, such as which software developers depend on which other software developers for a given piece of code or a document through calling, using, or describing [7].

The relationship between information includes the syntactic and semantic dependency among code parts that are linked through data flow, control flow or linear order. Code nodes in Fig. 4 can have different levels of granularity: code segments, methods, files, classes and packages. Documents are related to code through multiple dimensions. For example, a code node implements a portion of a design document; the design rationale of the code is described in a series of email discussions; a bug report is fixed by modifying several nodes of code; or a document describes the functionality of reusable code components.

The relationship between a developer and information includes who writes or changes the code, who has commented on the code, and who has reused the code component in his/her own programs.

The knowledge network in Fig. 3 is an actor-network that consists of actants (both human and artifacts) [20]. The knowledge embedded in each node as well as the links constitutes the group knowing of a project. The network, as well as the group knowing, changes as new actants are brought into or removed from the network (e.g. new information is added or a developer leaves), and as new relationships are developed, strengthened, or weakened (e.g. another developer started working on a module, a link between documents were discovered). An individual's capability about the project progresses as he/she develops more relationships with other actants.

4.2 A Continuum of Technical Support and Social Support

Using external expertise can be viewed as a software developer's activating the links in the actor-network in Fig. 3, and engaging in collaboration with actants. To do so, a software developer are faced with the following challenges:

(1) He/she might not be aware of where the expertise is located: what is the relevant information, and who has the expertise on this particular problem?
(2) When the actants are peer developers, how should he/she approach them, without causing too much communication cost of interruption?
(3) Whether the human actants are willing to engage in providing help?

Accordingly, the Dynamic Community approach (Fig. 4) provides three kinds of support for in situ knowledge collaboration. Assume a developer (A) is dealing with a task (α) and needs external expertise.

First, it employs both information access and information delivery mechanisms [27] to help developers find task-relevant information in the repository that models the actor-network of the knowledge ecosystem of a project (Fig. 4). *Information access* includes browsing or searching, in which the developer articulates what he/she needs through either traversing the links between the information (browsing) or formulating a query (searching). Contrary to information access that has to be initiated by the developer, *information delivery* proactively provides information by watching what the developer is writing, inferring what his/her information needs are, and then recommending the needed information without user initiated search activities. Information delivery is able to make developers access external expertise in the repository whose existence they are not even aware of [41].

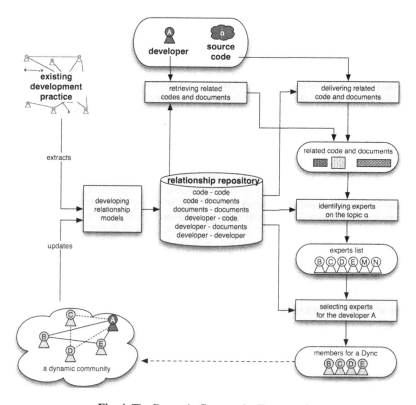

Fig. 4. The Dynamic Community Framework

When the relevant information retrieved or delivered from the repository is not sufficient for the developer to obtain the expertise, he/she need to access knowledgeable peers. In the Dynamic Community framework, a developer can post a question about the topic he/she is currently interested in, and a sub-network of developers is dynamically formed by activating the links in the actor-network of Fig. 5 through two processes: *expert identification* and *expert selection*.

The expert identification process traces the link between a developer and information, and identifies peer developers that are related to the set of relevant information nodes (i.e. α, β and γ in Fig. 3 where β and γ are related to α). Depending on the definition of the relation, those peer developers might have expertise or hold special interest in the set of information nodes. For brevity, we refer them as experts. The experts list obtained in this phase is *{B, C, D, E, M, N}* because they are linked to either α, β or γ in Fig. 3.

From the above experts list, the expert select process selects those who have good social relations with the developer A, which is *{B, C, D, E}*. The relationship between developers is derived from their previous interaction history and represents the affinitive relationship existing among them. A link from developer B to A indicates a high possibility that B is likely to help A when B's expertise is needed for A's task.

An ephemeral mailing list (called a DynC) is then dynamically created for the selected experts and A on the topic α (noted as *DynC(A, α) ={A, B, C, D, E}*), and A's question is sent to the members of DynC(*A, α*). DynC(*A, α*) members who reply to the question posted by *A* is also sent to all the members. When the developer *A* thinks there is no more need to discuss about the topic, he/she needs to terminate the DynC, and the associated dynamic mailing list dissolves. All the discussions, however, are archived in the repository so that other developers who have similar questions can benefit by either browsing or searching the repository.

4.3 Cost Reduction Strategies

The Dynamic Community approach attempts to reduce the overall communication cost in knowledge collaboration in a globally distributed project by utilizing the following strategies.

First, it considers social support as a costly transaction, and encourages software developers to explore the technical support afforded by the rich knowledge repository that weaves together the code, document and previous discussions. All the discussions in DynC mailing lists are archived and linked with the related information so that repeated DynCs can be avoided. The combination of sophisticated search, browsing and delivery mechanisms is employed to make locating relevant information easier for software developers. The Dynamic Community framework requires a developer to initiate a DynC from the search results, ensuring he/she has at least spending some time exploring the related information. Social support is very costly and should not be used as the main resources for expertise.

Second, the automatic identification of experts relieves a software developer from gaining an awareness of who the experts are, and thus reduces the cost of finding the location of expertise and asking the question. Knowing the experts is one of the major obstacles faced by developers in offshore outsourcing projects due to the lack of informal and spontaneous communication available in collocated projects.

Third, it reduces the cost incurred on expertise providers by limiting the recipients of the question only to those who are both able to (through the expert identification process) and very likely to willing to (through the expert selection process) to answer the question. Other developers who either do not have the necessary expertise or whose relationships with the expertise seeker are not strong enough to be motivated to engage in knowledge collaboration with the seeker are not disturbed. The strong social relationship also increases the intensity of the engagement and therefore the effectiveness of knowledge collaboration among participants [6].

Fourth, the DynC mailing list follows the principle of *asymmetric disclosure of information* [26] to conserve further the attention and good will of experts. On one hand, when the question is posted to a DynC, the members selected to the DynC are not made public either to the expertise seeker or to other members; only a receiver of the question message knows that he/she is selected as a member of the DynC. Only when a DynC member sends a reply message, his/her identity is revealed. A DynC member, therefore, may leave the DynC (a social equivalent of saying "no") at any moment without being publicly known. Due to this principle, no participation does not constitute the violation of social norms, which is punishable by the "iron hand of social pressure" of enforcing required individual behavior in a social unit [31]. On the other hand, because replying to the DynC reveals the identity of the sender of the message, the DynC members' contribution is publicly acknowledged and can lead to the improvement of motivation [9]. This socially aware communication mechanism that allows unwilling peer developers exit socially safely has two implications. The remaining peers are the participants of willing, and hence the expertise sharing becomes more effective. From the perspective of the expertise seeker, knowing that other developers could easily exit, he/she feels less pressured to post a question because the choice of participation is controlled by the experts.

5 System Development

To illustrate how the Dynamic Community framework supports knowledge collaboration in distributed software projects while reducing the overall cost of communication and collaboration, we describe two systems: CodeBroker [40] and STeP_IN [28] that we have developed. The two systems in combination provide continuous support for accessing external expertise. In the following usage scenario, which illustrates the functionality of the two systems, we use the Lucene-java (http://lucene.apache.org/java/docs/index.html) project as the data (the source code and its mailing list archive from 2001 to Aug. 2006) to populate the repository.

Suppose a developer (*lu1283*) needs to write a program that processes a stream of token extracted from a document in an information retrieval system, which uses the third-party open source library (Lucene-java). He first needs to normalize each token by lowering its cases, but he is not aware that a method already exists in the library. He sets to create his own program and writes a doc comment in the editor to describe his task (Fig. 5). As soon as the doc comment is written in the editor, CodeBroker automatically delivers a set of task-relevant library methods in the lower buffer of the editor. *Lu1283* finds the second method probably does what he needs, and clicks the method name in the buffer.

The document for the method is shown (Fig. 7). Now he knows this method is what he wants but he is not sure how it can be used. So he clicks the *Examples* button, and looks at the example code (Fig. 8). Now he wonders if this method does more than lowering the case. He clicks the *Discussion Archive* link and reads previous discussions on this method (Fig. 9) but could not find answers to his question. He thinks that other developers in the team might have used it before, so he clicks the *Ask Experts* link and posts a question (Fig.10).

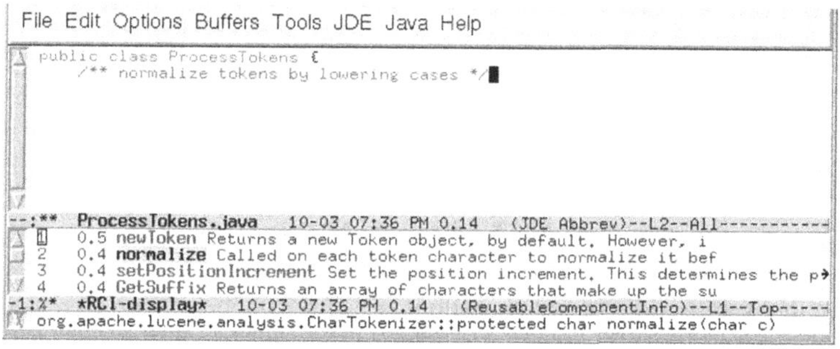

Fig. 5. CodeBroker: An Enhanced Emacs Editor for Java Programming

Fig. 6. Enhanced Javadoc documentation

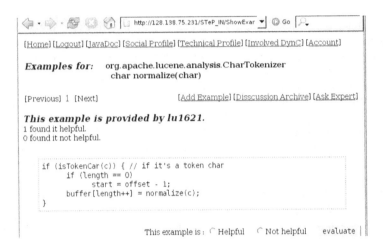

Fig. 7. Example code

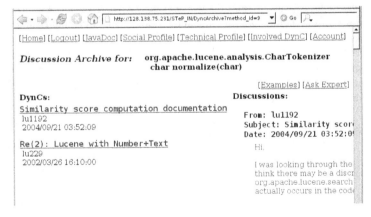

Fig. 8. Discussion Archive

Upon the submission of the question, a DynC mailing list is created by the STeP_IN system. Five members (*lu292, lu1192, lu229, lu953* and *lu1953*) are selected, regardless of their physical locations. They all have used this method before (5, 4, 2, 2, 1 times respectively) in their previous programs and have expertise on this method. In addition, all five members have affinitive social relationships with *lu1283* and the community, and they are very likely to help *lu1283*. *Lu292* and *lu1953* have sent emails to *lu1293* before, so they should have known *lu1283* by certain degree. *Lu1192* and *lu229* have got helped in the community by others more than they have helped others; therefore, it is their turn to fulfill their social obligations to reciprocate the favor they have received. *Lu953* is an eager helper [15], and had helped others more than 101 times, so he might also offer help this time.

The members, however, are not forced to help because lu1283 as well as other members do not know that they received this question due to the design principle of asymmetry of information disclosure. If some of the members are currently busy and do not have time to offer help for *lu1283*, no body would notice; and they will not face social consequences of being non-cooperative in this case.

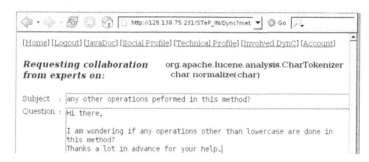

Fig. 9. Ask Experts

6 Discussions

The two systems introduced in the paper are meant to illustrate how the conceptual framework of Dynamic Community can be applied to support knowledge collaboration in globally distributed software development while reducing the cost of communication. The conceptual framework can be applied to support different tasks in distributed offshore projects. To illustrate its potential, we briefly sketch its possible application in maintenance support and agile development.

After a software system has been developed and deployed, the original developers are often assigned to other projects and the maintenance work is handed over to other members. Under such conditions, maintainers often do not know who are the original designers and developers of the module under maintenance and do not know who to approach for design rationales. The dynamic community can be applied to deal with this situation. Suppose a maintainer A needs to modify a module α. It is quite possible that many programmers have used or changed module α during its lifecycle. All those programmers can be considered experts on α and they can be identified from the configuration management systems such as CVS used during the development phase [23]. Because those original programmers have new assignments as their current work, they might not be readily available to help A. Using the two-phase selection of experts in the Dynamic Community framework, a list of experts who have knowledge and are most likely to assist A can be selected to form a DynC for this task.

Communication can be limited to those selected members and the results archived for later use.

In agile development, document-based formal coordination mechanisms are replaced with frequent, intensive, and informal communications. As systems are incrementally developed, the dependency of code changes accordingly; and the related developers that need to be involved in communication and coordination change, too [37]. Currently, developers have to decide by themselves who they should engage in collaboration. If we apply the Dynamic Community framework to this, a system can be developed to identify automatically the subgroup of developers that should be involved based on the social dependency derived from the dependency of code that each developer is developing, and create a DynC mailing list for their communication. As a developer moves his focus of development, different DynC mailing lists can be created accordingly in an automatic manner to reduce the cost of communication by limiting the number of communicants to the concerned members and by reducing the cost of determining communicants.

7 Concluding Remarks

In this paper, we conceptualize a distributed software project as a distributed knowledge ecosystem, and model it as an actor-network. This modeling enables us to view software artifacts produced in the development process and developers as knowledge actants, which constitute the organizational knowing of the project, and which should be engaged equally as knowledge resources for the indispensable knowledge collaboration in software development. Based on this conceptualization and modeling, we proposed the Dynamic Community framework as a new communication mechanism for knowledge collaboration. The framework reduces the cost of communication in offshore outsourcing software development by (1) using information delivery and search mechanisms to allow developers locate relevant knowledge from a knowledge repository that consists of code, documents and discussions in order to reduce the frequency of collaboration with other developers; (2) automatically selecting experts to mitigate the difficulty of finding the experts and initiating contacts; and (3) forming an ephemeral DynC mailing list that consists only of developers who are both technically capable and socially willing to engage in collaboration with a particular developer on a particular topic.

The ephemeral DynC mailing list resulted from the Dynamic Community approach is neither a direct emails, nor a mail list, it is something in between with persistent storage similar to discussion forums. It is similar to mailing lists in that the email is sent to unspecified members, and the participation in knowledge collaboration is completely controlled by its recipients. It is not mailing lists in that the recipients are not determined by their own subscriptions but by their social relationships with the initiator and their technical expertise on the topic. The latter point makes DynC mailing list similar to direct emails because they are intentionally targeted recipients who have already established social ties with the sender. However, it differs from direct emails in that recipients remain anonymous to the sender and other members, leaving the control of participation to the recipients, and in that the recipients are automatically identified and chosen.

In offshore outsourcing software development, many development activities need to be coordinated and collaborated through communication channels. To reduce the communication cost, it is important for a project team to be able to operate within a communicative economy with a variety of communicative resources at its developer's disposal [33]. Both the unique structure of each communication channel and the socio-technical relationships among developers determine the collective cost and benefits of each communicative act. To reduce the cost of communication and coordination, developers should be able to choose the most appropriate channel for their needs. The Dynamic Community framework provides a new communication mechanism that has its special niche. It is not meant to replace any of the currently dominating communication channels such as face-to-face, direct emails or mailing lists, but as a complimentary one. For example, if a developer happens to know who are the experts on a topic of interest, and is socially comfortable to directly approach the experts, he/she can use the face to face or direct emails (if not collocated). If the developer feels that the topic is important enough to be known by all members of the project, he/she can send it through project-wide mailing lists. If the developer thinks that his/her question only concerns a few, but does not know who they are, the DynC mailing list is a perfect match for that.

References

1. Allen, T.J.: Managing the flow of technology. MIT Press, Cambridge, MA (1977)
2. Arguello, J., et al.: Talk to me: Foundations for successful individual-group interactions in online communities. In: Proceedings of conference on human factors in computer systems (chi06)., pp. 959–968. ACM Press, Montréal, Canada (2006)
3. Brooks, F.P.J.: The mythical man-month: Essays on software engineering, 20th edn. Addison-Wesley, Reading, MA (1995)
4. Brown, J.S., Duguid, P.: Organizing knowledge. Society for Organizational Learning Journal 1(2), 28–44 (1999)
5. Coleman, J.C: Social capital in the creation of human capital. American Journal of Sociology 94, S95–S120 (1988)
6. Cross, R., Borgatti, S.P: The ties that share: Relational characteristics that facilitate information seeking. In: Huysman, M., Wulf, V. (eds.) Social capital and information technology, pp. 137–161. MIT Press, Cambridge, MA (2004)
7. de Souza, C.R.B., et al.: How a good software practice thwarts collaboration: The multiple roles of apis in software development. In: de Souza, C.R.B., et al. (eds.) Proceedings of the 12th acm sigsoft twelfth international symposium on foundations of software engineering (fse04), pp. 221–220. Newport Beach, CA (2004)
8. Dorina, C.G: Distribution dimensions in software development projects: A taxonomy. IEEE Software 23(5), 45 (2006)
9. Fischer, G., Scharff, E., Ye, Y.: Fostering social creativity by increasing social capital. In: Huysman, M., Wulf, V. (eds.) Social capital, pp. 355–399 (2004)
10. Goldberg, A.: Collaborative software engineering. Journal of Object Technology 1(1), 1–19 (2002)
11. Goldhaber, M.H.: The attention economy. First Monday, vol. 2(4) (1997)
12. Herbsleb, J., Grinter, R.E.: Splitting the organization and integrating the code: Conway's law revisited. In: Proceedings of international conference on software engineering (icse99), pp. 85–95 (1999)

13. Herbsleb, J., Mockus, A.: An empirical study of speed and communication in globally-distributed software development. IEEE Transactions on Software Engineering 29(3), 1–14 (2003)

14. Herbsleb, J.D., Grinter, R.E: Architectures, coordination, and distance: Conway's law and beyond. IEEE Software, 63–70 (September- October 1999)

15. Hoff, B.v.d., Ridder, J.d., Aukema, E.: Exploring the eagerness to share knowledge: The role of social capital and ict in knowledge sharing. In: Huysman, M., Wulf, V. (eds.) Social capital and information technology, pp. 163–186. MIT Press, Cambridge, MA (2004)

16. Hollan, J., Hutchins, E., Kirsch, D.: Distributed cognition: Toward a new foundation for human-computer interaction research. In: Carroll, J.M. (ed.) Human-computer interaction in the new millennium, pp. 75–94. ACM Press, New York (2001)

17. Illich, I.: Deschooling society. Harper and Row, New York (1971)

18. Kraut, R.E., et al.: Informal communications in organizations: Form, function, and technology. In: Oskamp, I.S., Spacapan, S. (eds.) Human reactions to technology: The claremont symposium on applies social psychology, Sage Publications, Beverly Hills, CA (1990)

19. Kraut, R.E., Streeter, L.: Coordination in software development. CACM 38(3), 69–81 (1995)

20. Latour, B.: Reassembling the social: An introduction to actor-network-theory. Oxford University Press, Oxford (2005)

21. McDonald, D.W., Ackerman, M.S.: Just talk to me: A field study of expertise location. In: McDonald, D.W., Ackerman, M.S. (eds.) Proceedings of conference on computer supported cooperative work (cscw'98), pp. 315–324. Seattle, WA (1998)

22. Meyer, B.: The unspoken revolution in software engineering, pp. 121–124. IEEE Computer Society Press, Los Alamitos (2006)

23. Mockus, A., Herbsleb, J.: Expertise browser: A quantitative approach to identifying expertise. In: Proceedings of 2002 international conference on software engineering, Orlando, FL, pp. 503–512 (2002)

24. Mumford, E.: Socio-technical system design: Evolving theory and practice. In: Bjerknes, P.G., Ehn, P., Kyng, M. (eds.) Computers and democracy, pp. 59–76. Averbury, Aldershot, UK (1987)

25. Nahapiet, J., Ghoshal, S.: Social capital, intellectual capital, and the organizational advantage. Academy of Management Review 23, 242–266 (1998)

26. Nakakoji, K.: Supporting software development as collective creative knowledge work. In: Nakakoji, K. (ed.) Proceedings of ase workshop on supporting knowledge collaboration in software development, Tokyo, (in press) (2006)

27. Nakakoji, K., Fischer, G.: Intertwining knowledge delivery and elicitation: A process model for human-computer collaboration in design. Knowledge-Based Systems 8(2-3), 94–104 (1995)

28. Nishinaka, Y., et al.: Please step_in: A socio-technical platform for in situ networking. In: Proceedings of the 12th Asia-Pacific Software Engineering Conference, pp. 813–820. IEEE CS Press, Taipei (2005)

29. O'Reilly, C.A.: Variations in decision makers' use of information sources: The impact of quality and accessibility of information. Academy of Management Journal 25(4), 756–771 (1982)

30. Orlikowski, W.J.: Knowing in practice: Enacting a collective capability in distributed organizing. Organization Science 13(3), 249–273 (2002)

31. Pentland, A.: Socially aware computation and cmmunication. Computer 38(3), 33–40 (2005)
32. Perlow, L.A.: The time famine: Toward a sociology of work time. Administrative Science Quarterly 44(1), 57–81 (1999)
33. Reder, S.: The communication economy of the workgroup: Multi-channel genres of communication. In: Proceedings of cscw1988, pp. 354–368. ACM Press, New York (1988)
34. Sengupta, B., Chandra, S., Sinha, V.: A research agenda for distributed software development. In: Proceedings of 2006 international conference on software engineering, Shanghai, pp. 731–740 (2006)
35. Szoestek, A.M., Markopoulos, P.: Factors defining face-to-face interruptions in the office environment. In: Proceedings of conference on human factors in computer systems, pp. 1379–1384 (2006)
36. Tyler, J.R., Tang, J.C: When can i expect an email response? A study of rhythms in email usage. In: Proceedings of the eighth european conference on computer supported cooperative work (ecscw2003), pp. 239–258. Helsinki (2003)
37. Wagstrom, P., Herbsleb, J.: Dependency forecasting. CACM 49(10), 55–56 (2006)
38. Walz, D.B., Elam, J.J., Curtis, B.: Inside a software design team: Knowledge acquisition, sharing, and integration. CACM 36(10), 63–77 (1993)
39. Weinberg, G.M.: The psychology of computer programming. Van Nostrand Reinhold, New York (1971)
40. Ye, Y., Fischer, G.: Information delivery in support of learning reusable software components on demand. In: Proceedings of 2002 International Conference on Intelligent User Interfaces (IUI'02), pp. 159–166. ACM Press, San Francisco (2002)
41. Ye, Y., Fischer, G.: Supporting reuse by delivering task-relevant and personalized information. In: Proceedings of 2002 international conference on software engineering (icse'02), pp. 513–523. Orlando, FL (2002)

Survey on Japan-Oriented Offshore Software Development in China

Lei Zhang[1], Meiping Chai[1], Xuan Zhang[1], Shigeru Miyake[1], and Ryota Mibe[2]

[1] Hitachi (China) Research & Development Corporation, 301,Tower C Raycom Infotech Park, 2 Kexueyuan Nanlu, Haidian District, Beijing 100080, China
{leizhang,mpchai,xzhang,smiyake}@hitachi.cn
[2] Hitachi, Ltd., Systems Development Laboratory, 292, Yoshida-cho, Totsuka-ku, Yokohama-shi, Kanagawa-ken, 244-0817 Japan
mibe@sdl.hitachi.co.jp

Abstract. In order to find out the main features and the existent problems in the Japan-oriented offshore software development in China, a survey was conducted in 24 Japan-oriented offshore companies. The questionnaire included the company information, the project information, the software development process, and the existent problems and expectations. The survey results were classified and analyzed according to the company scale and the project style. The analysis results showed that almost all of the basic features of the projects, the software development process and the existent problems had close relations with the company scale and the project type. Finally, based on the survey results some solution suggestions were proposed for the Japan-oriented offshore software development.

1 Introduction

In the recent several decades, outsourcing software development has become a popular way to decrease the software development cost and improve the core technical competence for many companies in the world.

China, as a big country with the huge manpower, is playing a more and more important role in the global offshore market. Furthermore, from the survey results of the market share of the offshore development in China [1], we found that Japan occupied 59% of the China offshore market, which was much more than the share of Occident (Europe and US). On the other hand, from the survey results of the market share of the outsourcing development in Japan [2], it could also be seen that China occupied the highest share (38%), which was higher than India, Philippine and other countries. In a word, Japan and China are the most important partners for each other in the offshore market. Therefore, researching on the offshore software development between Japan and China is significant to both Japan and China.

In recent years, some surveys on the offshore software development between Japan and China have been conducted by some organizations in both Japan and China. In Japan, some researchers [2][3] conducted the surveys on the Japanese outsourcing

B. Meyer and M. Joseph (Eds.): SEAFOOD 2007, LNCS 4716, pp. 170–181, 2007.

companies and the Japan-oriented offshore companies in China. They found out some existent problems of the offshore software development between Japan and China from the viewpoint of Japan side. In China, several consulting companies or research firms also conducted some surveys on the Japan-oriented offshore companies, but mainly focused on the market information. Therefore, it is necessary to conduct a survey on the Japan-oriented offshore companies in China to find out the existent technical problems from the viewpoint of China side. This is the consideration of the present paper.

This paper concludes the survey results based on 24 samples, which was conducted in China during July and August in 2006. The questionnaire mainly consisted of four parts: company information, project information, software development process, existent problems and expected solutions. Detailed results of this survey will be described in section 2. The main conclusions will be drawn in Section 3.

2 Survey Results and Analysis

2.1 Sample Introduction

The samples included 24 companies in Beijing, Shanghai, Dalian and other three cites, because there are many Japan-oriented offshore companies in these cities. The employee number and the number of the finished Japan-oriented projects of these companies are relatively larger compared with other offshore companies in China. Therefore, it can be said that these samples were representative. The scale and the employee structure of these companies were analyzed as follows.

(1) Company scale

The surveyed companies were classified into three kinds of scales according to their employee number or the number of finished Japan-oriented projects in Table 1. We can see that 24 samples were mainly large or small companies. Only about 20% were middle companies.

Table 1. Classification of Company Scale

Company scale	Employee Number (or Project Number)	Percentage
Large	>500	41.67%
Middle	100 – 500	20.83%
Small	<100	37.50%

(2) Employee Structure

All of the companies had the similar employee structure and bachelors were the main manpower in these companies. Masters and above were more in large companies than those in other companies (see Fig. 1). This states that the technology level of the employees in large companies were relatively higher.

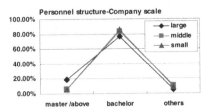

Fig. 1. Employee Structure

2.2 Basic Information

(1) Project style

The styles of the outsourced projects from Japan to China were divided into three types: (a) Whole project development; (b) Module development; (c) Maintenance or upgrade of an existent project. The survey results showed that the whole project development and the module development were both main styles of the offshore projects (Fig. 2). Furthermore, there was no obvious relation between the project styles and the company scales.

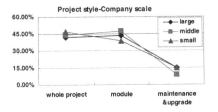

Fig. 2. Project Style

(2) Service mode

The service modes of the offshore companies include three types: (a) On-site; (b) Near-site; (c) Off-site. The results showed that off-site was the major service mode in the offshore market. Moreover, the larger scale the company was, the more off-site mode and the less near-site mode were (see Fig. 3(a)). This might be resulted from the higher technology level of the larger companies and their less dependency on Japan side.

In addition, the module development had higher proportion of the on-site mode compared with the whole project development, due to the higher dependency of the module development on Japan side (see Fig. 3(b)).

(3) Software form

Software form was divided into three types: (a) application software; (b) embedded software; (c) support software and other special software form like the ported software. The survey results obviously demonstrated that the software form was

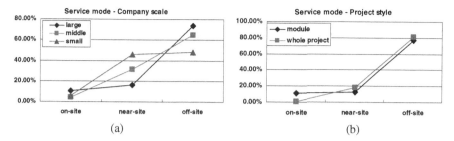

Fig. 3. Service mode

mainly application software. However, in the large and middle companies the proportion of the application software was lower than that in the small companies, while the proportion of the embedded software was higher (see Fig. 4(a)). This is because that the development of the embedded software is more difficult than the application software. Therefore, generally only the larger companies have the ability to complete the embedded software. In addition, the embedded software was mainly developed in China as modules, because the hardware part of the embedded system generally was done by Japan side (see Fig. 4(b)).

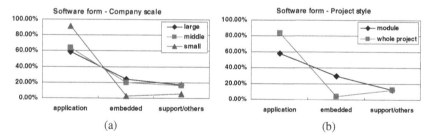

Fig. 4. Software Form

(4) Project scale

We classified the project scale into four kinds of scales: (a) Small (≤6 person-months or code size≤10K); (b) Middle (≤240 person-months or code size≤100K); (c) Large (≤1440 person-months or code size≤500K); (d) Oversize (>1440 person-months or code size>500K). In average, the middle-scale projects occupied the highest share in the Japan-oriented market. Moreover, generally the larger the company was, the larger the project was (see Fig. 5(a)). In addition, in the module development, the project scale was mainly small or middle because the development work was partly done by Japan side or other companies (see Fig. 5(b)).

2.3 Software Development Process

(1) Software development process

According to the survey, the large or middle companies mostly used the waterfall process in the offshore development, while the small companies applied the spiral

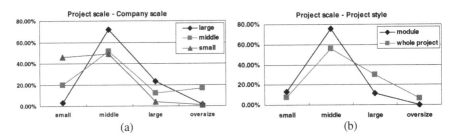

Fig. 5. Project Scale

process more often (see Fig.6 (a)). This maybe is caused by the higher flexibility and the higher acceptability of new software development process in the small companies.

On the other hand, the module development mostly applied the waterfall process, while the whole project development used more new software development processes, such as the iterative process and the V type process (see Fig.6 (b)). This is because the system design was mostly completed by Japan side in the module development, which resulted in the less flexibility of the module development process. However, the whole project development was easier to adopt the new software development processes.

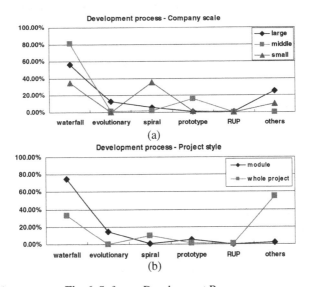

Fig. 6. Software Development Process

(2) Task assignment between Japan side and China side

The life cycle of software development mainly includes five steps: RS (requirement specification), system design, programming & unit test, system test and acceptance test. From the survey results, we found that in the Japan-oriented offshore development, RS was always provided by Japan side and the work of programming &

unit test were always completed in China side. However, the task assignment of system design, system test and acceptance test between Japan side and China side were not constant.

Averagely, the system design was mainly completed by the cooperation of both Japan side and China side. Furthermore, there was not obvious relation between the task assignment of system design and the company scale (see Fig. 7(a)). However, for the module development the system design was mainly done by Japan side or both sides, while for the whole project development, the system design was mainly done by China side or both sides (see Fig. 7(b)).

On the other hand, generally the system test and the acceptance test were mainly completed by China side and Japan side, respectively. However, for the large companies, the acceptance test was often done by China side (see Fig.8 (a)). This maybe is due to the higher reliability of the large company in China for Japan side. In addition, half of the acceptance tests of the module development were executed by Japan side.

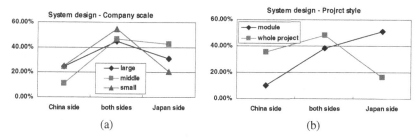

(a)   (b)

Fig. 7. Task Assignment of System Design

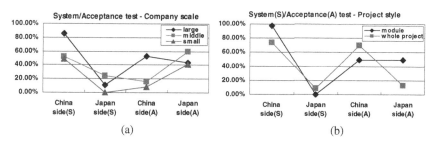

(a)   (b)

Fig. 8. Task Assignment of System Test / Acceptance Test

2.4 Existent Problems

(1) Existent Problems

The severity rank of the existent problems in the large or small companies was delayed delivery, overspent cost and bad software quality. While the rank for the middle companies was different (see Fig. 9 (a)). However, due to the limited sample number of the middle companies, it was difficult to explain the reasons. On the other hand, the problem of the whole project mainly focused on delivery (see Fig.9 (b)).

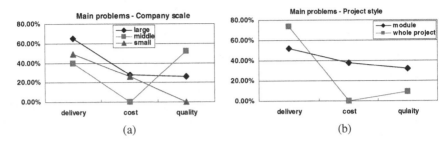

Fig. 9. Main Problems

The reasons of the above existent problems were also analyzed and showed in Fig. 10. In the large companies, bug fixing was the most important reason while the Japan side's factors had little impact. This is because the projects were developed more independently in the large companies and they paid more attention to the quality problems. However, this also demonstrated that in the large companies it was needed to strengthen the progress and quality management to reduce the time of bug fixing and shorten the delivery time.

In the smaller companies the Japan side's factors had more impact, such as the requirement change, the misestimating of the delivery and cost in Japan-side, Japan side's delayed feedback and the inconsistent understanding of RS between Japan side and China side. This showed that the small companies should communicate with Japan side more closely and frequently.

On the other hand, in the module development, the existent problems were mainly related to Japan side. While in the whole project development, the problems were mainly caused by China sides' abilities, such as bug fixing.

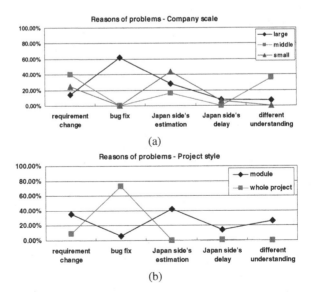

Fig. 10. Reasons of Existent Problems

(2) Requirement change

From the survey results, it was found that 96.7% of the projects' requirements were changed frequently during the development process. Moreover, the frequent requirement change usually led to the delivery and the cost problems.

The experiences of dealing with the requirement change in the offshore companies and the detailed proportion of each experience are showed in Fig. 11. It can be concluded that communicating timely with Japan side was the most effective way to deal with the requirement change.

Fig. 11. Experiences of Requirement Change

(3) Communication ways

The communication ways between Japan side and China side were ranked according to their application frequency as follows: Email, TV meeting, telephone, instant messenger and face to face. We can see that Email was the most popular communication way in the offshore development. Although face to face is most effective, it was seldom used due to the high cost (see Fig. 12).

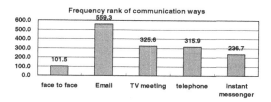

Fig. 12. Frequency Rank of Communication Ways

In order to keep full communication between Japan side and China side, the companies proposed four suggestions, which were shown in Fig. 13. It can be seen that more frequent face to face communication was most expected. In addition, sending progress and quality reports to Japan side more frequently or sending BSE (Bridge Software Engineer) to Japan side were also effective. Of course, if the employees could master Japanese, it also would be helpful.

2.5 Information of the Most Successful Projects

The survey results showed that 62.5% of the most successful projects were the whole project development (Fig. 14). Because compared with the module development

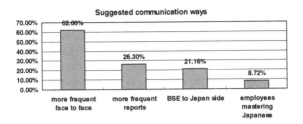

Fig. 13. Suggested Communication Ways

which was distributed in different companies, the whole project development was easier to be managed, especially when the design or the requirements were often changed.

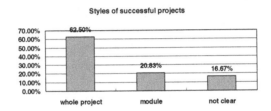

Fig. 14. Styles of Successful Projects

In addition, 79.17% of the most successful projects were middle scale, which were also easier to be managed compared with the large or oversize projects (Fig. 15).

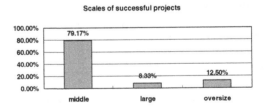

Fig. 15. Scales of Successful Projects

From the survey results, it was found that the success factors of these projects included four aspects (see Fig. 16): (a) Full communication of both sides; (b) China side's abilities, including the accurate estimation of delivery and cost, the suitable task assignment and the developers' technology level; (c) Japan side's ability, including the good design, the project management and the detailed RS; (d) Iterative process.

In the modules development, Japan side's factors were most significant, especially the design of Japan side. However, for the whole project development, the full communication was the most crucial success factor.

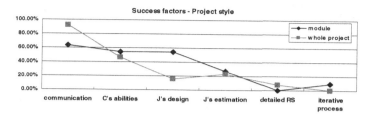

Fig. 16. Success Factors

2.6 Suggestions to Japan Side

In this survey, the suggestions to Japan side mainly focused on the more detailed RS, the better design and the special manager. However, the more detailed RS was more important for the large or middle companies, while the special manager was more expected by the small companies due to their more dependency on Japan side (see Fig.17 (a)).

On the other hand, the suggestions to Japan side for the module development mainly focused on the more detailed RS while those for the whole project development mainly focused on the special manager (see Fig.17 (b)). This is because for the module development the system design was mostly done by Japan side, the correct understanding of the requirement from Japan was most important for China side. However, for the whole project development, the system design was mostly completed by China side and more communication was needed. In this case, the special manager in Japan side was more significant.

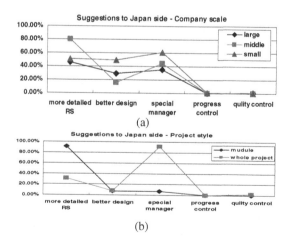

Fig. 17. Suggestions to Japan Side

3   Conclusions

Based on the survey results, it was found that almost all the basic features of the projects, such as the service mode, the software form and the project scale, had close relation with the company scales and the project styles. Furthermore, the software development process and the existent problems and expectations also had different tendency for different company scales and project styles. Some main conclusions were drawn as follows:

- The large offshore companies had higher technology level and less dependency on Japan side, so the large projects and the embedded projects were more than the smaller companies, and the projects were mainly completed by off-site mode. Waterfall process was mostly applied and the system and acceptance tests were also mostly done by China side. The software quality was paid more attention and the delivery was often delayed due to bug fixing. This showed the need to strengthen the progress and quality management in the large companies. In addition, the more detailed requirement from Japan side was mostly expected by the large companies.
- The small offshore companies had lower technology level and more dependency on Japan side, so their projects were mostly small and application software. Both near-site and off-site were main service modes. New software development process seemed more easily accepted by the small companies. However, the acceptance test was mainly done by Japan side. The delivery and quality problems were mainly caused by the requirement change, the misunderstanding of the requirement and the misestimating of delivery time in Japan side. This demonstrated that the small companies should communicate with Japan side more closely and frequently. Therefore, the special manager in Japan side was mostly expected by the small companies.
- For the module development, the system design and the acceptance test were mainly done by Japan side. Therefore, the good design from Japan side and the correct understanding of the requirement were important for China side. The proportion of the embedded software was higher and the project scale was mostly smaller compared with the whole project development. Due to the less flexibility of the module development, the waterfall process was mostly applied.
- For the whole project development, the system design and the acceptance test were mainly done by China side, so the full communication with Japan side and the ability of China side were crucial to ensure the project successful. The special manager in Japan side was mostly expected for the whole project development. In addition, the application software and the large projects in the whole project development were more than the module development. New software development process was more often applied.

Furthermore, based on these companies' problems and successful experiences, some solution proposals were presented as follows:

- Firstly, in order to ensure the offshore project successful, Japan side should assign the special manager who is responsible for providing the detailed and exact RS, the good design and the fast feedback. China side should improve the technology level and strengthen the progress and quality management.
- Secondly, due to the frequent requirement change and the different understanding of RS between Japan side and China side, it is suggested to apply new software development process and practices. For example, applying the iterative process

[4][5] to more flexibly adapt to the requirement changes and applying the XP practice of Customer Test Driven Development [6] to keep the consistency of RS understanding between Japan side and China side.

- Finally, the suitable assistant tools should be applied to improve the development efficiency and help the project managers find the potential problems. For example, some software configuration management tools can be used to collect the progress and quality information, the requirement management tools can track the requirement changes, and etc.

Of course, 24 samples maybe seem limited from the viewpoint of statistics, so further survey is needed to collect more detailed information and verify the above conclusions. Moreover, the above solution proposals should also be verified and improved by the application in the real offshore software development. In the near future, an experiment will be conducted to evaluate the effect of our new offshore software development process, which is based on the iterative process and the customer test driven practice.

References

1. http://www.analysis.com.cn
2. S-open offshore development seminar, Guide of Offshoring, Nikei BP Press (Japanese) (2004)
3. Software oversea supply seminar, Guide of Offshore Development in China, Computer Age Company (Japanese) (2005)
4. Beck, K.: Extreme Programming Explained: embrace change. Addison-Wesley, London, UK (2000)
5. Kruchten, P.: The Rational Unified Process: An Introduction. China Machine Press, Beijing (2004)
6. Jeffries, R., et al.: Extreme Programming Installed. Addison-Wesley, London, UK (2002)

Toward Visualization and Analysis of Traceability Relationships in Distributed and Offshore Software Development Projects

Cleidson R.B. de Souza[1], Tobias Hildenbrand[2], and David Redmiles[3]

[1] Departamento de Informática, Universidade Federal do Pará
Campus Universitário do Guamá, Belém, PA, 66.075-110, Brazil
cdesouza@ufpa.br
[2] Lehrstuhl für ABWL und Wirtschaftsinformatik, Universität Mannheim,
Schloss, D-68131 Mannheim, Germany
hildenbrand@uni-mannheim.de
[3] Department of Informatics, Donald Bren School of Information and Computer Sciences,
University of California, Irvine
Irvine, CA 92697-3430, USA
redmiles@ics.uci.edu

Abstract. Offshore software development projects provoke new issues to the collaborative endeavor of software development due to their global distribution and involvement of various people, processes, and tools. These problems relate to the geographical distance and the associated time-zone differences; cultural, organizational, and process issues; as well as language problems. However, existing tool support is neither adequate nor grounded in empirical observations. This paper presents two empirical studies of global software development teams and their usage of tools. The results are then used to motivate and inform the construction of more useful software development tools for offshore projects. This research focuses on issues that are tool-related but have not yet been solved by existing tools. The two software tools presented as solutions, Ariadne and TraVis, explicitly address yet unresolved issues in global software development and also integrate with prevalent other solutions.

Keywords: Traceability Relationships, Dependencies, Visualization, Distributed and Global Software Development, Offshore Software Development.

1 Introduction

Software development is one of the most common examples of collaborative work. Software developers interact face to face and through different artifacts to reach their common goal. To support this effort, several approaches and tools have been proposed. For instance, software processes [1] establish the sequence of activities that software developers need to perform, and modularization techniques [2] allow a software system to be decomposed and developed in pieces (artifacts) that can be later

B. Meyer and M. Joseph (Eds.): SEAFOOD 2007, LNCS 4716, pp. 182–199, 2007.

reintegrated. Tool support has also been adapted, ranging from simple tools such as instant messenger systems and email, to configuration management tools [3, 4], and to even more specialized collaborative tools such as Ariadne [5, 6], Augur [7], Jazz [8], and Palantír [9], among others.

More recently, due largely to economic considerations [10], engineers from different countries and continents have collaborated in *global* software development (GSD) efforts—software projects that span countries, time zones, and even continents [10]. Therefore, projects involving organizations from other continents are called "offshore" projects. However, these projects bring additional problems to the collaborative endeavor of software development: the geographical distance and the associated time-zone differences; cultural, organizational, and process issues; as well as language problems [11, 12]. Despite the commonalities in such global efforts, adequate tool support for these activities has not yet been fully realized. Furthermore, the few existing tools that have been proposed for offshore scenarios are rarely grounded in empirical data. The contribution of this paper is exactly that—it presents two empirical studies about GSD teams in offshore scenarios and their utilization of tools. The results are then used to motivate the construction of more adequate and useful software tools in this context. The empirical studies identify persistent problems in organizations conducting GSD projects. The focus is on issues that are tool-related but have not yet been solved by existing solutions. These particular issues are used to motivate the construction of two novel software tools, Ariadne and TraVis, which explicitly address yet unresolved issues in global software development and complement existing tools in practice.

This paper is organized as follows. The next section presents the empirical studies and section 3 then describes the tools that were developed grounded on the analysis of the empirical data. A discussion section about the tools specific usefulness and value added follows. Finally, conclusions and suggestions for future work are presented.

2 Empirical Studies

This section presents the two empirical studies that were conducted. The first one is a qualitative study that aimed to explore the advantages and disadvantages of offshore software development (OSD). The second one is an analysis of feature and change requests for a collaboration platform aimed at collaborative and distributed software development teams.

2.1 The MBL Offshore Software Development Project

This empirical study describes a qualitative investigation of an offshore software development project that took place in a large software development organization. A qualitative approach was adopted because it allowed us to investigate our own research questions while it also offered the flexibility to explore issues from the perspectives of the informants [13].

2.1.1 Setting and Methods

Our fieldwork was conducted in a large software development company we will call LAR (a pseudonym). LAR is one of the largest software development companies in the United States, with products ranging from operating systems to software development tools, including e-business and tailored applications. The project we studied, MBL (another pseudonym), was responsible for developing a mobile application that had not yet been released during the period of the study. The project staff was divided into three major groups: user interface (UI) designers, software developers, and the quality assurance (QA) team. The staff was distributed over five different sites spread in three different countries: North Carolina, US; Massachusetts, US; Beijing, China; Shanghai, China; and Taipei, Taiwan. To be more specific, user interface design and evaluation was performed by six professionals in North Carolina, and the implementation was performed in all other sites distributed as follows: nine developers in Massachusetts, five in Shanghai, five in Beijing, and four in Taipei. The quality assurance team was divided between the US and Chinese sites: three engineers were located in Massachusetts and six engineers in Beijing. The main coordination of the project and the project manager for this project were located in Massachusetts, where all the data were collected.

Data were collected through document analysis and semi-structured interviews [14]. Among other documentation, we collected artifacts, emails and instant messages exchanged among the software engineers. We were also granted access to shared discussion databases used by the software engineers. All of this information was used in addition to notes generated by the interviews. We conducted 17 semi-structured interviews with members of all teams from the different sites: some interviews were conducted face to face, and others were conducted by telephone, with one interview conducted by using instant messaging. The interview questions were designed to encourage the participants to talk about their everyday work, including work processes, problems, tools, communication, collaboration, and coordination efforts between their collocated and distributed colleagues. Interviews also aimed to explore the relationship between software dependencies and the coordination of software development projects, or, to be more specific, the potential usage of dependency information to facilitate collaborative software development. Interviews lasted between 20 and 70 minutes. All the material collected has been analyzed using grounded theory techniques [13]. The following sections describe the results of this analysis.

2.1.2 MBL's Software Development Process

As expected, user interface designers wrote specifications in the very beginning of the process. These specifications were aimed at managers and contained high-level descriptions of the functionalities of the application. Detailed specifications, also called design documents, were written by software developers and contained parts of source code (method calls, Java interfaces, etc.). The goal of these specifications was to allow the reader to learn how to use the software component being implemented; that is, they provided as much detail as possible about how the specifications would be implemented without actually coding them. UI designers and software developers reviewed the initial versions of these documents, which were stored in shared folders accessible to all team members.

Specifications and design documents were used to develop test plans, which would be shown to the developers once they finished their implementation work. In fact, testing had already started: the QA engineers tested the software, and when they found an issue, they filled a request in the bug database that would automatically generate an email to the developers. It was the developers' responsibility to find out where in the architecture the bug was to be found because the testing was performed from the point of view of the user. At the time, most issues were simply ignored by developers because they were aware that the issues reflected either things that were not implemented yet or things that they already knew were not working. Based on the specifications, software developers created methods in the source code but without actually providing an implementation for them. When the data collection was conducted, UI designers had just started opening issues in the database for problems in the software. Previously, they informed the developers about issues by using email or instant messages.

2.1.3 Changes in the Specifications and Notifications

UI designers performed usability tests in the specifications even before the implementation was finished. The results of these tests could lead designers to propose changes to the specifications they had created, and as a consequence could impact software developers' work. Indeed, according to one of members of the test team, the specifications changed fairly often. Another software developer reported overhearing his colleagues mentioning they had finished implementing a particular feature and then UI designers requested a change: "Well, I just implemented it this way and now they want us to change it" (informant 16). Other informants also reported not being notified about changes in the specifications. Another reason that led to changes in the specifications involved requests from the software developers. They requested changes to the UI specifications, arguing that some of the UI designs were not technically feasible in the amount of time they had.

Changes in the specifications also impacted the quality assurance team. Members of this team had to write test plans and rewrite them every time the specifications were updated. According to a tester: "it [the process of re-writing test plans] is a very boring job" (informant 09). To minimize this problem, QA engineers broke the test plans into two parts—the test design and the test data—so that only one of them had to be changed when the specification changed. The QA manager in China reported that QA members could not wait for the specifications to be finished to write their test plans because, if they did, they would not have enough time to write the test cases.

In any of these cases, changes in the specifications were preceded by discussions between the UI designers and the software developers through conference calls, emails, instant messaging, or even meetings (informants 14 and 16).

2.1.4 Notification of the Changes

A relevant aspect that came up in the data regarded change notifications, that is, notifications that were sent because of changes in the different artifacts. A software engineer in China reported that he would not receive notifications from his "contact person" in the US. In contrast, the UI designer interviewed reported that she would notify developers and testers of changes in the specifications. Whenever notifications were received, however, they overwhelmed developers because they were not tailored to them, as a developer in the US properly put it (informant 03):

> I will never go into one document trying to figure out what other people did. ... But I also wouldn't like it—the way that—I get a ... ten million different email messages just because somebody did over something that had nothing to do with me.

This quote also illustrates the importance to developers of change management systems that track the changes in artifacts.

2.1.5 Dependency Analysis

As mentioned in the previous section, one of the goals of the interviews was to investigate the usage of software dependency information to coordinate distributed projects. One informant mentioned that by inspecting configuration files of the project, he could find out which *components* depended on the component he was developing. With that information, this developer could find out which *developers* depended on his code, another piece of information that could be used to guide the notifications to be sent whenever artifacts changed.[1]

Another software developer reported a similar interest in finding out who the developers were that were calling her code: "There is no really ... good way to keep track of who's consuming your code." The distributed nature of this project was particularly relevant in this case, as the conversation below attests:

> Informant 03: ... local people like Mike [pseudonym]. It's easy just to say, "Well, have you tried this? Have you tried this as well?" ... "I didn't have time. I'm going to try it tomorrow." And then the second day I bumped into him again. I would bug him and say, "Well, have you tried it? How did it go?" [He would] say, "Oh, that didn't work. I would send you the exception." It's much easier at this point, but let's say the ... people in Taiwan ... I don't actively go ahead and chase them around and say, "How many—this interface, how many methods have you exercised?" You don't need this. I don't—I mean I don't have time, simply I just don't have time to do that. So ... is so much harder.

> Researcher: Would you like to know that information?

> Informant 03: I definitely would have liked to—would love to—have that information as early as possible ... because that makes my life much easier. For example, Mike [a local colleague] starts to use my stuff so late and we have ... builds supposedly by 23rd. That's when we have all of the ... work. And he only starts to test my stuff on the 21st and by [the] 22nd he realized there are two methods [that are] not really doing what I want it to do. And he told me on the 22nd and I only have one day—actually, not even one day ... to do it because we do build like once a day. Well, I would have had like any other build ... have to get up at four. ... So, of course, I would love to hear them telling me, "Okay, I have ... I did all of testing, [and it] worked."

---

[1] We will illustrate in the following section that this is exactly the principle used in Ariadne.

The quote above illustrates how it is important for developers to know *who* is consuming their codes and *when* this integration with their codes starts. This information is useful because it allows the developer to anticipate the work that will be requested of them before the deadline. This information is necessary from both collocated and distributed colleagues. The informal conversations that are afforded by the collocation simplify this process among local colleagues; in contrast, however, developers are not able to find this status information when their colleagues are distributed over different countries. This is again made clear by informant 03:

> With Mike [a collocated developer], I can say, "Can you please try …?" With Taiwan, I don't do that. I don't really know them that well. I talk to them, but unless something … unless something [is] really important, you don't …

In fact, this informant reported that in one occasion a developer in China was already using her code and she did not know it.

Developers in China reported the exact same problem during the interviews: the Shangai team was developing a software component already in use by the Beijing team for two months and by the US team for only a week. According to the Shangai team leader, his distributed colleagues were giving low priority to his component, and that could lead to problems in the end of the implementation phase for his team because they would have only a short time to fix potential problems. This happened with both the Beijing and the US teams. In fact, he reported having to email his colleagues in Beijing asking them to integrate his component into their code and requesting a deadline for that. During weekly "checkpoints," he would confirm how the integration was going. This team leader trained the Beijing developers on the usage of his component. During the period of data collection, a Beijing developer was in the United States, training the developers on the same component. To accompany this process, the Shangai team leader and the Beijing developer who was in the United States had weekly "checkpoints." It was through one of these checkpoints that the Shangai team found out that the US team had started using his component.

These results are not surprising (the effect of distance on the coordination of the work has been known for decades); however, the possibility of using software dependency information to minimize the coordination problems is an important result of this study. This will be discussed in more detail in the following section.

2.2 Feature and Change Requests for Offshore Collaboration Platforms

Collaborative software development platforms (CSDPs) comprise and unify not only source code management, but multiple software development and knowledge management tools. CSDPs include build management systems, issue trackers, Wikis, and discussion forums [25]. These tools have often been successfully used in distributed open source software development projects as well as offshore software development scenarios [24, 25],. Using a CSDP is state-of-the-art in OSD [26] and also serves as a method for capturing and maintaining more relevant traceability and rationale information [23, 27]. Therefore, in a second empirical effort, customer feature and change requests of one of the market-leading collaborative software development platform vendors, VCI (pseudonym), have been investigated and analyzed for evidence about yet open tool–related issues in distributed and offshore software development.

2.2.1 Settings and Methodology

VCI has a broad customer base, ranging from large producing companies and financial service providers to software development companies. In fact, most companies use VCI's tool for globally distributed development projects. VCI's collaboration platform supports most common collaboration features such as a document management system (DMS), a Wiki system, issue trackers, reporting, Wiki-enabled discussion forums, and chat rooms, as well as code-related features such as source code and build management (cp. [25]). The platform is not a stand-alone solution for software development, but also integrates various established tools (e.g., the Eclipse development environment, CVS, and Subversion), as well as numerous other tools. The platform does not prescribe one particular development process, which can be an advantage with several heterogeneous sites involved.

Customers are allowed and encouraged to post their requests concerning the platform directly to VCI's change request tracker. This tracker is based on VCI's own tool and establishes something comparable to a community of practice among its customers. The tracker also supports an item-related discussion among users and support personnel. Moreover, users can link change requests to other requests and artifacts and refer to those.

The data inspected was extracted from the change request tracker and contained 183 items from 34 different customers. Each item has a unique identification (ID) number, a brief summary in addition to a more detailed description with comments from different users, as well as responses from VCI's support team, a time stamp, a resolution status, and an issue category.[2] Table 1 shows the distribution of these feature requests over different categories and users. These figures illustrate that besides many unspecified items, the design of the Internet-based (Web) user interface and the lately added Wiki system drew most of the attention from customers. However, many unspecified issues also revolved around UI and Wiki.

In a second analytic step, 232 already resolved items were also investigated because some of those were not yet incorporated in the latest release of the software or were only partly implemented so far. Moreover, some customer needs could not be implemented due to time restrictions, but were valid expressions of their requirements as well. The distribution of categories is comparable to one of the unresolved issues (cp. Table 1) and thus complements the initial data set.

As for the interpretative analysis, each tracker item was investigated, including its cross references and the customers involved[3]. This in-depth analysis revealed that there are currently three major fields of interest among the CSDP users: *artifact change propagation, artifact linking and traceability*, and *relationship visualization*.

---

[2] Please note that the categories have been set by the vendor and several other attributes were not considered for this particular analysis.

[3] In the following sections, different customers, as representatives of their companies, will be coded with capital letters starting with "customer A."

Table 1. Distribution of Feature Requests over Categories and Users

Category	#Requests	#Users
Client	1	1
Communication	4	4
Database	15	4
Documentation	5	4
Eclipse Plug-in	3	1
Release	2	2
Remote Interface	12	2
Run Time	2	2
Server	11	7
Web User Interface	29	12
Wiki	22	5
Unspecified	77	23
TOTAL	**183**	**34** (unique)

2.2.2 Artifact Change Propagation

Many customers referred to the default notification mechanism for artifact changes as being too exhaustive or not fine-grained enough (e.g., customers C and D, among others). As one customer put it, "there [sometimes] is a mail flood" produced by the platform. In offshore software development (OSD) projects, however, an automated subscription and notification mechanism is critical for global change propagation and management [15]. VCI's collaboration platform already provides capabilities to adapt the propagation and notification patterns, but customers still bring up very special requirements, such as the "ability to subscribe individuals to be notified for a particular task" (customer E) and being able to configure the notification content in order to "quickly decide whether it could be important or not" (customer D).

Regarding distributed change management, there is also a demand for an automatically generated "change history" for certain artifacts or aggregated sets of artifacts. Examples include "a compilation of all changes in a whole subtree [of artifacts]" (customer A) and a more complete presentation of related notifications as a whole because they do not want to have "two separate systems, [the CSDP] and the email system" (customer B). This leads to issues of traceability of development processes and rationale, which are discussed in the next section.

2.2.3 Artifact Linking and Traceability

Capturing and managing traceable information about artifacts, processes, and development rationale seems to be a major issue among VCI's customers. Many issues were related to this problem, half of which are still unresolved in the current version of the platform.

Customers like the idea of being able to link related artifacts by using either Wiki links or the standards association mechanism incorporated in the CSDP. They use Wiki pages and Wiki comments attached to various other artifact types to create a project-specific traceability network (as stated by customers A and F). However, various customers mention sophisticated ways of linking artifacts not yet supported by the platform. Customer A asked for a unified way of linking different types of artifacts and even automatic synchronization between Wiki links and associations: "The Wiki-description of documents and tracker items should be scanned for inter-Wiki links to tracker items or documents, and those should figure in the [association] tab automatically."

This suggests that an easier and more concise way of capturing and managing links is required. Other customers also required easier and semi-automated linking of external artifacts, such as Internet, intranet, and Wikipedia resources. This requirement has been explicitly stated by customer A and confirmed by the VCI management in another tracker issue: "We need to be able to configure our own [CSDP] extensions."

The concept of rationale management is deeply related to that of artifact linking. Customers use the platform to capture their rationale for decision processes in different software development disciplines, such as requirements engineering, architectural design, and implementation. For instance, customers postulate their need to export the full contents of a tracker into their process reports. Customer G, for instance, expressed a need for a "way to export the full contents of a tracker including the comments."

Even though many requests revolved around Wiki-related issues, this seems to have spurred the general thoughts on different means of linking artifacts and retrieving this information from the platform. When analyzing the dates of committed requests, the discussion about traceability networks established by Wiki webs has apparently ignited more general requests pertaining to artifact linking. For example, customer A requested automatic synchronization of Wiki links with other association mechanisms: "[links] need to be [automatically] added to the [association] tab and removed."

Instead of just providing listed links to certain artifacts or resources, as customer A did, several parties demanded alternative ways of representing the network of links. VCI, as represented by their customer support, responded to this in the following way, according to VCI management: "In the first step we provide the relationship visualization with a quite simple GUI. In the next releases we will add graph, hypergraph, [and] MindMap visualization." VCI regards these features as complementary to the existing reporting functionality of their CSDP.

2.3 Brief Summary of Empirical Findings

As has been shown in the empirical studies in section 2, tool-related issues in offshore software development revolved around change management and traceability issues, in addition to the more general issues of distributed collaboration and asynchronous communication, which have been improved by the use of a CSDP in the VCI study. Both studies showed that change propagation and notification are still major issues in different tool settings. The MBL study also revealed many issues pertaining to dependency analysis and management, whereas the VCI customers had problems with linking different artifacts and visualizing these relationships.

3 Tool Support for Offshore Software Development

This section describes two different tools created to support OSD. The first, Ariadne, is an Eclipse plug-in, whereas the second tool, TraVis, is built on top of the same collaborative software development platform VCI used in our second empirical study. More important, the designs of both tools were informed by the empirical data described in the previous section. Both tools focus on the identification, analysis, and visualization of dependency and traceability information that exist among the software development artifacts. With this information, it is possible to identify software developers associated with these artifacts and provide tailored notification of changes and proper impact analysis. Furthermore, it is also possible to perform social network analysis to identify developers who play special roles in the software development process.

3.1 Ariadne

3.1.1 Functionality and Features

Ariadne is designed to perform automatic dependency analysis on software projects shared in configuration management repositories, and to generate visualizations of social dependency information. Generating social dependencies involves three types of dependency information. Initially, Ariadne identifies the technical dependencies in the source code by constructing call-graphs. According to Callahan and colleagues, a call-graph "summarizes the dynamic invocation relationships between procedures" [16]. Second, by describing dependencies in the source code, a call-graph potentially unveils dependencies among software developers responsible for the software components [17, 18]. In order to reveal dependencies among developers, it is necessary to populate the call-graph with "social information." The ultimate goal is to create a data structure that describes which software developers depend on which other software developers for a given piece of code. An example of this data-structure, called a social call-graph [17]. Last, because social call-graphs describe both technical dependencies and authorship information, they can be used to generate sociograms describing the dependence relationship only among software developers. That is, they can show social dependencies among developers that exist because of dependencies in the source code on which they are working. A sociogram, as used in social network analysis [19], is a graphical representation of a set of items, vertices, or nodes connected to one another via links or edges. The sociogram of the Tyrant project is shown on Figure 1.

The sociograms generated by Ariadne can be used by software developers to identify two important pieces of information: who they depend on and who depends on their work. As the MBL data indicate, this information is very important to facilitate the coordination of distributed software development projects. We have also used these sociograms to understand free/open source software development [20].

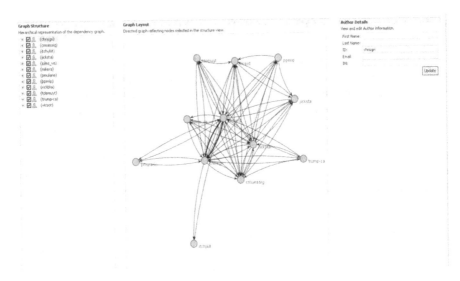

Fig. 1. Tyrant's Sociogram

3.1.2 Architecture

Ariadne is implemented as a Java plug-in to the popular Eclipse IDE. As such, Ariadne is integrated into this environment and makes use of Eclipse functionality and its plug-in model. The dependency processing functionality is encapsulated in a main control plug-in that delegates source-code analysis, annotation of the source-code analysis data, and visualization of the created data structure to sub-plug-ins. As a result, Ariadne offers users the flexibility to use dependency generators for a diverse set of source languages, configuration management repositories, and methods of visualization.

Ariadne automatically selects (while offering users the ability to override this choice) appropriate plug-ins for analyzing the user's project based on the project's context. Once the control plug-in has located appropriate sub-plug-ins to analyze the project's source code and query the project's configuration management, the control plug-in automatically generates social dependencies for that project. By using one of the installed visualization plug-ins, it is possible to display all three types of dependency information to the user: technical dependencies, social call-graph, and sociograms.

Our current implementation can present call-graphs and social call-graphs at three different levels of abstraction, based on the programming language's hierarchy (e.g., packages, classes, methods in Java). Essentially, information is aggregated at each hierarchy level to, potentially, average the different results provided by diverse call-graph extractors [21]. For instance, class dependencies are displayed as the aggregation of method dependencies (i.e., the call-graph).

Ariadne was initially implemented to analyze only Java projects and extract information from CVS repositories. Later, we redesigned it based on a layered architecture to be general enough to support various programming languages, configuration management (CM) systems, and visualizations. The configuration management and dependency management parts of the API are used to isolate the programming language and configuration management tools from the visualizations provided by Ariadne. Through this approach, independent developers can contribute new plug-ins (configuration management tools and programming languages) to Ariadne while reusing previous visualizations. It is also possible to easily design new visualizations to already supported programming languages and CM tools. Ariadne has default graph and tree view visualizations built in. Note that although Eclipse has a generic Team API for accomplishing simple tasks involving version-controlled files, programmers must use the internal (unpublished) API to accomplish more complicated tasks. The inability to directly manipulate remote resources motivated us to create our own remote resource API.

To facilitate the understanding and usage of Ariadne's API, we utilize the façade design pattern [22] to aggregate methods to be used to query program dependency, authorship information and both types of information combined (the social call-graph). For example, developers may query the classes that depend on a particular class, the authors of a particular piece of code, all the authors of a file, how the ownership of a class changes from one release to the next, and so on.

3.2 TraVis – Trace Visualization

The TraVis (Trace Visualization) tool leverages the use of dependencies among distributed assets unified in one CSDP and their users by allowing the visualization and analysis of these different relationships. The traceability and rationale information is captured as distributed CSDP users develop and document their processes in OSD projects. The artifacts are then annotated and connected with their respective descriptions, discussions (e.g., design-related), as well as inter-related process steps represented as issue tracker items. TraVis captures both traces explicitly modeled as associations and more implicit links as built by Wiki systems integrated in the CSDP.

This way, they form a heterogeneous network of information. Managing all this information on one single CSDP allows linking all the artifacts, activity descriptions, and responsible users, consequently establishing the actual "traceability network," as described by [23]. This network is complemented by capturing rationale information, that is, making decision processes (e.g., design or code-related changes) traceable by storing the history of artifacts and users' justifications behind decisions (see [27]). TraVis provides advanced visualization and analysis capabilities for traceability networks, including several logical filters for displaying certain aspects (e.g., particular artifact types, process categories, or user groups). Thus, different role-based views, e.g. for source code developers, designers, and project managers, can be defined. Moreover, TraVis is able to display networks originating from particular artifacts, activities, and users (see Figure 2).

This allows analyzing the graphs that grow around one particular entity (in Figure 2: task 1195), for instance in order to conduct impact analyses centered on certain artifacts that are subject to change. Moreover, the latest version of TraVis displays artifact nodes according to their user value (*value-based software engineering*, VBSE, see [28]). Because OSD projects contain a plethora of linked information, we implemented methods like VBSE to reduce and enrich the network information in order to be more useful to both developers and managers (see [29]). To

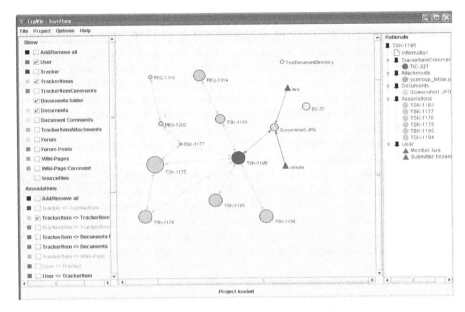

Fig. 2. Value-Based Trace Visualization with TraVis

this aim, not only the node but also the edges contain additional information, such as the type of relationship (i.e. link semantics) or the rationale for linking one artifact with another or replacing it by a changed version. Rationale information (e.g., comments on committed code or changed artifacts) is displayed in one context with the related artifacts (see right column in Figure 3).

Technologically, TraVis extracts traceability information from CSDPs over their remote APIs (e.g., via Web Services) or directly from their Web interfaces. TraVis stores this information internally and so far, no redundant persistent storage is implemented. TraVis then constructs the traceability network structure from the CSDP information. Artifacts, such as documents, code, Wiki pages, and tracker items, as well as related users are graphically represented as nodes, whereas their relationships are stored as edges. For visualization purposes, the open source software "Java Universal Network/Graph Framework" (JUNG)[4] was chosen. It enables many helpful features such as zooming as well as manual and automatic graph reorganization according to pre-defined patterns and algorithms.

4   Discussion

The most important aspect that can be identified in both the MBL and the VCI studies is the possibility of using dependency information to facilitate the coordination of OSD activities. Being able to find out when a dependency started to exist between software artifacts is an important aspect raised in the MBL study. Providing that information can facilitate the coordination of software development projects through

---

[4] http://jung.sourceforge.net/ (09/30/2006)

the awareness of other developers' work status [4, 30]. This aspect is deeply embedded into both Ariadne and TraVis. In fact, Ariadne supports the *automatic* identification of dependencies among software components. By doing that, Ariadne allows software developers to determine the set of developers who are using their codes as well as when this usage started. Ariadne is limited to source code to allow the automatic creation of dependency links because the source code can be properly parsed. Ariadne finds the dependency links automatically, so developers do not have to worry about manual artifact linking and trace capturing. As postulated by several VCI customers, Ariadne's automatic extraction of dependencies addresses the issue of extensive exports of traceability network information—at least for code-related artifacts and their authors.

In contrast, TraVis is based on the *manual* creation of dependency relationships. Its information base is not limited to source code only, however, and it supports all ranges of software development artifacts. TraVis also provides a real-time view of the project's traceability network of artifacts and users, which contains valuable information about dependencies between software developers (similar to Ariadne) and therefore supports better awareness for what other people work on. TraVis thus allows for real-time graphical representations and analyses. TraVis is also able to display the current status of inter-related tasks represented as tracker items. This allows for even better awareness in OSD scenarios. By providing a finer-grained dependency and tracking analysis of artifacts produced by distributed teams, both TraVis and Ariadne permit individual users to understand their roles in the broader software development process with respect to other users and the artifacts that they produce. This understanding is crucial to the coordination of collaborative software development efforts [31].

Once the dependency information is available to our tools, it is possible to tailor the notification messages that are sent due to changes in the artifacts; that is, notifications about the changes can now be sent only to the subset of developers who are interested in the changes. We assume that this subset is basically the set of developers who depend on the artifact being changed, but that assumption is grounded on our empirical data (see sections 0 and 2.2.2). The goal here is to reduce the number of notifications that software developers receive because a common problem in both the MBL and VCI studies was the overwhelming flood of notification messages initiated by other software developers or software tools due to changes in the artifacts. TraVis's role-based views and filtered visualization can also be used to alleviate this problem. TraVis can also help information brokers in offshore settings, as in the MBL study (section 2.1), to manage their immense workload of emails. By providing information about other users related to networks of artifacts and the possibility of starting an instant messaging session or Voice-over-IP conversation using the collaboration platform interface, TraVis supports self-selection of relevant users and an easy communication process. This, in turn, should relieve the brokers in their dispatching tasks. Again, the filters and the value-based software engineering perspective provide a better overview of the project to both managers and developers. In some ways comparable to TraVis, Ariadne also facilitates the management of notifications by providing visualizations of technical and social dependencies. The developers are thus able to actually see who is working on code artifacts related to theirs and contact these persons purposefully.

As mentioned before, notification messages are necessary because of changes in the artifacts. Often, these changes are preceded by discussions. However, these discussions were not visible to all interested parties (section 0) due to the distributed nature of the project. TraVis addresses issues related to unexpected changes in software development artifacts (including specifications) as follows: rationale information from a Wiki-based software development platform allows one to notice whenever there is a discussion going relating to a certain artifact of interest. For example, if the specification is assembled using a Wiki or the specification document is annotated and discussed through the Wiki, TraVis can display this correspondence with the affected artifact. By doing that, the relevant information is accessible to everybody entitled to read it according to the roles defined on the CSDP. In short, software developers who depend on a particular artifact can find out that this artifact is likely to change and therefore impact their own work by accessing the discussion that takes place about the artifact.

Finally, a relevant aspect of both Ariadne and TraVis is the focus on visualizations. Visualizations shift the load from the cognitive system to the perceptual system, capitalizing on the human visual system's ability to recognize patterns and structures in the visual information [32]. In terms of relationship visualization, Ariadne provides different types of network graphs (i.e., call-graphs, social call-graphs, and sociograms (see section 0)). As discussed in the previous paragraphs, these representations can be utilized to facilitate team communication in distributed and collocated settings.

TraVis visualizes all possible artifact relations and is thus able to provide traceability and rationale information to different project stakeholders. Role-based filters and the value-based perspective guarantee the appropriateness of the traceability network for diverse users. The integration with Wiki-enabled CSDPs ensures that capturing and managing the network information is easy and concise. TraVis also includes a set of predefined views and filters (see section 3.2.1) in order to enable alternative visualizations of relationships. As can be seen in Figure 2, different network compositions and layouts can be chosen. By means of a Wiki plug-in, it is also possible to include TraVis snapshots in a Wiki page, for example, for better communication. Due to TraVis's component-based architecture, an easy transition to other network representations, such as semantic networks and topic maps, is assured. In short, TraVis provides increased awareness within offshore software development projects based on a broad range of traceability and rationale visualizations that are created with information extracted from the collaborative development platform.

TraVis supports artifact change propagation as well as linking and the visualization of these relationships in multiple respects: First, it supports change histories (see section 2.2.2) by providing rationale information for each artifact. Hence, TraVis users can always check the artifacts' history and related discussions. Like Ariadne, TraVis creates better overall awareness through visualizations of the artifacts' dependencies and their related users. As has been concluded before, this enables more targeted communication processes complementary to the CSDP's notification engine.

5   Conclusions and Future Work

When comparing the issues arising in both studies, one can notice that they mostly deal with problems of change management and propagation as well as dependency management in traceability networks. These issues are analyzed in distributed and OSD contexts in order to empirically ground our requirements for tools to support these processes.

In addition to commonplace source code management and CSDP solutions, the analysis and visualization tools Ariadne and TraVis are designed and presented. The discussion in section 4 shows that these tools provide advanced functionality as demanded by practitioners in real-world offshore projects. However, in doing so we take a rather tool-centered perspective on OSD issues, deliberately not addressing social and inter-cultural problems in the first place.

Our future work basically includes two streams of research: First, further empirical studies will be conducted with other companies developing software in distributed and offshore scenarios. Second, a deeper integration of the two tools, Ariadne and TraVis, is planned to allow Ariadne to read other than code-related information from CSDPs. Because CSDPs are evolving as state-of-the-art in OSD, however, TraVis will be the basis for further tool development and will be enhanced by *automated* link extraction and social network analysis capabilities from Ariadne.

In addition to continuing our empirically informed design, the tools will be evaluated in various settings, such as open source software development (OSSD) projects. OSSD projects already use CSDPs and are therefore comparable to OSD settings from a tool-based perspective. They contain freely available data than can be applied to show the usefulness of our approaches in large-scale distributed projects. We also intend to have OSSD practitioners evaluate our various visualizations in order to determine the most useful ones. The tools will also be evaluated within globally distributed student projects involving universities in Brazil, Germany, Puerto Rico, and the United States.

Acknowledgments. This work was supported in part by the National Science Foundation under awards 0205724 and 0326105; by IBM through the Eclipse Innovation Program; and by the Brazilian government under CAPES Grant BEX 1312/99-5 and CNPq grant 479206/2006. This work is also a result of the project CollaBaWue supported by the German state of Baden-Wuerttemberg. CollaBaWue is part of the research association PRIMIUM. The authors would like to thank Li-Te Cheng, David Millen, and John Patterson for their comments on earlier versions of this paper.

References

1. Garg, P.K.: Process-Centered Software Engineering Environments. IEEE Computer Society Press, Los Alamitos, CA (1996)
2. Parnas, D.L.: On the Criteria to Be Used in Decomposing Systems into Modules. Communications of the ACM 15(12), 1053–1058 (1972)
3. Dart, S.: Concepts in Configuration Management Systems. In: Proceedings of the 3rd International Workshop on Software Configuration Management, Trondheim, Norway, ACM Press, New York (1991)
4. Grinter, R.: Supporting Articulation Work Using Configuration Management Systems. Computer Supported Cooperative Work 5(4), 447–465 (1996)

5. de Souza, C.R.B., et al.: From Technical Dependencies to Social Dependencies. In: Workshop on Social Networks for Design and Analysis: Using Network Information in CSCW, Chicago (2004)
6. Trainer, E., et al.: Bridging the Gap between Technical and Social Dependencies with Ariadne. In: Eclipse Technology Exchange, San Diego, CA (2005)
7. Froehlich, J., Dourish, P.: Unifying Artifacts and Activities in a Visual Tool for Distributed Software Development Teams. In: International Conference on Software Engineering, Edinburgh, UK (2004)
8. Cheng, L.-T., et al.: Building Collaboration into IDEs. Edit -> Compile -> Run -> Debug ->Collaborate? In: ACM Queue, pp. 40–50 (2003)
9. Sarma, A., Noroozi, Z., van der Hoek, A.: Palantír: Raising Awareness among Configuration Management Workspaces. In: Twenty-fifth International Conference on Software Engineering, Portland, Oregon (2003)
10. Carmel, E.: Global Software Teams: Collaborating Across Borders and Time-Zones. Prentice-Hall, Englewood Cliffs (1999)
11. Herbsleb, J.D., Moitra, D.: Global software development. IEEE Software 18(N2), 16–20 (2001)
12. Meyer, B.: The Unspoken Revolution in Software Engineering. IEEE Computer 23(1), 121–124 (2006)
13. Strauss, A., Corbin, J.: Basics of Qualitative Research: Techniques and Procedures for Developing Grounded Theory, 2nd edn. SAGE Publications, Thousand Oaks (1998)
14. McCracken, G.: The Long Interview. SAGE Publications, Thousand Oaks (1988)
15. de Souza, C.R.B., Basaveswara, S.D., Redmiles, D.: Supporting Global Software Development with Event Notification Servers. In: Workshop on Global Software Development, Orlando, FL (2002)
16. Callahan, D., et al.: Constructing the Procedure Call Multigraph. IEEE Transactions on Software Engineering 16(4), 483–487 (1990)
17. de Souza, C.R.B., et al.: How a Good Software Practice Thwarts Collaboration—The Multiple Roles of APIs in Software Development. In: Foundations of Software Engineering, Newport Beach, CA, ACM Press, New York (2004)
18. de Souza, C.R.B.: On the Relationship between Software Dependencies and Coordination: Field Studies and Tool Support, Department of Informatics, Donald Bren School of Information and Computer Sciences, University of California, Irvine. p. 186 (2005)
19. Wasserman, S., Faust, K.: Social Network Analysis: Methods and Applications. In: Structural Analysis in the Social Sciences, Cambridge, UK, Cambridge University Press, Cambridge (1994)
20. de Souza, C.R.B., Froehlich, J., Dourish, P.: Seeking the Source: Software Source Code as a Social and Technical Artifact. In: ACM Conference on Group Work (to appear)
21. Murphy, G., et al.: An Empirical Study of Static Call Graph Extractors. ACM Transactions on Software Engineering and Methodology 7(2), 158–191 (1998)
22. Gamma, E., et al.: Design Patterns: Elements of Reusable Object-Oriented Software. In: Addison-Wesley Professional Computing Series, Reading, MA: Addison-Wesley (1995)
23. Lindvall, M., Sandahl, K.: Practical Implications of Traceability Software—Practice and Experience, vol. 26, pp. 1161–1180. John Wiley & Sons, Inc., New York (1996)
24. Augustin, L., Bressler, D., Smith, G.: Accelerating Software Development through Collaboration. In: Proceedings of the 24th International Conference on Software Engineering (ICSE'02), pp. 559–563. ACM Press, New York (2002)

25. Robbins, J.: Adopting Open Source Software Engineering (OSSE) Practices by Adopting OSSE. In: Feller, J., Fitzgerald, B., Hissam, S.A., Lakhani, K.R. (eds.) Tools Free/Open Source Processes and Tools, Cambridge, MA, pp. 245–264. MIT Press, Cambridge (2005)
26. Rodriguez, F., Geisser, M., Berkling, K., Hildenbrand, T.: Evaluating Collaboration Platforms for Offshore Software Development Scenarios. In: Proceedings of the First International Conference on Software Engineering Approaches For Offshore and Outsourced Development, Zurich, Switzerland (2007)
27. Dutoit, A.H., McCall, R., Mistrik, I., Paech, B. (eds.): Rationale Management in Software Engineering. Springer Verlag, Heidelberg (2006)
28. Boehm, B.: Value-Based Software Engineering Software Engineering Notes, vol. 28, pp. 1–12 (2003)
29. Egyed, A., Biffl, S., Heindl, M., Gruenbacher, P.: A Value-Based Approach for Understanding Cost-Benefit Trade-Offs During Automated Software Traceability. In: Proceedings of the 3rd International Workshop on Traceability in Emerging Forms of Software Engineering (TEFSE '05), pp. 2–7. ACM Press, New York (2005)
30. Heath, C., Luff, P.: Collaboration and Control: Crisis Management and Multimedia Technology in London Underground Control Rooms. Computer Supported Cooperative Work 1(1-2), 69–94 (1992)
31. Grinter, R.E.: Doing Software Development: Occasions for Automation and Formalisation. In: Fifth European Conference on Computer Supported Cooperative Work (ECSCW'97), Lancaster, UK, Kluwer Academic Publishers, Dordrecht (1997)
32. Robertson, G.G., Card, S.K., Mackinlay, J.D.: Information Visualization using 3D Interactive Animation. Communications of the ACM 36(4), 57–71 (1993)

Author Index

Lecture Notes in Computer Science

Sublibrary 2: Programming and Software Engineering

For information about Vols. 1– 4111
please contact your bookseller or Springer